TRUTH PROOF 3

Bringing Down The Light

by
Paul Sinclair

Truth Proof 3: Bringing Down The Light
by Paul Sinclair

Paperback edition published in the UK by PBC Publishing 2019

© Copyright Paul Sinclair 2019

Unless otherwise stated, all photographs by Paul Sinclair.

All drawings by Paul Sinclair
- except the Wharncliffe Woods scene; drawn by Gemma Sinclair.

Free Press news articles courtesy of and copyright of Johnson Press Plc

Cover image and additional artwork by Chris Turner.

All rights reserved. No part of this work may be reproduced, stored in a retrieval system, or transmitted in any form or by any means, electronically, mechanically, photocopied, or otherwise without prior permission of the copyright holder, nor be otherwise circulated in any form other than which it is published.

ISBN: 978-1-9999165-3-4

Also available as an e-book

TRUTH PROOF 3
Bringing Down The Light

Whitley Strieber: Best-selling author and renowned lecturer.
"Paul Sinclair continues his convincing and exacting research into strange events in the United Kingdom, most especially his native Yorkshire, a true zone of strangeness.
In Truth Proof 3 he develops an amazing variety of cases with great skill, opening a door into the unknown that is present in East and North Yorkshire and even farther afield.
Truth Proof 3 is a mind opening journey into an unknown that isn't even supposed to exist, but is very real and very much a part of the world we live in. Chilling, thought provoking and mind opening."

Peter Robbins: Author, researcher and international lecturer.
"In Truth Proof 3, the tenacious Yorkshire-based investigative writer Paul Sinclair yet again proves his worth and takes his readers on the dark and at times unnerving journey he first introduced them to in his two previous volumes. Well done Mr. Sinclair!"

Nick Pope: Author and former Ministry of Defence spokesman for unexplained phenomena.
"The third volume of the Truth Proof series of books cements the reputation of East and North Yorkshire as being a 'hotspot' for UFO sightings and paranormal activity...Truth Proof 3 shows Paul Sinclair to be a determined, boots-on-the-ground investigator, looking at a wide range of mysterious events including UFOs, missing time, werewolf sightings and animal mutilations.
Truth Proof 3 also explores allegations of strange rituals that may link some of these phenomena, providing some clues about the bigger picture. This is a fascinating account of mysteries that can be both intriguing and sinister - as one would expect when an investigator shines a light into the dark spaces that exist where the occult and the paranormal intersect."

John Hanson: Retired UK police detective and author of the '*Haunted Skies*' series of books.
"Paul is acknowledged as being a specialist in his own field of investigation from his base in North Yorkshire and I am proud to say that I would have been honoured to have worked alongside him as a police detective. He is the only man I have met who possesses such unique detective skills and is to be congratulated for his commitment to preserving the history of something that should be taken seriously rather than the opposite! Well done Paul."

Howard Hughes: Broadcaster, journalist and presenter of '*The Unexplained*' podcast.
"Paul Sinclair does primary research into modern mysteries. He goes to places and talks to people. He follows up. Paul does not rehash the findings of other people...he comes up with his own. Compelling and credible. Paul did his first radio interview with me and it was clear even then that he'd become known worldwide. A real investigator."

Derek Tyler: Author of the '*Alien Contact*' series of books.
"Paul Sinclair is one of the most courageous and unfailingly-accurate researchers and authors in the field. His personal integrity and credibility are beyond question, and he often delves into unsolved cases and events which are all but unknown to most members of the public. I consider him to be Europe's leading authority when it comes to the topic of UFOs, and one of the [most] reliable authors in the world.
In a world which is filled with delusions and disinformation, Paul provides a welcome breath of fresh air! He puts an enormous amount of time and effort into checking and re-checking his facts, something which is a great service to the reader. When he says something occurred, you can be sure it really did, and in precisely the way he described it. Mr. Sinclair is my favourite author in the field, and his books are not to be missed.
Paul has earned a well-deserved reputation among his peers for his personal courage, integrity, accuracy and the highly-detailed clarity of his writing. I consider his books to be 'must-haves' for my personal library and recommend them highly. Fascinating, informative and painstakingly researched, Paul Sinclair's manuscripts are second to none!"

Daniel Loose: Author for Nexus Magazine (Germany).
"Since paranormal research is - in contrast to traditional science - primarily based on witness accounts, its success largely hinges on the researcher's integrity. Given that he has to discern interpretation and delusion from what has actually been experienced, to grasp subtle details, and to gain the witnesses' trust, this might be one of the reasons for the growing attention that the 'Truth Proof' book series by English author Paul Sinclair is attracting."

Anna - Professor of Medieval Studies, UK.
"Paul Sinclair is a researcher who has shown his grasp of the immense importance of [telling] stories...His Truth Proof series utilizes many sources, ancient to modern, in the dedicated quest to find some structural order...in the universe.

He has had the bravery to share his own stories with an often dismissive and misunderstanding modern world, and the courage and generosity to provide a voice for the stories of others who have experienced the anomalous: those strange and wondrous events which have always been so much a part of the human experience, from the earliest recorded history into the present day.

Unafraid to question reality itself - always a terrifying proposition for any species which relies so much on order - he has brought forth, through careful study and a profound respect for individual experience, not only new data to fit into an established pattern, but compelling evidence which demonstrates how enduring and universal that pattern truly is.

From 10th century carvings to 21st century emails, he has patiently sifted through the facts presented, questioned every source, and examined every possible explanation, from the most stolidly traditional to the most radically novel, seeking every step of the way a more comprehensive understanding of the world and all its wonders...he has unearthed a wealth of experience - a treasure-trove of stories; often mysterious, sometimes frightening, always invaluable for what all of us can learn from them - and has in turn produced these marvellous documents of his own, which future generations can turn to in their own enduring quest - the drive of all humanity to understand."

Also by Paul Sinclair :

TRUTH PROOF 1
The Truth That Leaves No Proof

TRUTH PROOF 2
Beyond The Thinking Mind

CONTENTS

AREA MAP
ACKNOWLEDGEMENTS
PREFACE
INTRODUCTION
DEVILS, DEMONS AND BLOOD SACRIFICE
TRIANGLES AND ELECTRONIC WEAPONS
Earth Sample
Is High Strangeness, Drawing In Or Releasing The Incredible?
Five Days Later
Big Interest On A Small Lane
THE ALL SEEING PHENOMENA
Sub-Surface UFOs
Two Days Later
A Walk Along Blake-Howe Lane
The Hum of Social Media
Paul Prince - Fisherman
THE WATCHERS
Bob Brown's First Warning
7 Days Later: The Warning Is Real For Bob Brown
SHEEP MUTILATIONS
Echoes of the Skin Walker
Similarities Miles Apart
BACK TO BEMPTON
TERROR-FIRMA
COUNTING SHEEP
LIGHTS ABOVE, EYES BELOW
Lightforms
Eyes In The Darkness
BODY IN THE COVE
FLARES OR INTELLIGENT LIGHTFORMS?
Pyrotechnics
No One Knows
Cliff Lane - Christmas Day 2018
BRINGING DOWN THE LIGHT: The Bempton Missing Time
It Never Stopped, It Just Waited
Deer In The Hawthorn
Further Investigations
What Predator?

ROAD KILL OR SATANIC SACRIFICE?
June 2018
No Ordinary Cat
A Clean Cut
INCIDENTAL UFOS
UFO Bigger than a Battleship
UFOs at Christmas
With A Little Help From Social Media
THE PHENOMENON IS ELUSIVE
An Average Day
From Terra Firma To Terror Below The Waves
Porpoises Found
THE COUNTRY PARK DEATHS
An Expert Opinion
WHAT IN THIS WORLD IS GOING ON?
Historic UFO Sighting Off Bempton
Six Miles Off Bempton
Land Lights
A Highly Unusual Night
MORE FLARES THAT NEVER WERE
The Maritime and Coastguard Agency Logs
A Visit To Flamborough Lifeboat Station
IAN RICHARDS' PREDATOR
The Christ Church Ghost
SIGHTING OF THE CAYTON PANTHER
The Filey Lightforms
A Visit to Star Carr
More Big Cat Clues
The Cayton Panther Revisited
UFO at the Carrs
All the Strange Creatures
FILEY'S GOLDEN SANDS
The Filey Lights
A New Contact
Suicide Vehicle
The Filey Dragon
The Tumbling Lightforms
THE WEREWOLF OF FOX WOOD
THE CAYTON CARRS WEREWOLF
MONSTERS ARE REAL

Foxholes Werewolf Sighting on the B1249
Some Things Are Better Left Undiscovered: The Towthorpe Beast
More on the Foxholes Werewolf
WALLABIES AND GIANT LEAPS INTO THE UNBELIEVABLE
The Coffs Coast Connection – New South Wales
The Wallaby Deaths at Sewerby Park Zoo – East Yorkshire
More Australian Animal Deaths
The London Wallabies
The Shell Cove Swamp Wallaby
More Thoughts
Human Understanding
Did the Suspect Change in 2012?
An Unknown Something
THE MONSTERS OF WHARNCLIFFE WOODS
BRITISH BIGFOOT
Growls and Howls in the Night
The Ivy Den Creature
Howls, Figures and Footprints
A STRANGE OWL AND AN UNKNOWN TRUTH
Recent Email From a Reader

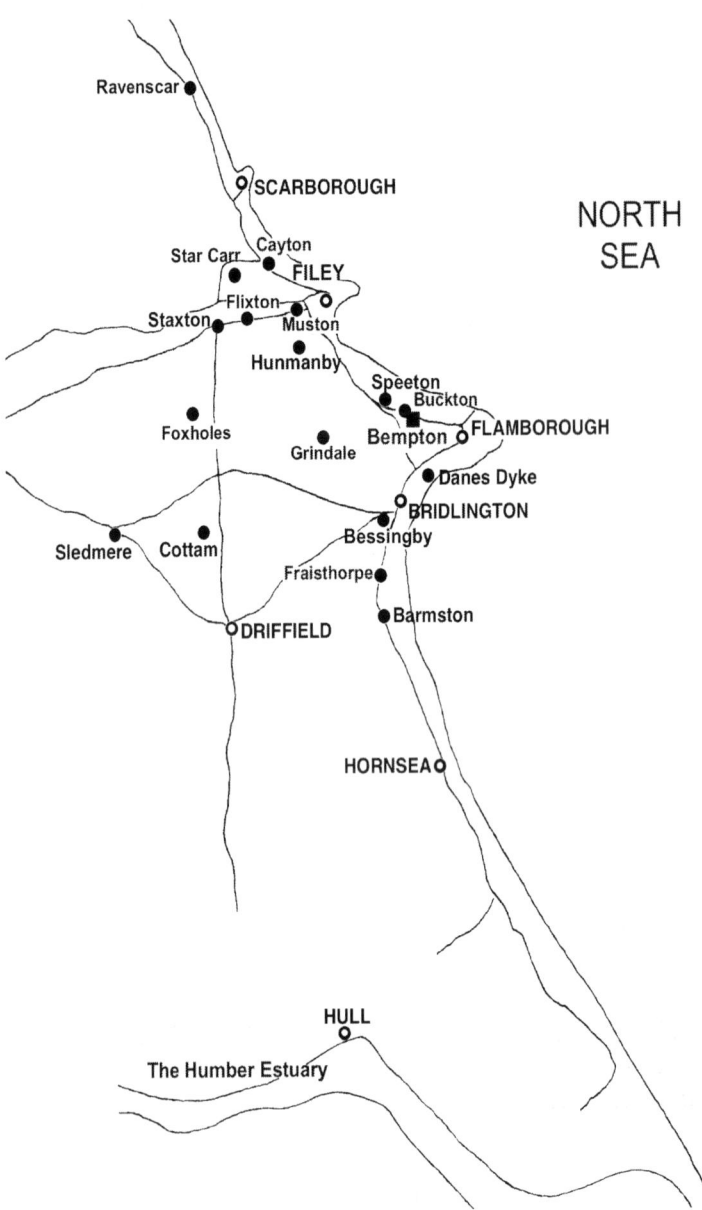

ACKNOWLEDGEMENTS

Truth Proof 3 is not just about my work as a researcher, it is about everyone who has shared their personal accounts and stories with me. I know how hard it is to tell the world about experiences that many people think are impossible; experiences that are often deeply personal and sometimes disturbing. But for me, you did this and I am grateful.

Many people have contributed to the writing of this book, and I want to say thank you to each and every one of you.

To my wife Mary, for putting up with me and allowing me the space and time to devote to the *Truth Proof* research, and to my girls, Sarah, Gemma, Jessica and Laura, who are always there to help in any way that they can.

To my good friend Karl for carefully editing and proof-reading the book, we make a good team. Even when the work goes slowly, the end result is always worth the time invested.

I want to say a few words of thanks to my friend Al Carter, who has helped enormously by also proof-reading the book. Al is always on hand if I need any help or advice, and for that I am very grateful.

Thanks to my good friends Bob Brown, Steve Ashbridge and Andi Ramsden, who have spent so many hours with me in cold and remote locations over the years, I say thank you. Few people understand better than these men, what a thankless task it can be, standing on a cliff-top facing the north sea on a late December night.

Thank you to Les Drake and Christopher Turner for believing in my work; both of these men have been an enormous help. My grateful thanks go to researcher Peter Robbins, who has always supported and encouraged my work. And to author Whitely Strieber, for his continued encouragement and interest.

My special thanks go to radio and talk show host Howard Hughes, who has supported my work from the earliest beginnings, through his many radio shows and podcasts.

Thank you to Deborah Crossley Hatswell, the British Bigfoot researcher, for supplying additional information and sightings of strange creatures seen in the UK, and my grateful thanks go to Professor Robin Allaby for sharing his invaluable views and opinions on the UK wallaby deaths of 2011.

Thank you to all of the witnesses who came forward and shared their experiences with me; in various interviews, emails and discussions over the last few years. Without their input and patience, there would be no book.

Much of *Truth Proof 3* could not have been written without the help and cooperation of local farmers and landowners in my area. Although their exact locations and names have not always been revealed, I thank them all for their invaluable cooperation.

Thank you also to the many people who have travelled from all parts of the country, to spend time in East and North Yorkshire, on the strength of the *Truth Proof* books. I consider many of them as friends, although I dare not mention any names, for fear of missing one out, but they know who they are.

PREFACE

Truth Proof 3 covers many new and exciting accounts from the around East and North Yorkshire. The book also steps out of this local *zone of strangeness* and into other parts of the UK.

This is something that had to happen eventually, partly due to the amazing reports I have received from other parts of the country. Even though they are outside of the locations that I usually research, some of the phenomena seem to be linked to other parts of the UK and even to other parts of the world.

There are locations in East and North Yorkshire where every type of unexplained activity is reported: from UFOs and sightings of big cats and werewolves, to people who experience missing time while walking the cliff-tops of Bempton and Flamborough. Everything is presenting and overlapping, as part of an exotic science that mainstream media and academia fail to understand.

The information I have gathered leaves me in no doubt, that everything seen, experienced and reported is connected. Extraordinary events, however detached they may seem, are repeating time and time again – and I believe location is the key.

Truth Proof 3 highlights the fact that sheep, deer and even porpoises, have all been found in the affected locations, with devastating injuries. My research into these animal mutilations has developed into a much bigger story - a story that is still gathering pace. These terrible crimes against livestock and wild animals highlight the fact that highly unusual events happen at the same time. They leave clues that no one ever thought to look at before, because, at first, they appear so detached from one another.

We may not know how or why, but there appears to be an invisible thread of paranormal life working together within the locations that I call multi-phenomena areas.

In my previous books I wrote about satanic activities that were alleged to have taken place at the former RAF base in Bempton. I now know, without doubt, that the activities that took place in that underground bunker between the 1970s and 1990s were real. Such dark rituals, performed in a multi-phenomena location, may even have enhanced the exotic science that produces some of the things we are seeing today.

I do not claim to have the answers to these mysteries, but *Truth Proof 3* opens up more disturbing avenues of research than ever before.

INTRODUCTION

I did not discover all of these amazing stories until 2018. They appeared to have been happening in connection with each other throughout 2017 and into the new year, and all within a five-mile radius of each other.

They read like some disjointed carnival of the strange. There were strange lights under the sea, mutilated animal carcasses, visits from men in black and even more lightforms seen over land and sea. And I still knew very little about the body that was discovered in the sea cave in November 2017, or what kind of animal had been watching us in the darkness.

All this had been going on throughout the year; but I had to find out for myself, such is the secrecy of people involved, that no one would say a word.

I felt sure there was a link from one to the other, but so far the only link I could find was *location*. And I have always said that 'location is key'.

I never realised, when I was taking soil samples from a farmer's field, that animals were being found mutilated around the area. And why were there American pickup trucks parked on Blake-Howe Lane? They were loaded with military equipment and positioned right in the centre of all the activity.

An aerial map showed just how close these strange events were to one another, but how did they all fit? And if the military were there observing, how did they know? Whatever sophisticated equipment they had brought with them, had to be there for something. Or was that just another coincidence?

I knew that if I wanted to find out what was behind all this, I would be heading into a nameless *outer nowhere*, where exotic phenomena hovers on the fringes of our reality.

For now all I could do was gather information and watch the story develop as the events began to unfold.

DEVILS, DEMONS AND BLOOD SACRIFICE

In the first two *Truth Proof* books, I wrote about satanic practices in and around RAF Bempton - the old radar base near Flamborough on the coast of East Yorkshire. Gathering information was difficult, but it can be found if you look hard enough.

It is an interesting observation that all the people I interviewed about these dark practices at the disused base wanted their real names and identities to be kept out of anything that I published. Does that sound like the normal reaction to something that allegedly never happened? It suggests to me that nothing good ever came from this underground location during those highly secretive years after the RAF finally left in 1972. And now, almost fifty years later, fear and silence still hold people back from talking openly about what took place below ground at RAF Bempton. It is apparent that whatever happened there still makes people feel very uneasy.

I wonder if some of those who were originally involved had lived locally. I'm sure they must have done. The original members of the cult would be quite old now; some of them may have passed away - but their memories still hold power. I find it amazing that, although these dark practices supposedly ended sometime during the mid to late 1990s, twenty-five years later people are still frightened to talk. I am sure there is more information out there still waiting to be discovered.

In early 2018 I was contacted by a 38-year-old woman named Ann who grew up in Bempton village. She told me that during her teenage years she had seen and experienced strange things below the disused radar base. She also put me in touch with several other people who confirmed some of the information she shared. Ann talked about seeing dead animals and birds deep inside the bunker; animals that, in her opinion, had been sacrificed. None of this surprised me.

Years before, I had been told by a very reliable witness about a dog that was found nailed to a crucifix deep inside the bunker. The same witness also spoke of finding a pentagram on the floor, painted in something resembling blood.

I soon realised that agreeing to change the names of witnesses was the only way to guarantee anyone would ever talk to me. Even after all these years the Bempton bunker still had the power to create fear. The effects of whatever happened down there still echo in the minds of those who remember it. I had several conversations with Ann and came away convinced that she was telling me the truth.

Ann:
"Some really weird things were going on inside that bunker in the 1990s and that still makes me feel very nervous - even talking about it today. I don't think it's ever gone away Paul. It's just not a nice place, I'm not sure it ever has been."

Ann has not been back to the village for at least fifteen years, and she could not tell me with any certainty whether the people who knew about the activities still live there.

Ann:
"We were teenagers when we first went into the tunnels; we were kids searching for thrills and adventure. Growing up in the village we all heard little bits about what was happening up on the old RAF base. Our parents would talk about it from time to time, I suppose we all thought it was exciting. 'An underground bunker where people went to do devil worship!' That's what we thought anyway. Our parents weren't joking though when they told us never to go there."

Ann told me that even though her parents had warned her never to go near the base, she said lots of kids from Bempton and Flamborough were drawn to it. It was almost like a rite of passage for them. The village had nothing to entertain its youth and the old RAF base was an exciting place to explore. It is interesting to note that most of the people I have spoken with about the strange activities at RAF Bempton no longer live in the village. I'm not sure what that tells us, but very few people who still live there are willing to talk.

One of the people Ann put me in touch with was a man named Joe, who now lives in Scarborough. He told me that he went to the base many times during his teenage years, and that he once found real evidence that something connected with the occult was happening there.

Joe:
"The whole village was nervous in those days. No one really knew exactly what was going on or who was involved, you could do anything around those cliff-tops and no one would ever know. We went up there once in the winter, me and a few mates. We intended lighting a fire and drinking cider, but we didn't hang around for long. There was people already down there, deep inside. We couldn't hear what they were saying, but it sounded like a chant or a repetitive song. Someone I was with shouted the swear word 'w*nkers' - at least I think that's what he shouted - and the voices suddenly stopped.

We expected to see torchlights and hear people approaching, but we heard nothing. Everything just fell silent. It was really weird, but knowing there was people down there was even scarier than if we had been chased out. It felt like we were in a horror film. We hung around a good distance away, half-expecting someone to emerge, but nothing happened.

Another time we found an old steel box in one of the rooms and when we opened it, it was full of robes and hoods. They had even made an altar. We also found knives and candlesticks. It's scary just thinking about it now. Most of the village knew about the devil worshippers, but no one ever dared to speak about them openly because no one knew who was involved."

These types of stories have come out from the 1970s to the mid-1990s, from people of all ages; some who were teenagers at the time and others who will now be very old. All of them share one thing: fear. It is a fear borne of knowing something dark and sinister was happening.

For a few years Joe's family kept animals on some rented land close to the base. This meant that spending time near the base was unavoidable. Joe told me that the landowner was always very guarded and defensive whenever they spoke about anything connected to the base. He warned Joe to never go near it, under any circumstances. He even told him that it was extremely dangerous below ground, because the floors had been destroyed in various places to discourage unwanted visitors. Joe told me that his father was also very suspicious of the landowner and thought he knew much more than he ever let on.

The underground bunker was still accessible as late as 2010. I will never understand why the entrance was never fully sealed. Sealing it would have been the best solution to stop these activities, which had been going on since the 1970s. I wonder why that never happened?

Joe had recalled entering a room in the tunnels beneath the base and finding robes and hoods stored in a steel chest on the floor. His account is very similar to another I wrote about in TP2 where the witness also found a well-made robe and hood. Joe also told me it was not uncommon to see people walking towards the base during the night. While groups of teenagers from the village would sit drinking alcohol close to the base, Joe said they would sometimes see groups of people entering the underground bunker.

The strangest part of these accounts is the fact that not one person living in the village has been recognised as being involved. But perhaps this is because everyone seen entering the bunker appears to have done so under the cover of darkness.

Joe is of the opinion that the bunker was at one time connected by a long passageway to the nearby RAF base at Speeton. This is something I have heard on numerous occasions from other people. It is also interesting to note that both bases are in a line with RAF Staxton Wold, which, as the crow flies, is about ten miles away from the old Bempton base. In fact I have also been told, by a contact who still works in an official capacity, that the two bases *were* once linked. They said that below ground, the passageway linking the bases was sealed by sixteen metres of concrete. If this is true then it must have been done prior to 1970, whilst the RAF were still on the site.

I think it is interesting that they said 'metres' and not 'feet and inches'. At that time in the UK we only used imperial measurements, so people would have used feet and inches and not metres. However, this should not detract from the fact that I have been told about the underground passageway on more than one occasion, by people totally unconnected to each other.

Another contact of mine, an ex-military police officer who was there in the years when the base was operational, also confirmed that many rooms and passageways below ground were bricked up and rendered over before the RAF left Bempton.

But while on the subject of Staxton Wold, another interesting story worth mentioning was told to me many years ago by a plumbing engineer who once worked there as a private contractor. He told me he was amazed to see trucks arrive at the base and they were carrying large coils of plastic tubing. He said that there was miles of the stuff and he saw it unloaded from the trucks and taken into a small single story building that had no windows. To this day he still cannot understand where all of the tubing he saw taken into that tiny building had disappeared to.

Someone who once worked at Staxton Wold, told me that he worked there on 'level six' and said there were other levels below that. So although information about other rooms and levels below these military installations was never meant to be known, the puzzle remains. Of course, none of this has anything to do with the subject of satanic practice at RAF Bempton, but the information does suggest there is much more below ground at these bases than first appears.

Discovering dead animals, robes and hoods; along with knives and candlesticks, in pitch black rooms hidden deep below the earth is a long way from anything considered normal. Unless the residents of Bempton and the surrounding villages were lying, something unnatural took place throughout this twenty-five year period. I wonder if the people, who used the bunker in this way, knew that the area was already charged with high strangeness? Did their activities somehow attract even more of the phenomena from the place I call the outer nowhere?

I think everything around the area has the potential to be touched by the phenomena. Perhaps we are victims of our own emotions, or victims of circumstances, trip-wiring the silent intelligence that walks in high strangeness?

There must have been a reason for these blood rituals and animal sacrifices. They are a taboo someone obviously thought was worth hiding if the end result was an otherworldly experience. No one seems to know how many people were involved. I don't think a group of people from outside of the village could have done this alone. Someone local to Bempton must have been involved. Perhaps it could even be a secret handed down through one family; a family that is still local to the area?

Various words have been used to describe these dark activities over the years, but what do these descriptions actually mean? A 'satanic cult', a 'band of devil worshippers', people 'practicing witchcraft'? Was it any of these or was there something else entirely going on? Do any of these descriptions fit the people who practiced their dark art below ground at RAF Bempton? The word occult is derived from the word 'occultus'; a latin word meaning hidden or disguised. It also describes the pursuit of supernatural knowledge, power and dark magic.

No one has ever told me exactly what type of magic was practised at Bempton, if it even was magic, but pockets of these highly organised groups are found all over the world. The secretive nature of this most dark of human pastimes has made finding any information relating to it virtually impossible. That changed in September 2018 after I met a middle-aged man from Scarborough who told me that the Bempton bunker was used as a 'Temple of Thelema'. He said the people who used it were practising sex magic. He would not say if this happened between the 1970s and 90s, but he was sure the group were active at Bempton for a number of years.

My knowledge of this subject was limited, but I learned that it was something to do with the occultist Aleister Crowley, who wanted to develop Thelema as a new religion in the early 1900s. This information was a new development, but my contact was very protective of the information he shared and at times seemed quite frightened to tell me the true extent of what he knew. He believed that some who frequented the bunker went further down the path of black magic than others. He spoke about the creation and use of a skin-covered book called the 'Black Pullet of Satan', and suggested that in the right hands many strange things could have been evoked and brought into reality below the earth at Bempton.

I am not sure what to think about all this talk of bizarre rituals and black magic, but the part of me that has seen and experienced incredible things knows not to dismiss anything out of hand. Perhaps something that started out as an experiment turned into something much more spectacular and dangerous. The ingredients of high strangeness have always been present around this part of the country, so adding a magical element to the mix could have enhanced an already potent phenomenon.

Imagine the reaction of someone who had gone to the cliff-tops at Bempton with the intention of 'summoning' a UFO, then finding a row of orange orbs appear over the sea. They might think they were responsible for this appearance. But what if something like that *had* happened in the early years for the people using the Bempton bunker, something that was so incredible that they continued going there for decades? Their use of a magical book of talismans may have just been a placebo, but it might have been enough to give them the impression they were involved in a phenomenon that has always been there.

In TP1 and TP2 I looked into how people involved in a satanic cult at Bempton might have gained access to the bunker, but managed to remain undetected. The nearby RSPB nature reserve is in close proximity to the old base and is usually devoid of people after 6pm. If the cult was real, and I believe it was, turning up at the nature reserve, especially under the cover of darkness, would give the easiest route to access the base.

On May 21st 2018 I received piece of information that added another twist to the story; the suggestion of a second entrance to the Bempton bunker via a hidden sea-cave.

My contact holds a position of importance within the *Maritime and Coastguard Agency* (MCA) and I believe they are highly reliable. But I need to be extra careful about how I describe what I was told, for two reasons; 1: I intend going with them to this secret entrance when they are next in East Yorkshire. 2: it appears to be in a very dangerous place, and if I gave away its approximate location I would not want anyone to risk their own life trying to find it.

The geology of the coastal landscape at Bempton certainly supports the possibility of sea caves that begin at the cliffs and extend miles inland. There are literally hundreds of these caves along the Yorkshire coast;

some were even used for smuggling in years gone by. One of them is known as the 'Rudston church cave' which sits underneath the foghorn station at Flamborough and is said to extend inland many miles. My good friend, an angler named Andy Barmby, has been into the entrance, but he could not get very far because it has a deep channel full of water. Locals say it runs inland right up to All Saints Church at Rudston. If this is correct then it stretches ten miles inland.

The cave I would like to find is said to have been used by the Ministry of Defence as an auxiliary weapons storage area. I am told there is a heavy steel door at the back of the cave and from there it is said to connect to the Bempton bunker. It was recently rediscovered sometime during 2016 by urban explorers during the making of a movie.

Local fishermen agree that the cave exists, however, I don't think it is a viable place for regular entry to the inland bunker. The tiny cove where the cave is found can only be accessed by boat, or on foot during an exceptionally low tide, and the sea around this stretch of coastline is very dangerous and unpredictable. I doubt anyone would risk taking out a small boat so close to the rocks and to venture there at low tide would almost certainly mean being cut off by the rising tide on their return journey.

I guess time will tell whether I discover if this cave exists or not, but I don't think it is an impossibility.

Examples of the occult symbols found below ground at the old base

TRIANGLES AND ELECTRONIC WEAPONS

On Monday June 15th 2017 I had received a phone call from my good friend of many years, Ian Wilson. Ian lives on the outskirts of Bempton in a village called Buckton. He had called to tell me about a strange triangular formation he had seen in a field during his early morning walk that same day. He was puzzled by its sudden appearance and said that whatever caused it must have done so over the weekend, because he could not recall seeing it there the week before. He had suggested that I meet him and see for myself. Unexplained phenomena in a pea-field didn't really sound that inspiring, but looking back I see this was the start of a much more detailed picture of events beginning to emerge.

Three weeks later I was told about a flying black triangle, seen by a dog walker on the cliff-tops at Speeton, just three miles up the coast. The Speeton sighting was a strange one. The witness says she only saw the object for a few seconds as it passed between the cliffs of a cove. She claimed to have seen enough to confirm that it was triangular, but said it was flying so low and so close to the cliff-face that she never got to see it again.

Impression of the black triangular-shaped object shown here below Speeton's 400ft cliffs - July 2017

15

Could this sighting and the shape seen in the pea-field be connected? The Speeton sighting also had an extra element that I have never heard anyone report before; the witness said she saw the object from above. When people usually report seeing UFOs they only ever see the underside, but the dog walker had been on the cliff-top and was looking down on it. She described the object as looking like black Teflon and completely flat with angled edges. I wonder how many other people have observed a UFO from above?

Earth Sample
June 16th 2017

Ian Wilson had not actually seen anything in the sky that morning in June, but his description of the triangular shape in the pea-crop intrigued me enough to want to see it.

I arranged to meet up with him the next day, and at 5.30am on the dot I pulled up outside Ian's house with Wolfy, my little dog. Ian was already waiting outside and a short time later we were heading in the direction of Cliff Lane. The field in question is close to Bempton Chalet Park, a caravan site off Cliff Lane. It is a big field that sweeps up and down in gentle slopes.

Ian:
"Wait 'til you see this."

Ian stopped in front of a large gap in the hedgerow and he pointed towards the top of the field.

Ian:
"It's up there Paul, near the top. Can you see it?"

I could see it instantly. The thick green pea-crop was about twelve to fifteen inches high, but in the middle of the field, for all to see, was a large brown triangle of bare earth. It was sharply defined and exactly as he had described it. It looked as though someone had cut a shape, clean out of the crop. I took a few photos and decided that I would go back the following day to collect a soil sample.

Ian:
"All I can say Paul, is that I don't think it was there last week. If it was, I'm sure I would have noticed it.
You're going to think I'm daft now as well..."

Ian looked at me for a second or two. He seemed a bit unsure if he should speak.

Paul:
"What do you mean?"

Ian:
"Well, I keep feeling as though I'm been watched. Every time I come up here, around this part of the road and up towards the cliffs, it's like I can feel there are eyes on me."

Bare triangle of earth in the field of pea-crop, as photographed from a distance.

I didn't reply; for no other reason than I did not want to say too much and make him feel more unsettled than he already did. If I had, it could have also gone the other way around and he might have thought I was nuts. Ian knew I had written *Truth Proof*, a book about all things unexplained, but I had never gone into any detail with him about my own paranormal experiences during childhood. If I had said he should always trust his own instincts, I would have probably had to answer more questions. At that moment it was a path I did not want to go down.

I looked up towards the top of the field. He was right about the distinct triangular shape imprinted in the earth. I could not imagine how the crop could have grown like that, but it was enough of a mystery to make me want to investigate further. Something must have caused or affected the soil so much that nothing would grow, so I knew I had to collect a soil sample.

At first light the next day I found myself back in Bempton. I parked up near to the White Horse pub and proceeded to walk up Cliff Lane; armed with a bag, a small trowel, my camera, and Wolfy the dog. By about 5.35am Wolfy and I were standing at the edge of the pea-field. I remember looking up towards the barren triangle of earth in the field closest to Blake-Howe Lane and thinking I would be up there in no time. That was the first mistake I made that morning. The field was deceptively huge. I could clearly see the clean-cut shape close to the top and began walking along the hedgerow which separated the pea-crop from the adjoining chalet park. The large hawthorn hedge ran all the way along the site so I doubt anyone in the caravans would have noticed me. However, by the time I reached the pea-field I realised I had misjudged the height of the crop.

I discovered it was closer to two feet high and very dense. That was my second mistake. I looked around and could see no sign of Wolfy, but I could see slight movement in the crop. He was struggling to keep up. I'm sure he wouldn't have been able to see a thing in the dense vegetation and would eventually have got lost. He is my wife's dog and I dare not risk losing him. I think if she had to make a choice between me or little Wolfy, she would pick the dog. I say that with a smile, but I had not come this far to turn around and go home because of him. I reached down into the crop and picked him up.

With Wolfy safely tucked under my arm I continued to walk up the side of the field. I am always respectful of crops and I did not have permission to be on the land, so rather than walk through the plants, I ploughed on through the nettles and thistles until I reached the top of the field. Once there my eyes scanned the tops of the pea-crop; I could not see anything resembling a triangle of earth. The field rises up on a gentle slope and the shape of bare earth I was looking for must have been lost in the contours of the land. I decided to walk along the hedgerow bordering the top of the field, thinking it would come into view at some point, but it was hopeless. I couldn't see a thing.

I wish I had kept my eyes fixed firmly on the area. By carrying the dog and negotiating nettles, brambles and hawthorn I had lost sight of the triangle. I knew if I was ever going to find it I would have to walk back down the field until it came into view.

I made my way back down a tractor track in the middle of the field. I had avoided that route earlier because I did not want to be seen, but I was not about to not leave empty-handed. Half way down the field I could see the triangle of earth beginning to emerge from the crop, I would not lose sight of it a second time. But it was deceiving, because from Cliff Lane it looked very close to the top of the field. In fact, it was a considerable distance away.

It was now almost 6am and, to my surprise, I saw a large silver four-wheel drive pickup truck pull up on the road below. Two men, who I believe must have been farmers, got out of the vehicle and just stood there watching me. I must have looked an odd sight. As you can imagine, they were the last thing I wanted to see; as I stood in the middle of a pea-field at 6am with a little dog called Wolfy tucked under my arm. How was I going to explain this? I turned away from them and headed back up the field in the direction of the triangle of earth. I figured I was going to get caught anyway, so I might as well get what I came for. I decided to tell them that I was there because the dog had ran into the field and got lost. It was all I could think of.

When I looked back I could see that their pickup was pulling away; it took a right turn and went down the dirt track known as Blake-Howe Lane. They must have thought I intended to come out of the field that way. Wrong. I quickly gathered my soil sample, then turned and ran back down the tractor track and onto Cliff Lane. Looking back up the field, in the distance, I could see the roof of their silver pickup above the hedge on Blake-Howe Lane. I am sure they were waiting for me to emerge at the top of the field. I just had to hope I could get back to my car before they realised I had doubled back. It was hardly the crime of the century, but I wanted to avoid explaining why I was there.

Well I made it back to tell the tale, soil sample and all. In fact the soil is still in a filing cabinet at home; next to various other items of potential unexplained treasure. At some point in the future, I am sure an opportunity will arise to have the soil sample tested.

Ian's discovery of the triangle in the pea-crop was the first domino to fall in a succession of strange events around Cliff Lane - events that no one was ever supposed to connect.

The sighting of the black triangle travelling below the cliff-top at Speeton is similar to reports from the past. People have seen strange black triangles moving around these cliffs for many years. My question is: why Bempton and Speeton? What is unique about that area? We may never know for sure whether the Speeton sighting and the shape in the field were connected, but the two were seen around the same time and the distance between them is less than three miles, so I think both reports have to be considered.

The cliff-top sighting at Speeton brought to mind a conversation from February 2017, when I was told about a river that allegedly runs *beneath* the Yorkshire Wolds and meets the sea, somewhere below Bempton and Speeton. As unbelievable as this sounds, if there is even a single grain of truth to the story, then it might explain why there is more activity in this particular area. Perhaps this also connects with the lightforms I discussed in TP1 and TP2 and my suspicions that they travel beneath the sea to avoid detection.

I first heard about the underground river from Gordon Anderson who lives in Cayton. He told me that one of his friends, a lady named Gillian, had a story that she wanted to share. Gordon gave me a rough outline, along with the lady's age and background, and although it did sound a little far-fetched, I agreed to speak with her.

I called Gillian later that same day and what she told me was very interesting. I had certainly never heard anything like it before. I cannot say if there is any truth in what she shared, but I have no reason to doubt her. I also think the strange details of our conversation are worth including here because of their connection to Bempton and Speeton.

Gillian:
"When I was a little girl my father used to work on a farm for a large estate on the North Yorkshire Wolds. It was a close knit community where the men who worked the land rarely ventured out of their own area. People would talk about all sorts of things; mostly related to the land and livestock, but I can remember my father and other farm-hands talking about seeing small submarines."

Paul:
"What did you say?"

My eyebrows raised as soon as I heard her say submarines. The North Yorkshire Wolds are the last place I expect someone to have seen a submarine. I actually think you would have more chance of seeing a UFO than a small submarine. But no matter how unlikely it sounded, that was exactly what Gillian was telling me. I saw no point in questioning her claims at this early stage in our conversation so I just let her story unfold.

Gillian:
"That's what they said Paul. They had seen a small submarine surface in an area of water around Foxholes, just north of Langtoft. I am not that good at geography, so I don't even know if there are any large areas of water there, but I am certain they said it was around Foxholes.

My father did not lie and it was common knowledge amongst the local farming community. If he said he saw them then I believe him. I don't know the exact place, but it was in a lake or a pond. They spoke about seeing it on more than one occasion and it was a long, long time ago. I was about 8 years old when I first heard about it and I am 83 now, so it was a long time ago. I don't know when submarines were first invented, but the men always called them small submarines.

I am sure they were telling the truth. Why else would grown men talk about seeing such things? They said they came up from an underground river from the sea, somewhere close to Bempton Cliffs"

Paul:
"An underground river you say?"

Gillian:
"Yes. I never found out why it was there or how anyone knew about it, but I will never forget my father and other farmers talking about these small submarines that surfaced in the water. My father talked about it when I was a little girl and in later years. His story never changed. He talked about submarines that travelled along an underground river; a river that flowed into the sea somewhere around Bempton and Speeton."

This was quite an incredible tale and it was one that I didn't really believe. It is true that nothing would surprise me about this area, but a submarine, travelling at least fifteen miles inland from the sea and surfacing on the Wolds, took some believing. Could there really be an underground river flowing out to sea at Bempton?

The cliffs at Flamborough, Bempton and Speeton are littered with sea caves, so I suppose some of them must be under water. Objects have been seen leaving and entering the sea off this coast before, so could some of these secrets be subsurface?

Is High Strangeness, Drawing In Or Releasing The Incredible?

Collecting my soil sample from the triangle of earth in the pea-field was the start of a series of unusual events that I think were connected in some inexplicable way. I did not discover the full extent of what was happening until the very end of 2017; New Year's Day 2018 to be exact.

Some of the unusual events of 2017 had been deliberately hushed-up throughout the year. I am not saying they were being withheld from me specifically, because I very much doubt those involved even knew I was actively investigating the area, but those directly affected just did not want outsiders knowing what was happening. I am referring to some unusual deaths of livestock in the area, which I had no knowledge of at this stage in my investigations.

As usual, I was looking into a catalogue of the strange and just when I thought it could not get any stranger, I discovered that I was wrong. Something truly horrific was happening locally, something that only a few people in the area were aware of. It had been occurring alongside my own research throughout 2017, but all the while I had been totally unaware of it. The craziest part was that no one wanted to talk about it, outside of their own small circle of friends. Many of the strange incidents from 2017 were not immediately obvious, but they carried ripples of the surreal throughout the year. I was about to learn that they were components of an even larger unknown something.

Ian Wilson usually walked Cliff Lane most days of the week; morning or night, depending on the weather or his work pattern. After my triangle of earth adventure, I began doing more early morning walks in the affected area, alone and with Ian.

Many things that had seemed of no importance suddenly became interesting. One thing that Ian noticed was that as he approached the brow of Cliff Lane his phone went dead, even when he was only listening to pre-recorded music that did not need a signal. This was a new development that I admit I did not think much about at the time. Ian had always said that he got an uneasy feeling in that area, like he was being observed. But it would have been impossible for anyone to hide, with open fields on either side of Cliff Lane, so I wondered what had created those feelings of unease. It wasn't long before I understood what he was talking about.

On Thursday June 28th, Ian called me to say he had come across a deer carcass on Cliff Lane, close the RSPB nature reserve. I suppose it could have been hit by a car and nothing I can say would prove otherwise, but he had observed something that made me think a vehicle accident was not responsible for the animal's death.

Ian:
"The deer had a large neat three-inch round hole in its side Paul."

The description he gave later was that it looked as though a core drill had ran through it. Core drills are designed to remove a cylinder or plug of material, usually from masonry or timber.

Later that day I drove along Cliff Lane but couldn't find any trace of a deer carcass. I did find an area of flattened vegetation by an entrance to a field, but nothing to suggest a large animal had been lying there. There was no trace of blood or fur anywhere near the place Ian had said he found the carcass.

**Cliff Lane:
showing the site of the deer carcass
found by Ian Wilson**

Five Days Later
July 3rd 2017

The following Monday evening, Ian phoned me again. He wanted to tell me about something else that had happened to him on one of his morning walks. It was something that made him feel so uneasy that he could not talk about it in detail until we were face to face. He stressed that I would be very interested in this new development.

To receive so many calls from Ian was quite unusual. He has never been a man who makes unusual claims, so if he tells me something I take it seriously. I agreed to meet him at 6am the following morning; we could do the cliff-top walk and he could tell me what had made him feel so unsettled. Anyone who knows this man as I do, would realise that he does not get so easily rattled, and that is what makes his story all the more convincing. Plus, I still wanted to see the photo he had taken on his phone of the deer carcass. There is nothing normal about finding an animal with three-inch hole in its side.

Morning arrived and we found ourselves back on Cliff Lane. The sky was dull and overcast, and out to sea the horizon was lost in fog. We stopped at the entrance to the pea-field; the triangle of earth was just the same. The crop had grown thicker, but we could still see the patch of barren earth. I remember wondering what could have caused it, because at this point I had no knowledge of the flying triangle seen by the dog walker at Speeton cliffs.

I thought about the morning I had collected the soil sample and wondered which of the farmers in the area owned a large silver pickup truck. Why were they on the road at such an early hour? But then, I suppose they were thinking the same about me. I stood with Ian and we looked up the field towards where the farmers had stopped to watch me; I must have looked an odd sight that morning. I began retelling Ian what had happened. I was reliving the experience one last time before the crop was harvested and the triangle of earth was erased forever.

If it were not for my research, I doubt anyone except the people directly involved would ever know the full details. The happenings were so detached that no one would have ever made a connection.

We walked another quarter of a mile along the lane and Ian stopped.

Ian:
"This is where my phone cuts out every time now, just this spot Paul. It works fine if I walk on a bit."

He was right. The music on his phone suddenly cut dead when we reached the affected area. We walked a little further up the lane and Ian stopped again and then turned to the left. The skeletal remains of RAF Bempton loomed out of the mist like something from a horror film.

Ian:
"This is where I found the deer Paul, it was laying in the side of the field. I don't think it had been there long. I suppose it could have been hit by a car, but it didn't look like that to me. It just had a nice neat hole in its side. I saw no other injuries to suggest it had been in an accident."

He pointed down to the grass, which looked a bit flattened, but apart from that everything seemed normal. We searched for anything that might suggest a collision had occurred, but there was nothing: no blood, no fur, or any sign that something terrible had happened. The surface of the road was free of tyre marks and the place he found the deer was not even on the edge of the road; it was inside the entrance to the field. I would have seen it though, had it been there when I went to look. I suppose it is possible that the farmer could have moved it, or perhaps some of the staff at the RSPB.

Paul:
"If it had been knocked down by a car, that still would not explain the hole in its side."

Ian was right. I guess it is something we will never know, but I was still keen to see the photo he had taken. Ian had described a hole in the animal's body that looked as though a core-drill had ran through it. In his words, it was the size of cutter used for a gas boiler flue. If that is correct it would have been about three inches round. I cannot imagine how such an injury could occur from a collision with a car, and what kind of machine might do that to an animal on a remote country lane?

Paul:
"Well at least you got a photo of it Ian; I want to see that hole in its side for myself now."

Ian raised his eyebrows and shook his head.

Ian:
"Not any more Paul. I did have a picture, but I haven't got one now. That is part of the reason I called you last night. What I'm going to tell you next gets strange. I came up here as usual early yesterday morning and got roughly to where we are stood now."

Ian pointed to the RAF buildings in the distance.

Ian:
"I looked over towards the old base, I always do. I'm not sure why, but my eyes are always drawn to it. I could see something that looked like one of them big American motorhomes parked up there. It was very big and it looked out of place, but that's not the only thing that looked odd. There were men up there in white overalls; I saw at least three. I'm not sure what they were doing, carrying things I think, but that's only my guess. I was just shocked to see anyone on the base at that hour. And what happened next made me turn and head back home."

I looked to where he was pointing and wondered what people in white overalls could have been doing. There is nothing left of the former RAF base above ground, except for a handful of derelict buildings, and the underground bunker has been sealed off since the disappearance of a young man in 2010. It made no sense.

Ian:
"No kidding Paul. They were dressed in white overalls, just like those guys on a CSI clean-up operation."

I believed Ian, but could not understand how a motorhome could have got onto the base. In 2014 I remember contacting the farmer who owned the land, to ask if I could go up there to take pictures for my new book. He gave me permission as long as I told him when I was going to be up there. The road was in a terrible state when I visited.

It had deep water-filled furrows that would have been impossible to negotiate with anything less than a four-wheel drive vehicle. Something had definitely changed since I was last there. I suppose they could have repaired the road leading to the base, unless Ian was wrong about what he saw. I asked him what happened that was so unnerving that he decided to turn back and go home.

Ian:
"Paul, I remember you asking me to try and get some pictures if I ever saw anything out of the ordinary. So I got my phone out and decided to do just that. I aimed it towards the three men to take a picture, but all of a sudden, loads of lines appeared across the screen. A bit like you would get on an old television if you tried to tune it in. The next thing, I saw everything on my phone flashing up on the screen; pictures, texts, everything. No kidding. It was just like someone was going through my phone at lightning speed. Then it went dead and it was 100% flat. When I got home and put it on charge, I discovered that everything on my phone had been erased. Explain that one Paul."

Of course, I couldn't explain it any more than I could explain all the other things that were happening, but I did believe him. It was another twist in a fast developing mystery.

Everything and nothing about the location surprises me. It is almost like there is a sleeping giant that has gone unnoticed for a long time. Over the years the different things that have happened are rarely talked about, if ever. And if they are, they are soon forgotten. The area is so remote that you have to ask yourself; 'who even knows that anything is happening?'

A perfect triangle of earth in pea-crop, a dead deer with a perfect hole in its side *and* men in white overalls. All this was occurring around the same area within weeks and months of each other - and no one would have ever known if Ian had not taken the time to contact me. Something was unfolding in 2017, opening and closing like the wings of a butterfly, in short bursts of 'amazing' and no one, except those directly involved, had any clue beyond their own personal experiences.

Locations of the three men in white overalls seen on the deserted base at 6:10am

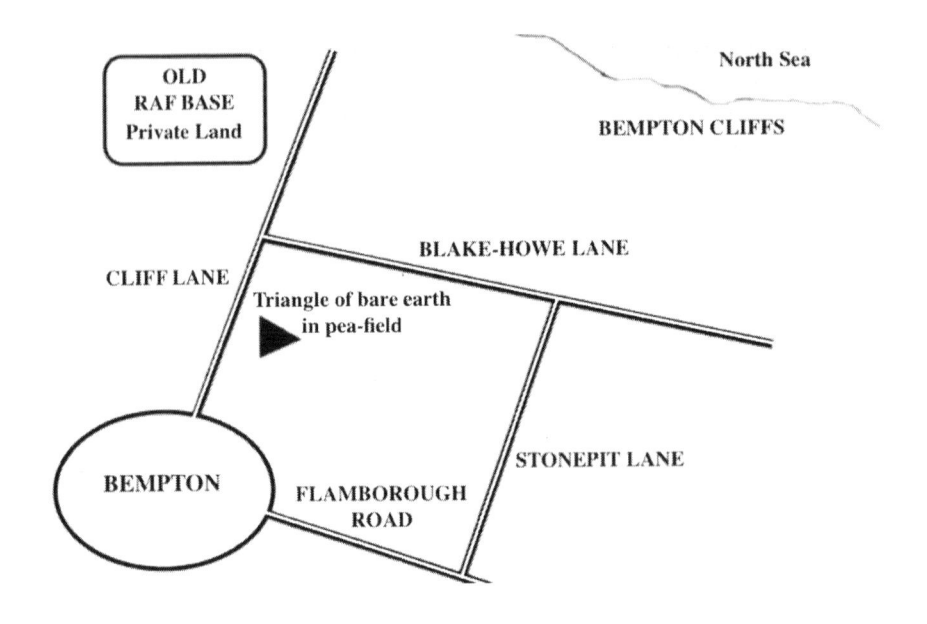

Big Interest On A Small Lane
July 25th 2017

Ian was not the only person to witness strange things around Bempton and Flamborough in July 2017. On Tuesday 25th I received a phone call at 11.30am from a local man named David Hinde. David wanted to tell me about an unusual vehicle he had observed, less than half an hour before calling me. He said it was on the back road between Flamborough and Bempton and stressed that it looked very unusual. He suggested that I should go and check it out before it left the area completely. After his phone call I jumped into my car and headed out towards Bempton. David's description of the mystery vehicle sounded like nothing I had ever seen before and I wanted to see it for myself.

Sure enough, when I arrived it was still parked up exactly where David had said, and he was right, it did look highly unusual. I did not expect to see a dark blue American pickup truck with German number plates parked on the back lane between Bempton and Flamborough. On the back of the pickup was a huge square box unit that was painted green, and the box had steel flaps around the top that were folded down. It had two narrow glass windows in the front and small triangles on its sides that were painted red. I found out later that these red triangles were stencils used by the US Air Force.

The two narrow glass windows looked yellow, unless the interior was slightly illuminated and they were glowing yellow from inside the box unit. Behind the pickup was a large trailer that looked fully loaded and it had a camouflage tarpaulin covering it. I was informed later that week that this was a generator. But that was not my main focus of interest with this vehicle. On top of the box unit was a large dish that was tilted towards the sky at an angle of about 45%. I want to say that it was a radar dish, but I don't think it was. I took a few random photos as I passed, then turned the car around and attempted to take a few more.

It had started to rain and it was difficult try and take photographs while I was driving, but I did the best I could. When I arrived back home I decided to send the images to some friends who are military and ex-military.

Their opinions were that it could have been some kind of microwave device. *"That's some serious shit"* was how one of the guys described it, adding that he also thought it was something to do with microwaves.

I went back the following day but the strange pickup and trailer had gone. However, I suspected the vehicles were still in the area and the only place they could have gone, if they wanted to remain discreet, was to nearby Stonepit Lane. It wasn't really rocket science, because this was the only other road close to where they had been the day before, and no one, except the farmers who work the land, ever use that road. Thankfully, my suspicions proved correct. The pickup and trailer had only moved half a mile, and they were parked at the other end of Blake-Howe Lane, which just happens to come out onto Stonepit Lane. Was it just coincidence that they were now in close proximity to the triangle of earth in the pea-crop?

Months later I purchased the November edition of Air Forces Monthly, a military aviation magazine. Page 92 was particularly interesting. One of their readers had sent in two images of a vehicle similar to the one I had seen and photographed. The pictures were taken near Staxton Wold, the RAF base near Scarborough, which is around twelve miles from Bempton. Whoever sent the images to Air Forces Monthly had asked if anyone knew what these vehicles were. The editorial staff responded by saying they believed they could be something called *SAM Emulators*, although they said they were not certain.

I have since been told there is a strong possibility that what I saw was an electronic weapon, although my highly qualified contact could not understand why they would have been on a back road near Bempton.

THE ALL SEEING PHENOMENA

Whenever I visit Bempton cliffs I am always quite focused on trying to obtain footage of the lightforms. After I had seen the strange American pickup truck, I found myself back at Bempton cliffs later that same evening. This time I took with me my good friend Bob Brown, the host of *Beacon of Light Radio*.

Bob is a few years older than me and was recovering from knee surgery, so I had no plans to walk miles and miles along the cliff-tops, like I usually do. Having said that, we did cover some ground as we made our way up past the old RAF base and on towards Speeton; where we stopped at the cliffs to take in the incredible views. Speeton cliffs are a sheer drop, four hundred feet down into the North Sea. This is the same area the dog walker had seen the flying black triangle. As we walked along, I told Bob about this recent sighting, since we were so close to the location.

We still had good light and the weather and sea conditions were calm. I remember pointing out an old ships boiler, which we could see resting on the rocks below. It was a sad reminder of how many ships had come to a tragic end off this stretch of coastline in the early part of the century. Perhaps one day I will write about some of these unfortunate vessels that have come to rest below the mighty cliffs.

Suddenly my mobile phone began to ring - which was unusual in itself, as I never normally get a signal at Speeton. It was a number I did not recognise.

Caller:
"Hello. Is that Paul Sinclair?"

I said yes and asked how I could help.

Caller:
"I found your name and number on the internet; you're the UFO guy, yes?"

I told the man he had the right person, and said I would love to hear what he had to say.

Caller:
"I need to tell you about something that happened yesterday evening. I live in Garton-on-the-Wolds. When my daughter arrived home she told me she had seen two UFOs. Paul, I need to tell you that I believe her 100%. She never says anything like this, she never has."

I wish I had been at home when the man called me, instead of standing on top of the cliffs at Speeton. I wanted to ask him if we could talk another time, but experience has taught me to gather as much information as possible when someone contacts me for the first time. I have spoken to so many people over the years, who are very enthusiastic about recalling a UFO encounter, but then decide they do not want to talk about it the next day. I realised that, despite my surroundings, I had to gather as much information as possible while the man was on the phone. Bob didn't mind. After all, he had come up to Bempton hoping to see or experience something unusual. I suppose this was unusual.

Caller:
"My daughter was driving from Sledmere back home to Garton when she saw them. I wouldn't normally call anyone but this really shook her up. She described one as a huge black cigar-shaped UFO with a glowing red line running through its middle. She said the red line was glowing or illuminated. She thought the other was the moon, until it moved and faded away."

It certainly sounded as though she had seen something amazing, and I told her father that I was very interested to learn more and maybe even see the photos. But I had to explain that I was out on the cliff-tops near the old RAF base at Bempton and only had a poor signal, so I said I would try and call him back if the phone went dead. I explained that his daughter's sighting might even tie in with things that had been seen locally in recent weeks, and that military-style pickup trucks had also been in the area.

Caller:
"Mmm...well, this was a really clear sighting Paul. She described them as looking huge. She was able to get a couple of pictures on her phone

*Two anomalies: not the moon, but a huge lightform
& above, the red light of the UFO seen by the caller's daughter.*

... But there is something else, not another UFO, but something odd that might be connected with what you have just mentioned. There is an American army jeep of some kind parked in a field just outside of Sledmere. It's a big pickup-type thing and it has a big box on the back with some sort of satellite dish or something on the top of it. I have seen it myself in a few different places this week. People in the village are talking about it. One resident even tried to take a picture and was told to stop by the people inside the pickup."

I told him a few other people had also seen these pickups trucks, and one had been seen somewhere between Bempton and Flamborough that same morning. I had no idea why U.S. military-style vehicles were being seen around the area. Their sudden appearance might just have been a coincidence, because I have nothing to link them directly to these other events that had been happening.

These strange vehicles were seen intermittently over a number of weeks around the area. There had been another sighting of them at nearby Gransmoor, close to Barmston, within the same time frame. All the locations are within fifteen miles of each other, and they are all close to areas of high strangeness. However, it is impossible to say whether their presence was due to UFOs or the other strange things that were happening - most of which, I was not even aware of until much later in the year. But this phone call was very interesting, especially since the caller had also referred to similar vehicles in the same conversation.

I spent so much time at Bempton in 2017, but for one reason and one reason only: I wanted to capture good clear evidence of the lightforms that are seen by many people off the coast and out at sea. I knew my chances were slim, but up on these cliff-tops I had a better chance of success than any other place I know of.

While I was writing the first *Truth Proof* book I received a phone call with a warning about going to Bempton alone at night. The caller told me to stop looking into events over the North Sea. This was the time I was researching the crash of ZA610; the RAF Tornado jet that crashed in December 1985. I think the call was designed to unnerve me. I try to remain as level-headed as it is possible to be when looking into these things, but I do wonder if people in high places have their eyes and ears fixed on these areas at all times.

Was it pure coincidence that Ian Wilson's phone data was somehow erased on July 3rd, just days after he discovered the mutilated deer. And could the triangle of earth and the flying triangle at Speeton all be part of the same sequence of events? Were they the reason there were military trucks in the area?

I thanked the man for calling me about his daughter's sighting, and assured him I would be in touch, then Bob and me decided to head back. We began walking down towards Big Railings; the large wooden viewing platform on the cliff edge. It is used in the daytime by bird watchers, but during the evening it rarely gets any visitors - except me, I think. It was about 8pm as we reached the perimeter of the old RAF base. My eyes were scanning the sky and the surface of the sea and we were discussing my phone call about the UFO sighting. That's when I saw them.

Sub-Surface UFOs

At first I thought I was imagining things, but the more I looked, the more I was sure that I could see lights. There were three white lights under the surface of the sea and they were in the shape of a large triangle. I told Bob and pointed into the distance towards them. Even though they were quite far out, I was sure about what I could see. My distance vision has always been very good and I had no problem seeing them. I stepped up the pace and told Bob that I would wait for him further down the cliff path. I had to get as close as possible to the lights if I was going to get any pictures.

Bob was still busy trying to focus on what I could see clearly, but this was not the time to hang around, so I headed off. I kept stopping along the path as I went, to make sure I was actually seeing what I thought I was seeing. I suppose I could not believe it at first; these were real glowing lights and they were under the sea. They were still quite far out to sea when I eventually stopped at the viewing platform, but I was as close as I was going to get. They were right ahead of me and I wasted no time in getting out my camera and taking a few pictures. This was where the Nikon P900 came into its own; its amazing zoom lens took me right out to the lights.

A few minutes later a breathless Bob Brown caught up with me.

Bob:
"Right mate let me have a proper look. Well, when I get my breath back!"

I didn't turn round. I just told him to focus on an area that I estimated to be about two miles out from the cliff-face. He could see the direction my camera was pointing.

Bob:
"*I can see 'em now matey. Bloody hell! What are they? What could be out there do you think? They're not moving. It can't be a submarine, not that shape.*"

In the water we saw three evenly-spaced and distinct circles of light. They were glowing and formed the shape of a huge triangle. I was so pleased that Bob could see the lights; it did not prove anything or tell us what they were, but the fact he witnessed them too helps to strengthen this account. I spend so many hours alone in these remote locations and sometimes I hold back from talking about some of the things I see. Sometimes I actually think I see too much and wonder if people think I imagine half of it. It is always difficult to talk about things that leave no proof, especially when there is often only one witness. At least now I felt happier knowing that someone as genuine and honest as Bob Brown could see the same lights that I could.

I think anyone who places themselves often enough in areas of high strangeness, will eventually have their eyes opened. And I place myself in these areas more often than most people.

I continued taking photographs of the lights as we talked. Bob's eyes and mine were now fixed on what looked like a perfect triangle of white circular lights beneath the sea. It is hard to say what size they were due to the distance, but for them to look as distinct as they did, I would estimate that each light must have been over fifteen feet in circumference. As we continued to watch I remember hearing Bob uttering the words 'bloody amazing' several times, plus a few other phrases that I will not type here. He also made an interesting observation.

Bob:
"*Am I seeing things Paul or is the sea steaming above the lights?*"

Bob wasn't seeing things. He was right. The seawater *was* steaming above each of these three patches of light. How far below the surface they were was impossible to say. I didn't even know how deep the water was in this part of the sea. I have since spoken with local fishermen who tell me it's at least eighty feet deep, but whatever was below the surface was creating enough heat to make the sea water visibly evaporate.

This was not a quick sighting where we made assumptions after the fact. We were discussing the lights and the steaming water as we watched them in real time. The lights formed a triangle, in the same way that any three objects would, and they did look evenly spaced. I cannot say whether they were all connected below the surface, but if they *were* joined together, then whatever this thing was must have been enormous.

I successfully obtained photographs, which clearly show the lights under the water. I have included one of the photos here, but it is impossible for me to offer any more proof of what we saw. I had heard people talk about seeing lights under the sea before. But to actually see them with my own eyes was a new development.

The three sub-surface lights seen from Bempton cliffs

I couldn't help but think that these sea-lights might be connected in some way to the events described to me in the call to my mobile earlier in the evening. The caller even mentioned seeing the military-style vehicles - which was interesting, because I had seen them myself that morning, before me and Bob went to the cliffs. So why were they there?

We kept watching the lights for about fifteen minutes, until they slowly began to move further out to sea and we lost sight of them. This was truly a significant sighting.

Bob and I talked about the phone call and how it might be connected to everything that was happening. Already there was a growing number of unexplained events, all following, one after the other: the triangle of earth in the pea-crop, the flying triangle at Speeton, the mutilated deer, the men in white overalls up on the old base, the new sighting of the black cigar-shaped UFO, the military trucks seen by multiple witnesses and *now* lights under the sea. This was quite a tangled collection of phenomena, which I think has to be more than a coincidence. There has to be a connection.

Even after all that had happened that day, July 25th was still not over. We were both still buzzing with excitement after seeing the submerged lights, but we could never have expected what happened next.

After the sea-lights had slowly moved out of sight, Bob and me turned to look to our right towards Flamborough Head. From our position at the overhanging platform of Big Railings we could see the white cliffs of Bempton and Speeton, which jut out to sea at various points up and down the coast. Then suddenly, about a mile away, we saw a strange rectangle of red light switch on and off, on a distant cliff-face. It was quite amazing and happened so quickly, that I think if one of us had blinked we would have missed it. It was still light enough for us to see the cliffs clearly and there was no mistaking what we saw. It was a huge red rectangle of light that covered a large area, just below the cliff-top.

I cannot even begin to understand what could have emitted so much energy that it was able to light the cliff-face so brightly for a fraction of a second. The area it covered was at least twelve by thirty feet and looked about the size of an articulated lorry container. We had no idea what it was, but we talked about it all the way back to the car.

Location of the rectangle of light seen from Big Railings

Two Days Later
July 27th 2017

The following Thursday I received a phone call from a lady named Susan Prince who lives in Ebor Flats in Bridlington. Ebor Flats are a small tower block of apartments on the sea-front, directly overlooking the sea. They have the best views of the bay in Bridlington. If the sky is clear you can see Flamborough Head to the left and Hull to the right, the views are amazing. Susan told me she had been looking out of her fifth floor window at 3am that morning and saw large ball of yellow light above Flamborough, six miles away.

She said it was very bright and thought it looked quite close to the lighthouse, but could have been further out to sea.

Like most people who have clear views out to sea, Susan is used to seeing all the usual air traffic; jets, helicopters, hang-gliders and so on, but she said this was different. She also told me there were two smaller balls of light below the large one. Although it was impossible to tell if these smaller lights were attached to the larger one, Susan stressed that they were very close to each other, but didn't appear to move the whole time she observed them. She remembers watching them for about ten minutes before they simply vanished.

It is impossible to know what Susan saw, but I think, since there was enough activity already presenting in 2017, her sighting is worth including here.

A Walk Along Blake-Howe Lane
August 1st 2017

After speaking with various people it appeared that the military-style pickup trucks were still around and taking a keen interest in something, they were just very low profile. I spoke with a mother and son who had been out walking their dog along Blake-Howe Lane. They told me they had actually spoken to the men the American pickup and asked what they were doing. They were told that some 'unusual planes' had been seen, so they were monitoring the area.

Nothing about unusual aircraft or American pickup trucks ever reached the local newspapers. However, I suppose we are in an unstable world and perhaps the public are not meant to know, but I am pleased I was able to take a few photographs to prove the vehicles actually existed.

Another witness from a farm close to Bempton told me that an American pickup had been parked out of sight on Blake-Howe Lane for a few weeks. He said he had seen them a few times in the early morning when he was out with his dog. I was a little surprised to hear this, because I had not seen the vehicle with its strange green box and trailer for over a week, so I assumed they had left the area. Obviously I was wrong; they had just become more elusive and moved further along the lane.

There are no restrictions on anyone walking Blake-Howe Lane and I had nothing to lose; so I decided to take our dog and walk the lane to see what I could find. I remain convinced that the triangle-shape of earth that I had investigated in the pea-crop was one of the reasons these vehicles were around. If not, it was an incredible coincidence they were there at the same time.

I parked my car in Bempton village and, along with Wolfy the dog, made my way up Cliff Lane. As I approached Blake-Howe Lane I could see the farmer. He was wearing dark blue overalls and his eyes were fixed on me as I got closer. I'm sure he was thinking, *'Here he comes again. I bet he wants to take pictures and ask more questions.'*
And he would have been correct, because I think he must have seen the military vehicles around the village and I'm sure he knows much more about some of the things I have been investigating.

Like so many people, their secrets go with them to the grave. Strange though, when you consider that some people just roll their eyes at the mere mention of anything paranormal, but still hold onto their secrets as though they were the Holy Grail.

The farmer nodded and I said hello and asked if he was busy working. He nodded again and said he was waiting for a lift up to the farm. I told him that Wolfy and me were going to take a walk along Blake-Howe Lane, then I told him I wanted to see the American pickup trucks and trailers that people were talking about.

Paul:
"Have you seen them? They have been parked on the back roads and on Blake-Howe Lane."

Farmer:
"I have heard about them, but I've not seen them myself. Not sure I'm that bothered."

I am always amazed how reluctant some people are to speak, but then, no one has to say anything if they don't want to. Even the ones with nothing to hide.

Before leaving him, I asked if he thought I might get permission to go onto the old RAF base to take photographs. I already knew the answer, but enjoyed asking. He shook his head.

Farmer:
"Not a chance. I doubt anyone would ever be allowed up there again. There is too much going on up there now."

That was a very interesting thing to say.

Above ground the old base is sealed off from prying eyes by huge slabs of concrete and steel. The dilapidated buildings contain nothing but cobwebs, cow dung and far-away memories of their former years. But he thought I would not be allowed to take pictures up there because there was 'too much going on up there at the moment'? Our conversation had been short but interesting. In fact, the lack of information told me everything I needed to know - that there really was more going on.

I said goodbye to the farmer and walked with Wolfy across the road to the entrance of Blake-Howe Lane. To the left of Blake-Howe Lane is the pea-field where the triangle of earth suddenly appeared on the morning of June 16th. Less than half a mile from the pea-field is the spot where the deer carcass was found on June 28th. If you stood there and looked left across the fields, you would clearly see the old RAF base where, on July 3rd, Ian Wilson saw the American motorhome and the three men in white overalls.

The farmer I had just stopped to speak to told me he knew nothing about any strange goings on, but he still thought I had no chance of gaining permission to go onto the former base to take pictures, because there was 'too much going on up there' at the moment.

I continued walking my dog along Blake-Howe Lane that morning and noticed there were no American or military-style vehicles anywhere to be seen. But that hardly mattered, I had already been given enough to think about.

The Hum of Social Media
August 2017

I don't usually search the internet when researching for my books, but I was told about something interesting that was being discussed on social media. It was something that could have linked into one, or all of the things that were happening.

A few people began contacting me on *Facebook* to ask if I had heard about a low-pitched humming sound that had been heard around Bridlington and Bempton. I had even heard the sound myself in the early hours of the morning on several occasions, but could not pin-point where it was coming from. It was one of those subtle sounds that was just there. At first you don't even hear it, then when you do tune-in, you just cannot get it out of your head.

After reading about it in lots of online comments, it seemed that I was not alone. The hum had been reported in many areas around Bridlington and Bempton in late August. It didn't seem to favour any particular time of day or night and no one seemed able to pin it down to a specific area. Below are a few of the comments, from August 22nd and 23rd, with opinions and theories from people who heard the noise - including my own. All other names and contact information have been removed.

Reply: 22nd August - 15:18
"Is it noise to keep birds off land? They have random hums or shots etc"

Reply: 15:20
Paul Sinclair: *"I heard it between 9 and 11pm. So not to keep birds off land."*

Reply: 15:22
"I don't know. I know the one near my parents is constant, it is noisy 24/7"

Reply: 15:26
"If you mean the random low frequency noise like a distant compressor (or diesel idling), then I have been hearing that for ages. At some times (or weather conditions) it is more noticeable than others. I did think it

must be something going on in my head, but others also say they can hear it. There is also a higher pitched but fairly steady noise, which comes from The Maltings."

Reply: 15:50
"It wasn't there after 8.00am and isn't there now J... and I've not heard it in Bempton before - so don't think it's The Maltings. This was a deeper, almost electrical sounding hum, but pulsating. Like R... indicated - it was hard to go back to sleep once I was disturbed by it."

Reply: 15:52
"The noise was in Bridlington at 10pm."

Reply: 15:55
"Awake between 4 & 7 couldn't sleep! (Not like me!) What the hell is it!???? Had a headache all day!! Fracking perhaps?? Maybe out at sea??"

Reply: 16:07
"Hope they were ours!"

Reply: 16:10
"ULF comms." [Ultra Low Frequency communications]

Reply: 16:13
"Fog horn..."

Reply: 16:14
"Are the pulses regular or irregular? Just trying to establish whether we are all talking about the same noise!"

Reply: 16:15
"No not a fog horn - was an electrical type of intermittent pulsating humming noise. Interesting what you say."

Reply: 16:16
"It's regular. Someone has suggested ULF Comms."

Reply: 16:33
"There are no ULF transmitters in the vicinity. Nearest location for a

transmitter of this type would be the GCHQ facility in Scarborough."
[Government Communications Headquarters]

Reply: 16:34
"Gas pipelines are another possibility, as we do live in the immediate vicinity of a gas substation (on Newsham Hill Lane)."

Reply: 16:35
"What about a mobile ULF transmitter/transmitters in the area?"

Reply: 16:36
"It's being heard in Old Town and in Bridlington Central too."

Reply: 23rd August - 06:53
"I was woken by the 'explosive thunder' this morning...I have heard this weird humming/whirling sort of a sound you describe. Until about 2 minutes ago, it 'wound down', whatever it is. Some sort of a mechanical sound, like a big machine spinning a drum of sorts. No idea what it could be or where it's coming from."

These were just a few of the comments made by people who heard the unusual humming sound in 2017. I was also told about a strange sound heard by one of the residents who lives in the remote sea-front flats at Wilsthorpe. The lady I spoke to was of the opinion that whatever was responsible for making the noise was, at one point, directly over her the roof of her home. She described it as a pulsing electrical sound that slowly got louder as it approached. She told me that she was too frightened to go outside or even to open the curtains to look.

The fact that the American pickups were also in the locality suggests to me that they may have been responsible for the humming sound. It was interesting that no one on social media mentioned any knowledge of a military presence in the area. To me, this confirms just how low-key they were.

Our home has CCTV and one of my cameras also records sound, the person who referred to the 'explosive thunder' in their comment at 06.53 was correct. Our CCTV actually recorded the sound and pictures of the sky as this 'thunder' broke. It was a sound that just came from nowhere, as people were hearing the hum. It came as one huge explosive sound, followed by silence.

It is not my intention to attribute unexplained phenomena to every strange occurrence that happened around this period in 2017, but in view of what had been seen and experienced, I think these comments from *Facebook* should not be disregarded. It may be a long time before we see how these things fit into the overall picture, however, I don't think adding them at a later date would help the research.

Paul Prince - Fisherman

On Tuesday August 29th 2017 Paul Prince was fishing off the harbour wall in Bridlington, something he loves to do whenever he has free time. At about 9:30pm that evening he became aware of a large ball of orange light that appeared over the sea out of nowhere. Paul was sure the object was not a helicopter as he continued to watch it, wondering what on earth it could be. He even managed to capture a bit of video footage of the object before it disappeared, but like most videos of lights filmed at night, it is pretty inconclusive. Full credit to Paul though, for having a go at filming the object. Unfortunately, all it shows is an orange dot on a black background.

The way Paul described the light; making a sudden appearance and its movements before disappearing, makes me believe he was looking at one of the lightforms. He described it as being a large bright orange ball of light, which just appeared out over the sea. He said it slowly moved from east to west, then vanished.

I had been spending lots of time up around Bempton and Speeton hoping to see similar lights to those Paul saw from the harbour wall. However, I was not the only person who was taking an interest in the area. On several occasions I saw a four-wheel drive pickup truck on the cliff tops between Bempton and Flamborough. It would have needed to travel over private land to get to its vantage point. I don't think I would have even noticed it, if it was not for a mobile phone suddenly lighting up inside the truck.

THE WATCHERS

Bob Brown's First Warning

On Thursday September 14th Bob Brown called at our home. He had a story to share with me about something that had happened on the previous night. I could tell from his body language that he was upset about something, which is out of character for Bob. He is usually full of smiles and very calm and collected. He sat down and began telling me what had shaken him up so much.

Bob explained that he was house-sitting for a good friend, who was away on holiday for a few weeks. He was also caring for his friend's dog, because they did not want it put into kennels. Bob had recently sold his own home and was looking for a new place, so these arrangements worked fine for him. His friend's home is a large detached house on Cardigan Road, an affluent area of Bridlington where the world-famous British artist David Hockney also owns a property. The house is alarmed and also has CCTV, he also said the property has a secure back garden; with a seven-foot fence around its perimeter and a gate that is locked at all times. He assured me the gate was locked on the night in question.

The lounge at the back of the house has patio doors that open into a narrow porch, with French doors that open out into the large garden.

Bob says that about 9.30pm on the previous night he was watching TV in this lounge, when he suddenly felt like he was being watched. At exactly the same time he noticed the dog lift its head then look towards the patio doors, so Bob turned around to look for himself.

The only light in the room was from the TV and as he turned to look at the doors he could see the shape of a tall man standing outside. Bob said that he could only see a dark outline, but his first impression of the figure was that it looked like the fictional character Zorro.

Bob:
"It bloody shocked me to be honest Paul. I jumped up and went to see who it was.

They were obviously up to no good and the dog was going nuts at this point. He was barking and jumping at the doors, desperate to get out. I didn't know what to bloody think, because whoever it was shouldn't have been there. I opened the doors and let the dog out into garden, he went mad running here there and everywhere. I cannot understand it Paul, because I don't know how he managed to get in, let alone get away. He definitely had something on his head - a weird hat. But all I could see was the black outline."

At that point I did not read too much into Bob's story. I certainly did not think it was anything to do with events at Bempton. I thought it could have been an opportunist thief checking out properties. I told Bob to call me if anything else happened and that I would help him if I could.

As well as hosting *Beacon of Light Radio,* Bob also works as a volunteer in a local charity shop for a few days each week. If I am in town I always like to call in and say hello. The shop is usually quite busy, but Bob always has a smile on his face and a few kind words whenever I call in.

On Tuesday the 19th I did just that, but to check that he was okay more than anything else.

Paul:
"Now then Bob, how things? Have you had a good weekend? I hope you haven't had anymore unwelcome visitors."

He shook his head and smiled.

Bob:
"No I haven't seen anyone else in the garden, thank God, but I am pleased you've called round, it saves me a job. I've seen a UFO Paul - at least I think that's what it was. I don't know how else to explain it. I saw big white ball of light over the sea the other morning, as I was walking to work."

I asked him if he could remember which day he saw the light.

Bob:
"It was last Friday morning...yes definitely Friday. I took a few pictures of it, but nothing showed up on the photos. And that's not all. A big black car keeps passing me. I've seen it in the mornings when I take my friend's dog down to the beach and I've seen it when I am coming home from the shop. All its windows are black as well. It's odd. I have seen it parked up and as I walk towards it, it pulls away. It passes me a few times. What do you think all that is about?"

If I was honest I could not give him an answer. At that point I had not linked anything he told me to the events that had been happening at Bempton. The only thoughts that ran through my mind were the recollections of Nathan and Steven that I had written of in TP1 and the black cars that followed them back in 2013. These two local researchers had discovered something on the cliff-tops; I will not go into detail, but they were looking into something sinister around Bempton and found more than they ever expected. But this happened in 2013 and had nothing to do with Bob Brown's recent experience, or did it?

7 Days Later: The Warning Is Real For Bob Brown

More than a week had passed since Bob had seen the intruder in the back garden at his friend's house. I was relieved he had not seen any more unwelcome visitors. The last time we spoke was in the shop, when he told me about seeing the light over the sea and the strange black car that passed him several times. Other than that, his life seemed to have returned to normal.

I got up at around 6am on Friday September 22nd and went through my usual routine: kettle on, teabag in the cup, bathroom visit, then a look through my emails. Everything clicked into place as any normal day. Then, sometime after 8am, my mobile phone bleeped with the sound that told me I had a text message. It was from Bob. *"Paul could you please call in at the shop this morning, I need to talk to you. It's urgent."*

I didn't like the sound of that, so by 9.30am I was closing our kitchen door and heading into town. I had a few books to post, but Bob's message kept on flashing up in my mind. What could be so urgent that he felt the need to text me? That might sound silly, because it was just a text message, but Bob never sends me a text.

At around 10am I reached the charity shop where Bob works. He has an uncanny knack of spotting people as soon as they enter and the habit of saying a long drawn out *"hello!"* when he sees you. This day was different however. Bob's head was tipped forwards and he was looking down at the counter as I entered the shop. His eyes though were straining upwards and were fixed on the door. I knew he had seen me, but it was most unusual for him not to smile and say hello.

As I walked towards the counter, few customers were browsing and another member of staff was putting a few items on a rail.

"Is everything alright Bob?" I asked in a quiet tone. He looked up and placed a finger on his lips and quietly told me to hang around. I could tell he did not want to talk in front of anyone, so I stood at the counter in an awkward silence. It was obvious he didn't want anyone to overhear what he had to say.

Bob:
"I had visitors last night," he eventually whispered.

Paul:
"Was someone in the back garden again Bob? You should have phoned, I would have come up right away, mate."

He shook his head and said no. When the shop became less busy he told me more.

Bob:
"At around 8pm someone knocked on the front door. I wasn't expecting anyone, so I stood in the hallway for a moment trying to work out who it was. All I wanted to do was sit down and relax. I could see the dark outline of two men through the frosted glass, and they were tall. I have to admit I thought they were police officers. The dog was barking like mad. I had just let him out into the back garden when they knocked. My immediate thought was, 'what do they want at this time?', but before I could open the door the dog came charging back through the house like a mad thing. While holding the dog by the collar and trying to work out who they were I shouted out, 'just a minute'. I managed to get the dog back into the garden and close the back door, so that was one problem out of the way."

The front door setup at Bob's friend's house is very much like the doors at the back, the only difference is the frosted glass on the inner door to stop people looking directly into the hallway.

Bob:
"When I finally opened the inner door and saw them through the glass of the outer door, I just didn't know what to think. I was shocked I suppose. I had never seen men like these two in my life before. For a start they had no eyebrows. A daft observation I know, but that was the first thing I noticed.

I asked them what they wanted and they just stared down at me. I know I felt nervous, but I couldn't just close the door and walk away. Its not in my nature. But they never even flinched when I spoke to them, so I opened front door and said it again. I wish I hadn't now.

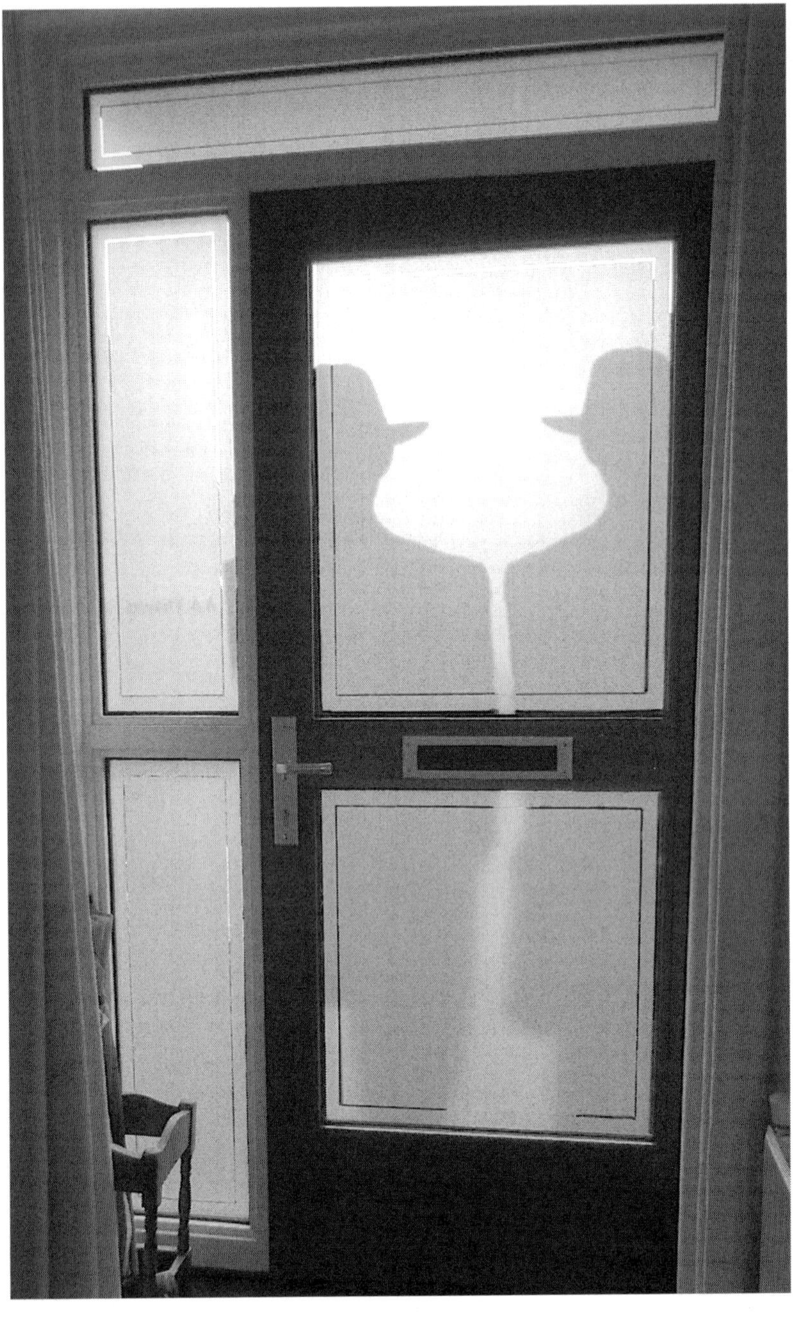

They were standing very close together. The one nearest to me leaned towards the doorway and bent forwards. He didn't tip his head forwards, it was as though all his body moved, tilted. Everything was wrong about these two. I could only see their faces, I don't remember seeing their hands, but their skin was smooth and pale. There was something else Paul: when he leaned forwards and spoke to me, I never saw his lips move. But I would have noticed this because I never took my eyes off him."

Stranger:
"We have been watching you."

Bob:
"What do you mean 'watching me'? Who are you? I have never seen you before. Why are you watching me?"

Bob told me that they paused before speaking and seemed almost robotic. He could not tell if they were bald-headed or not, but said they looked and dressed very similar. They wore fedora hats and black suits. Bob said they were dressed like old-time gangsters and looked totally out of place in 2017.

Stranger:
"You have seen something, something you should not have seen. We are here to warn you. Stop looking. We are watching you now."

Bob told me they mentioned the phrase UFO but he could not remember in what context or where in the conversation it came up. He just knows that he felt very scared. He told me that one of them whispered in his ear, but even though he can remember the nearest one leaning towards him, after that moment the situation became vague and fragmented. Bob Brown is a very down-to-earth man who is the first to admit that this was the first time in his seventy years of life that anything like this had ever happened to him. He did remember them saying:
"You should be very careful."

Bob:
"Look go away or I will call the police. You have no right to be here. Who are you?"

Strangers:
"We are watching you now. What you saw now sees you."

Bob slammed the door shut and gathered his thoughts. What had he just been involved in? Had that really just happened? He remembers the two strangers standing motionless behind the glass for a few seconds, then they turned and walked away.

Bob:
"Then I ran upstairs Paul, to see where they had gone. My heart was going like mad, they really scared me. I looked out of the upstairs window but I couldn't see anything. It was too dark"

I don't think Bob realised the importance of what he had just said: 'It was too dark.'

I had connected the dots immediately. He said the time was about 8pm when they arrived, adding that he could see them through the frosted glass. So when they arrived it was still light? But when they left it was dark. Yet Bob says they only spoke on the doorstep for a few minutes.

This revelation did not sit well in Bob's mind. What he told me was the truth, but there was a gap; a section of missing time between seeing them in daylight and looking out of the window a short time later and the street being in darkness. Bob does not recall much about the evening after the strangers left. He cannot even remember going to bed, although he must have done at some stage.

The strangeness for Bob continued into the new day - starting as soon as he opened his eyes and turned to the clock. That was his first problem, because the digital display on the clock was off, so he had no idea of the time. At that moment he hadn't yet remembered his visit from the strangers and he just rolled out of bed and got dressed. Once downstairs he was greeted by the dog in the kitchen and the strangeness continued.

"I went to put the light on Paul and nothing happened. All the bloody power was off. I looked at my phone and saw that it was 8:30. I had overslept by two and half hours. I was shocked, because normally I have been to the beach with the dog and am walking to work by that time.

I assumed the power had tripped out, so I found a torch and went down into the cellar. I knew where the consumer unit was, but it was weird. All the switches were facing up as though nothing was wrong. I just could not understand it. Well I began to flick each switch, one by one, and then back on again, but nothing happened. I mean, this just did not make any sense at all Paul. I tried it one more time, turning everything off and on again, then 'bingo' the power did come back on."

Bob has told me he has thought through this series of strange events every day since they happened. He has no explanation. I believe they fit in some indescribable way into everything that took place; from the shape in the pea-field to his warning from the 'Men In Black'. I had witnessed the same things as Bob had, up at Bempton, so I am not sure why I was never visited by these strangers. Perhaps I will be. Or maybe I am a different type of person to Bob Brown and need to be dealt with in a different way?

SHEEP MUTILATIONS

I first learned about the sheep killings from a vagrant named Andrew, who lives in Danes Dyke. He's a nice guy and we take him food from time to time, which was one of my reasons for visiting Danes Dyke that day on January 1st 2018. Andrew told me that two police officers had spoken to him earlier that morning. They wanted to know if he had seen anything out of the ordinary; in particular, any unusual looking dogs or animals stalking the woodland. When he asked what it was about, they told him that between ten and fifteen sheep had been killed in fields around Bempton and Flamborough in the weeks leading up to the New Year. He told them he hadn't seen anything, which wasn't entirely true.

In September 2017 Andrew told me he had seen a large black cat, slinking away from his camp early one morning. He was 100% certain that it was a big cat. The police officers had said they were looking for an unusual animal; like an extremely big and strange-looking dog. But what Andrew saw in September was no dog, so he told them he hadn't seen anything.

After our conversation on New Year's Day, I knew I had to look deeper into these sheep killings. I was 50,000 words into my fourth book *The Night People*, but the work would have to wait. I could not let an opportunity to discover what was happening in real time slip past me.

Over the weeks that followed I spoke to a few people about what I had been told, these were people I knew within the farming community. I remembered speaking with a farmer named Steve Barmby from Wilsthorpe in July 2017. Steve had told me about finding one of his own sheep that had been mutilated back in 2009. But from his description, it did *not* sound like his sheep had suffered the same type of injuries that were being inflicted on those found in 2017 around Bempton and the surrounding area.

Steve:
"We had our sheep in one field and the field next to it had been ploughed. It was undisturbed fresh earth. That's where I found a single sheep in the field, just laying there on the ground. The four-foot high barbed-wire fence between the two fields had no wool on it or damage,

no breaks, nothing. The rest of the flock were still in their field. But if one sheep gets out, they all get out. So I went towards this sheep and saw that it wasn't dead. I'd seen it move. It's eye was all ripped out and it was in a terrible state. It couldn't move and it was stressed to hell. It had a look of real fear on its face.

When my Dad came to see, I asked him, "how's that sheep got here in this empty field?" There were no sheep footprints anywhere on the ground near it. This was soft freshly ploughed earth, but there were no other animal prints or human footprints to be seen either. For the sheep to be in this condition you would think it had been hounded by a dog and run ragged and had just given up. It was 30 to 40 metres away from the other field and we could see all the other sheep huddled together. They were looking worried when we saw them. My Dad said it was just weird and we should call the police because there was definitely something wrong here.

So I stayed with the sheep until the police officer arrived. When he saw the sheep he just said, "I don't know what you mean." So I explained about the lack of sheep footprints and asked him why he thought its eye was hanging out. The police officer said the sheep must have jumped over the fence and got caught, but I told him there was no wool caught in the barbed wire and I've never heard of a sheep jumping a fence that high.

I told him to look at his footprints in the ground. We could see my footprints, my Dad's footprints and the police officers, but there were no sheep footprints anywhere in the field. Eventually the police officer said, "yes, I see what you mean. Well, we'll let you know if we hear anything."

When we didn't hear anything my Dad called the police station to ask if they had any news. They said what had happened to the sheep was nothing. It just got out, got its face caught on the fence and that's it. But they spoke to my Dad in a really nasty and sharp way. Why did they react in such a way? If they had only said they had heard nothing, we would have put it down to one of those things, something strange, but we would have accepted it. There was no need for them to be so nasty about it. The police officer seemed really nice when he was here. But they just don't want to know."

There is no denying that the circumstances surrounding the discovery of Steve's mutilated sheep at Wilsthorpe were highly unusual. But the livestock mutilations around the Bempton and Flamborough area were just as puzzling. For instance, many of the sheep had their ears and eyes removed, and the removal appeared to have been done with a very sharp implement. Their wounds were almost surgical in their precision. Most had their throats torn out, yet there was hardly any evidence of blood on the carcass or the surrounding grass. It was also noted that if a leg was missing from the animal, it was always the front left.

It also became apparent that mutilated sheep were something very few people wanted to talk about, outside of a close-knit group of farmers. But this is East Yorkshire, where saying nothing appears to be a power that some people enjoy exercising.

I also realised that people would eventually begin to talk, they had to. Insurance claims alone, against the loss of sheep, would mean that some kind of investigation had to be carried out. It is easy to say 'don't talk about what is happening' if you are not directly involved, but if you are the person suffering the loss of livestock it becomes impossible to remain silent.

Everyone involved had an opinion; the sad thing was that no one wanted to face the fact that sheep were being killed by an incredible predator that did not seem interested in consuming its victims. All sorts of 'expert' theories were being put forward as the cause of these animal killings. One Bempton farmer claimed that the sheep had died after receiving a wrongly-administered injection before spring lambing. He said that after the sheep had died, their carcasses were being eaten by foxes and badgers, but that suggestion later proved to be a load of rubbish. A wrongly-administered injection cannot remove an animals eyes and ears or strip the face of skin. Add to that, the killing continued throughout the year, long after spring lambing.

Fox and badger do feed on other animal carcasses if they are not discovered quickly, even flocks of crows are known to descend and scavenge, if the carcass is left exposed for any length of time. But none of the aforementioned are able to remove body parts with surgical precision. Another theory was that a large hunting dog could have escaped and gone feral. In this scenario the dog was said to have slept all day, only venturing out to kill after dark. If this really was the case, why were most of its victims left uneaten? And why did their wounds appear to have been done with a sharp implement?

One sheep carcass, discovered in the early morning in June 2017, had only been killed a short time before it was found. It died horrifically, after its throat had been completely torn out in the attack; the poor animal would have died almost instantly through massive blood loss. Incredibly, no other injuries were found on the carcass. This doesn't sound to me like any known predator here in the UK or the work of a feral hunting dog.

On February 2nd 2018 my good friend Dean Dealtry told me he had spoken to a farmer whose sheep were being killed. It turned out that he had been friends with the family for many years. This was my chance to gather some first-hand information, so Dean told the farmer about me and my research, adding that I would like to help investigate the mutilations if I was allowed. The following Saturday at 1pm: February 10th to be exact, I visited the farm owned by Dean's friend, on the outskirts of Bridlington. Driving my old Mazda 6 as carefully as I could along the bumpy road leading up to the farm, I wasn't sure what to expect.

I was greeted by the farmer who was waiting in the entrance of his home as I arrived. I never quite know how a meeting will go, sometimes it can be a strained five minute conversation and at other times it can be very rewarding. Thankfully this meeting turned out to be better than I could have hoped for. I need to stress that I did not go armed with phrases such as *UFOs* or *paranormal activity*, I simply wanted to offer my help to look into the killings with an open mind.

The farmer, who I will call John, spoke to me for a few minutes in his porch before I was invited inside. It was clear to me that he had been deeply affected by the killings. The financial loss to his livelihood, as well as the high strangeness surrounding the deaths, made the situation seem impossible to solve. John had no clue what was responsible and everyone he had spoken to seemed to have an expert opinion. I suppose they were doing what we all would do; trying to make these killings fit into something that could be understood, something that would make it all acceptable. The problem is, that no matter how hard we try, these things don't fit within the boundaries of human understanding.

I told John that I would like to help him investigate the mutilations. He already knew from Dean that I looked into the unexplained. He also realised that I would not just pin a label on what was happening without real proof. I asked him what had happened and what he thought was responsible for the deaths of his livestock. I also wanted to know whether he had found any clues that could tell us what kind of predator it was.

John:
"We found the first one in July 2017. At that point, we thought the sheep had died of natural causes and the foxes and the badgers had moved in on the carcass. All we found was a fleece and some bones, with the skull and part of its ribcage. Then over the weeks that followed, we found more dead sheep. That's when realised something else was happening.

Then one morning I found a fresh kill, and when I saw its injuries I knew instantly that it was not a fox or a badger. They are just opportunist scavengers that take advantage of a free meal, but the wounds inflicted on this other sheep were devastating. The poor animal would not have known what hit it, I mean it was incredible. The killings have continued throughout the year. The last one was found on the 18th of December [2017]. After that, we moved the sheep out of the area. I just could not risk leaving them in those fields."

The more I heard John's story, the more interesting it became. It is an amazing case, although if I discover that something perfectly explainable is responsible, it will still have been worth the time invested. John told me that in August 2017 he found another freshly killed sheep, with its throat torn out and its face stripped of skin, just like the ones before it. He told me that he decided to leave the carcass exactly where it was, in the hope that whatever had killed it would return to eat it the following night.

The next day, at first light, he went into the fields to see if the carcass had been touched during the night. John found a second dead sheep.

Its throat had also been torn out and its face stripped of skin, but the first kill remained untouched. Over a few months he discovered a pattern was forming. The predator would kill one sheep per night, for three or four days, then stop. Then a period of three to four weeks would pass without incident. Then it would kill another three or four sheep over consecutive nights, then stop.

To me this does not sound to me like the activity of any known predator. Even if we accept the suggestion that a big cat was in the area, it does not appear to be the behaviour of a big cat or any other hungry animal. The purpose of taking down a prey animal is, after all, to eat it, and most animals need to eat at least once a day, but the motives and methods of this killer are, at present, a complete mystery.

Echoes of the Skin Walker

After the August killing John decided to move his sheep into fields closer to the farmhouse. Because the grass was shorter there than in the surrounding area, the animals could be monitored more easily. While we were talking John remembered something else that had happened earlier in the year, and it was something that still puzzled him. By this point we had left the farmhouse and were talking outside, as John began telling me an amazing story - one that I believe is just as incredible as any of the strangest accounts in the world - including the paranormal happenings at the world-famous Skin Walker ranch in Utah.

John was showing me around the yard and we began walking towards a pile of galvanised panels, which are designed to be erected and dismantled fast. They are used to make corralled areas so the sheep can be managed more easily. He told me the panels can be combined to form a narrow passage with an upward sliding gate attached at each end. This panelled passage usually holds up to six sheep, nose to tail. The animals can then be tagged or moved through a foot bath if required, then released into a larger holding area.

John:
"Last year something happened on those fields Paul; something so strange that I still cannot get the image of it out of my mind."

He began assembling a few of the panels as he spoke.

John:
"I fixed these panels together myself, because I needed to tend to the flock. It's a 'right game' trying to heard them into it because they know what you're doing. They're not daft. They know that going into that holding area involves something being done to them and they don't like it. That's why it's so hard to believe what happened. If someone had told me I would not have believed them, but I saw it with my own eyes."

Paul:
"Saw what John?"

John lifted one of the steel panels and asked me to hold it, then he lifted another two panels and slotted steel rods into them to hold them together. It took us less than 5 minutes to build this narrow run that forms a corral designed to hold six sheep, nose to tail.

John:
"Right, now you can see what I am talking about. Now imagine walking towards this and finding it full of sheep. Its hard to believe, but that run had thirty sheep crammed inside it one morning last year.

Sheep runs, assembled from panels on John's farm.

The poor things were in a right state. They were piled up on top of each other, and in a right tangled mess. I dismantled the panels and began sorting them out, they were frightened to death. When I finally got them all untangled, four of them were dead. I think they must have suffocated or overheated. It must have been terrible for them.

I will never understand how they got in there in the first place. It's hard enough for me and the dogs to get them into the larger holding area in daylight, but this happened during the night. How thirty sheep ended up in that narrow steel passage I will never know."

We walked back to the farmhouse and I asked John if he had recorded the dates and times of these incidents throughout the year. Fortunately, he kept a diary and he told me he could check the dates. That was when we made an amazing discovery. We learned that John had found his thirty sheep, crammed into the corralled area, on June 28th. He showed me the page and I looked at the date for a moment, then quickly opened my notebook.

John was standing next to me as my fingers flipped through the pages. I stopped on the page that read: *"28th of June. Roe Deer found on Cliff Lane with 3-inch hole in its side."* It was a surreal moment. This was the exact same day that Ian Wilson had found the mutilated deer carcass on Cliff Lane. The distance between these two incidents is minimal, so what are the chances of them both occurring on the same date and them not been connected?

I have talked about this sheep incident on radio and at conferences, and on more than a few occasions people have drawn similarities to the events at the Skin Walker ranch in Utah.

One story about Skin Walker describes how the owners at the time, the Gorman family, passed a corralled area on their land which contained four of their prize bulls. When they passed by again, less than one hour later, those bulls had vanished. The family desperately searched the 480-acre ranch for the bulls, but could not find them anywhere. Inside the corral was a steel trailer with its door locked and secured by heavy metal wire. Looking inside the trailer was a last resort. They had searched everywhere else so decided to unlock the door and look inside.

They were amazed to find their four bulls crammed tightly inside the trailer. Even stranger, was that the bulls appeared to be in some kind of hypnotic trance; only stirring when Tom Gorman began shouting that he had found them. At that moment the huge beasts seemed to 'wake up', and begin franticly kicking and struggling, in an attempt to get out of the trailer. The Gorman family said that it would have been difficult enough to get just one of those bulls inside the trailer. They had no idea how four could have ever got so tightly packed inside.

Later I discovered that another Bempton farmer had found some of his sheep mutilated. They were in fields at the back of the pond close to the village of Buckton. The fields run parallel with Hoddy Cows Lane and form a valley, which leads to the cliffs of Bempton and Speeton. It is interesting that all of the affected areas where mutilated livestock have been found are close to the cliffs. Over a period of two months ten sheep were found dead at Buckton. Their throats were torn out and the skin had been stripped from their faces, in exactly the same way as the Bempton sheep.

I phoned various livestock auctioneers and cattle markets around East and North Yorkshire to enquire if anything similar had been reported from other farms. I discovered there *had* been similar attacks throughout 2017; one six miles away at Muston, another twenty-two miles up the coast at Ravenscar and others in Flamborough. In all these attacks a few things remain consistent: they all happened close to the sea, all the animals died from their injuries, their faces were usually stripped of skin, and each attack happened under the cover of darkness.

Is this UFO/Alien related? As much as I would like to say yes, I have to say that I don't have a clue and I have no proof that anything paranormal is responsible either. Could it be the work of some deranged man or woman, or even a group of people? I suppose it is possible, but I personally do not think so.

John had a few theories about what was killing his livestock. At one point he thought it could have been a large dog that had been trained to kill; one that had managed to escape and gone feral. He could be correct. However, I don't think so, but I have to stress at this stage it is only opinion. On every occasion this killer has not even left a footprint or made a sound. John also considered the possibility that someone with sadistic tendencies was responsible, or even members of a satanic cult.

The wounds inflicted on these animals are so horrific, that we can be certain all of the sheep must have died within minutes of coming into contact with the killer, due to massive blood loss. But then the mystery gets even stranger, when we look at the location of the kill and realise there is no sign of blood on any of the carcasses or on the ground where they lay. And does the strange pattern of the deaths tell us anything? From John's flock alone, three to four sheep were killed over a three to four day period, one a day. Then the killing suddenly stopped for three to four weeks. Why?

It is impossible to say what could be doing this other than it is something that exists. If it is a creature then it must be an apex predator; something large and powerful enough to instantly immobilise an 80 kilogram sheep. But where does it go in the three to four weeks between killing sprees, and why is it only killing its victims and not eating them?

Also, where is the evidence that it is consuming enough nourishment from its victims to sustain it during its periods of inactivity? I have not seen any, and, at this moment in time, I do not know if the killer is even a living, breathing animal.

Assuming we *are* dealing with a flesh and bones creature we should also consider the amount of calories needed to sustain such a killer. If we were to guess at this animal's body weight, and it can only be a guess, it would have to be at least 60 kilos to hit its victims with such a deadly force as to render them instantly incapacitated. Other farmers in the area are of the opinion that it is a trained hunting dog that has gone feral, I suppose such an animal could easily kill a sheep, but to kill and not consume its victim is not the behaviour of a true carnivore.

On February 15th 2018 I called John to give him an update. I had been working hard on his behalf all week. With all the information I had been given about how the livestock were being killed, my mind went back to the big cat sightings. If a genuine big cat was roaming the East and North Yorkshire coastline, could it be responsible? It was wild speculation, because nothing pointed to a cat being the killer, but I was running out of places to look. I always search for a logical explanation before looking into the possibility that genuine unexplained phenomena could be responsible.

At that moment anything seemed possible; even alien mutation of some kind. I have limited knowledge of this type of phenomena, but these animals appear to have died without a struggle, and the animals I found soon after death did not appear to have been killed for food - unless stripping the faces of skin and removing an ear and an eye are considered a meal by some predators?

I contacted John to inform him that I had called many of the livestock auctions around East and North Yorkshire. I assured him that I had been careful not to reveal any information about the locations that livestock were been found dead, but to paint a picture of what was happening, I told him I gave full descriptions of the condition the sheep were found in; thus giving them an idea of the killers capabilities. Without that knowledge, the people I told would have most likely formed the opinion that a dog was worrying the livestock.

Ryedale livestock auctioneers told me that they were aware of sheep being found dead in unusual circumstances. However, they knew nothing about the Bempton mutilations.

I told John I had also called a few independent farmers in the area, to ask if they had any knowledge of livestock deaths in unusual circumstances. That line of enquiry proved to be more enlightening. I had spoken with Ted Jones, a freelance builder, who works on different farms around the area and Ted's son works for one of the larger farming groups around East and North Yorkshire. Between the two of them they were better placed than me to ask the appropriate questions. They were able to inform me that a small number of mutilated sheep had also been found in Muston and Hunmanby during 2017.

I have no photographs of these animals, but, from what I can gather, the death toll was nowhere near as high as around Bempton - and the description he gave reads like a carbon-copy of the Bempton and Flamborough mutilations.

John listened to all of this with interest. I had no idea what he thought might be responsible for the killings, and although many experts within his circle of friends thought *they* knew, none of them could prove anything. They were all looking for something that would fit within their understanding, but if the answers were that easy to find, this mystery would have been solved long before now. I never asked John what he thought as I relayed all this information, and he gave no hint.

John:
"If this thing is what I think it is Paul, I want to know where it goes when it's not killing my sheep. I am more interested in the Muston and Hunmanby areas than anywhere else Paul. It sounds to me like it could be the same thing responsible for killing them all. As I see it, this thing is using the cliff-tops to move from place to place; using the thick cover where no one walks, and the cliffs have loads of sea caves that no one can get to."

I still avoided asking him what he thought was responsible for the mutilations at this point, because I knew this story would continue to unfold and gather pace. Instead, I told him what a sheep farmer, close to Cottam, had told Ted Jones earlier in the week.

Paul:
"A female sheep farmer told my friend Ted that while she was working in the valley, between Cottam and Octon, she saw a big beige-coloured animal that was definitely not a dog. She said it was very big and actually thought it was a mountain lion."

John just rolled his eyes. He didn't seem surprised at all by what I told him.

John:
"I have heard more than one person say they have seen a big cat in the area Paul, but it's always been black. Sometimes I share my workload with a farmer who lives just a few miles away, and he swears he saw a big black cat jumping over rows of freshly cut corn. This was up around Buckton Hall, and he said it jumped in the air and seemed to slip under the cut corn. He never saw it again after that, which is odd when you think about it. I mean, I believe him, but where did it go to after it jumped into the corn?"

John showed me some pictures he had taken of the dead sheep with his phone camera. The images were date-stamped, so it was clear that his sheep could not have been the same animals the police had been talking about on New Year's Day with Andrew, the vagrant living in Danes Dyke. All of John's sheep were moved away from the affected area on December 18th - almost two weeks before New Year's Day. I suppose it is possible the police only told the vagrant a tiny bit of what had been happening. Mutilated sheep had definitely been found throughout 2017, but they might not have felt the need to tell him that.

John was still at a loss to understand how thirty of his sheep came to be in the corralled area in June 2017 and he spoke about it every time we met. I also found out more about the sheep killings near Buckton village. It turned out that the ten sheep found in the field near the pond, were slaughtered over a period of two months; June and July. The carcasses were found in a very similar condition to those discovered just two miles away at Bempton. My guess is, this had to be the same killer.

These extra bits of information were leading me further and further away from the suggestion that the killer was a wild animal. Some of the sheep deaths at Muston and Ravenscar had occurred in the same months, so it seems unlikely that a land-based predator could be in so many places at once. Ravenscar is twenty-five miles up the coast from Bempton and Muston and Hunmanby sit in-between. Apart from the fact all these villages are close to the North Sea, I cannot find any other link at the present time. I cannot accept that a normal land-based predator would travel twenty-five miles north to strip skin from the face and remove the eyes and ears of its victim and then do the same twenty-five miles south.

Someone close to all of this believes that some form of demonic activity is responsible. I am not so sure. John believes it is a large dog that has escaped and gone feral. He may be correct. However, I don't think so. The farmers are looking for an answer that fits in with what they know and understand - even if what is being done to their livestock looks like nothing they have ever seen before.

We can be fairly certain that the sheep died within minutes of being attacked. But if the animals died from blood loss, we have to ask, 'where has all the blood gone?' Most sheep are white; admittedly, they are a dirty white, but if they have a main artery severed, their hearts would pump out blood at an alarming rate. Surprisingly none of the carcasses had any blood splatter on them, and neither did the surrounding grass or earth. And why, at one point, were three to four sheep killed over a three to four day period and the killing spree just stop for a few weeks?

If the farmers are right and an animal *is* responsible, then it must be an apex predator; a large, fast and powerful animal. But an animal fitting that description would need a large amount of calories, so why would it choose to leave the bulk of a carcass, after only stripping the face? And why leave gaps of three to four weeks between the killings? All this paints a picture of a highly unusual animal, to say the least.

I cannot understand why a large cat or a feral dog would not consume its victim. I could accept that a pet dog, which was running free amongst the flock, would leave a carcass untouched, but not a dog that had gone feral. It would effectively have become a wild animal.

Despite all of the claims from the authorities and wildlife experts, that no big cats are roaming free in the United Kingdom, should we not consider that a big cat *is* responsible? After the *Dangerous Wild Animals Act* of 1976 came into force, there were always rumours that big cats were released into the wild. I have seen paw-prints in Danes Dyke and on the Wolds that are clearly not from a dog, and despite what people say, sightings of big cats *are* reported all over the British Isles. Unless there are breeding populations, any cats released into the wild after 1976 should have died out by the 1990s. Yet we still get random clusters of strangeness cropping up.

There has to be something unique about specific locations. That is the clue. Usually, the cats appear in what I call 'repeat areas'; where other types of phenomena have been seen. Certain areas of the Wolds are renowned for the lightform phenomena, and likewise Flixton never fails to amaze with its stories of a werewolf. I am convinced that these repeat areas should be the focus of serious scientific study. But the phenomena is so difficult to untangle, perhaps even impossible. Our minds and words are not up to the job of accepting or explaining what presents in these areas. Nothing that is seen or experienced resembles anything our brains can process. This is a major obstacle blocking any chance of future understanding.

Continually trying to fit the phenomena into situations that work within our current scientific knowledge holds it in perpetual limbo. First we need to accept that it is real, even if we don't understand how or why - then establish the true locations. Those places of 'over-science', where there is a strong possibility that the phenomena can be studied.

As soon as the farmers realised the extent of what was happening, they began to monitor their livestock more closely - they also realised their sheep were not being killed for food. For me, this takes the emphasis away from the killer being a wild animal. For them, it has to be something natural, so they fall back on the idea that it is a dog trained to kill - even though the method used to kill is nothing like a dog attack. Until I see evidence suggesting otherwise, I am ruling out the suggestion that a dog is responsible.

The following 10 graphic images show the kinds of injuries seen on various sheep, deer and a badger, found dead in the area.

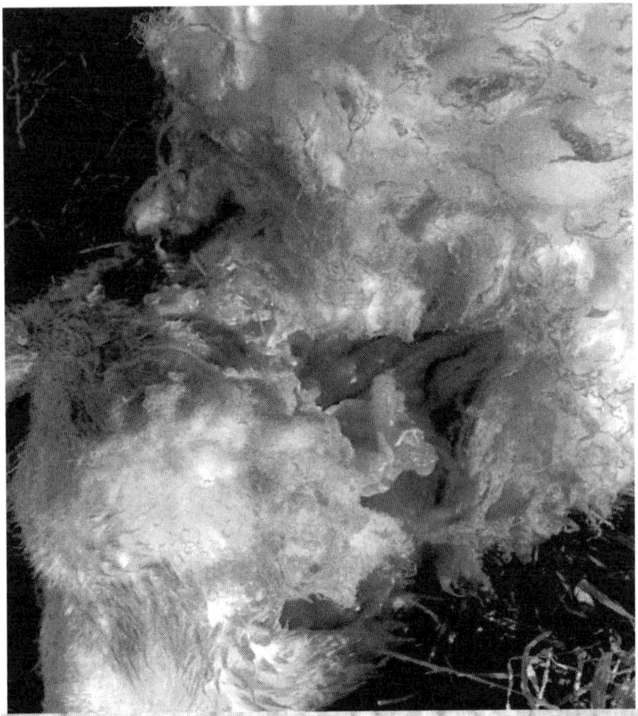

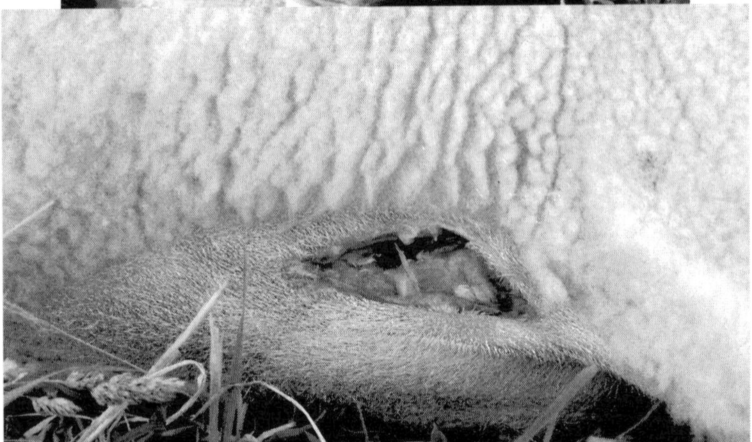

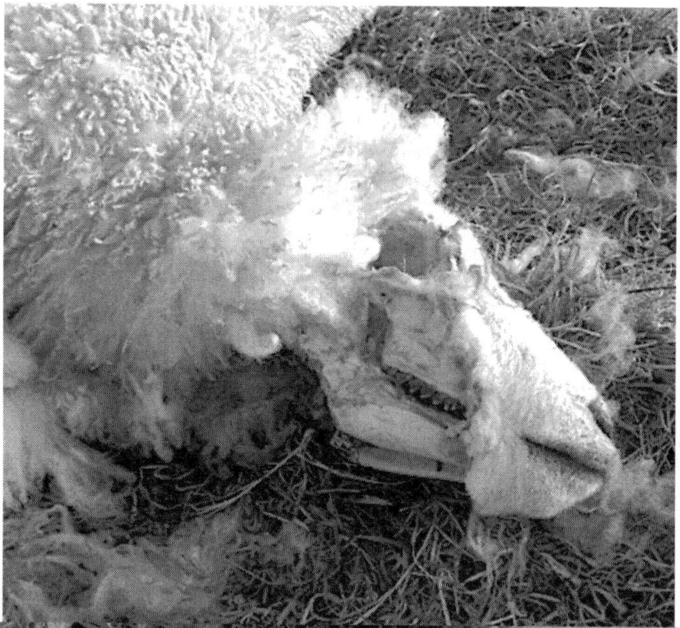

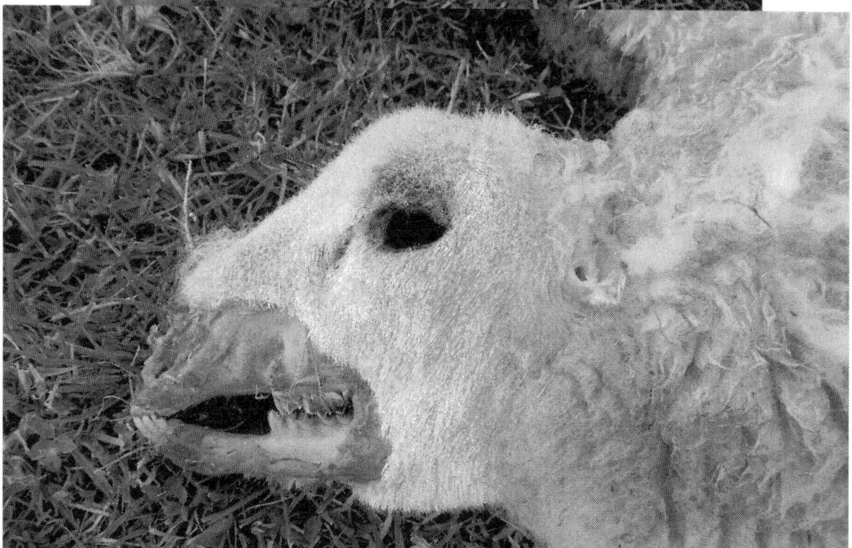

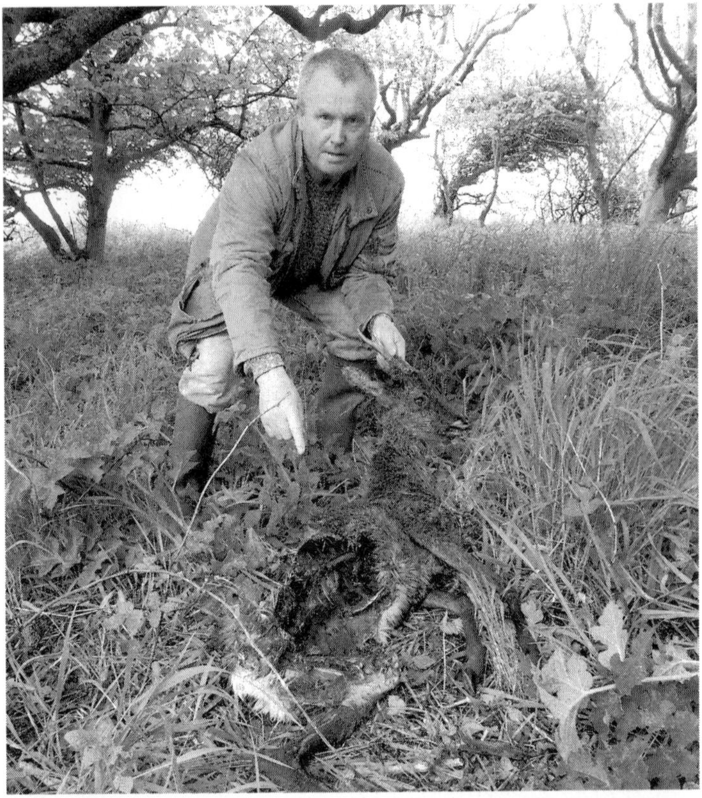

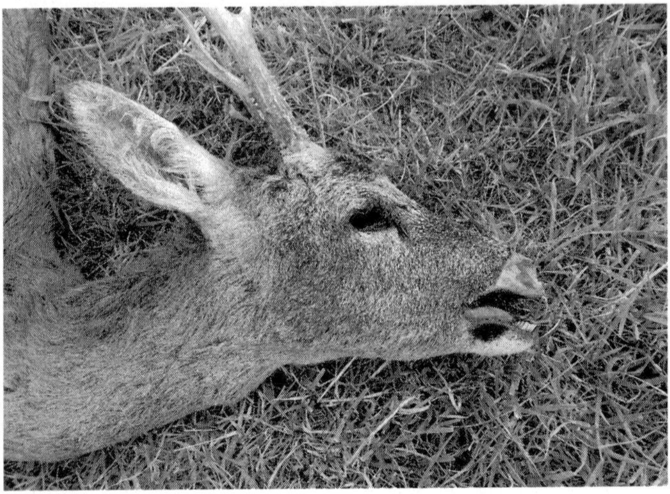

Above: The body of a headless deer. Below: A skinned badger carcass

Similarities Miles Apart

If a big cat killed a sheep or any other animal, it would remove fur or wool first, then eat the internal organs and the prime areas of meat. Cats will often drag what is left of the kill to a secluded area and come back to feed on it when they are hungry. The Bempton sheep were largely untouched and not injured to a degree that would indicate a kill for consumption. Domestic dogs kill for the fun of the chase, but they are usually well fed and, as a result, do not need to kill to eat. But evidence of a domestic dog attack is usually apparent by the amount of random bites inflicted on the defenceless victim. None of the sheep carcasses that I saw had multiple bite marks.

Was it coincidence that other areas in the UK were also targeted by an unusual type of predator in 2017? What I find fascinating is that the Bempton killings appear to have been happening around the same time, but no one could see a connection. If a big cat was responsible, it could not have been the *same* animal; because in some instances, the distances between the killings is over three hundred and fifty miles.

On Tuesday March 27th 2017 the news website *The Independent* wrote of a similar attack in the far north of Scotland: *"Mysterious 'beast' believed to be roaming Scottish Highlands stripping all the flesh off sheep and eating them."* The report stated that in the last five years about forty sheep had all been found killed in the same way. A large cat *"with a taste for mutton"* was blamed, which left no trace, except for bones and wool.

The most recent death was reportedly a healthy ewe that weighed around 50kg. The animal had been found less than 100 metres from a croft in the village of Swordly. Its skin had apparently been peeled off before it was eaten. The report went on to say that the ewe's owner was not the only Scottish crofter to suffer such a bizarre loss of livestock.

The report went on to share the findings of local researcher Jim Johnston, from the village of Bettyhill. He told them that forty sheep were found dead, *"apparently killed in one go"* and they were all *"neatly stripped of their skin before being eaten"* over a large area between the villages of Farr and Tongue. Mr Johnson went on to say that whatever killed these animals, *"skins the sheep in a most expert way"*, adding that *"it crunches through the bones and kills the animal very easily. It's a very interesting phenomenon."* He recalled an occasion where two animals were killed in exactly the same way, yet were found 200 metres away from each other. He had wondered if the killer could be a puma, although he was not certain.

Mr Johnson explained that between 1976 and 1981 numerous sheep killings in the area had been attributed to a big cat, and there had been a few sightings, but despite searches, the mysterious predator was never found. He said that the most recent sighting had been in 2012, but no one knows where the killer comes from. He said that when it was made illegal to keep exotic animals in London gardens, one man *"came up to the Scottish Highlands to release the creatures"*.

I was contacted in September 2017 by a man named Andrew Tonge, after he heard me talking about the strange mutilations on a radio show. Andrew claimed to have had an amazing sighting of a panther-like creature. With Andrew's permission I include his letter here:

"Hi Paul,
...as promised I'm writing to tell you about my own black panther sighting, which took place one early Sunday morning in February or March 2012, in the countryside outside of Redditch, in Worcestershire.

My Dad and I were en-route to a local farm, where he has stuff in storage. We were just outside the built-up part of town, close to the fields and woodlands of the surrounding area. Having just turned off from Windmill Drive onto Callow Hill Lane, we rounded a bend in an areas where the road is bordered on both sides by trees.

The animal was crossing the lane; it was huge. With its nose just off the left-hand side of the road, its long looped tail reached almost out to the white line in the centre of the lane. Its head was slung low, its shoulders were raised, and, as I already said, it had a long curved tail stretched out in its wake. There is nothing of this size - aside from possible stray dogs - which has any place roaming the UK countryside, and at this point the question became a simple one. "Andrew," I asked myself, "can you tell the difference between a cat and a dog...?"

The obvious answer to this was, yes I can. This was nothing less than a hugely up-scaled cat, out on the prowl. In just a couple of seconds it had disappeared into the trees. I felt no urge to shout "Stop the car...!" to follow it off into woods...

In an interesting afterword to this sighting, my Dad - who didn't fully register the black mass that had been in the road - went to the farm where his property is stored. The owner was then in his mid-eighties; a proper old rustic farmer, who was pragmatic and not given to tall tales or flights of fancy. When my Dad told the elderly farmer what I claimed to have seen, his first and sole reaction was one of concern for his sheep and lambs. As it was lambing time, he brought them all in from the fields. His lack of laughter or mockery, told me that he may well have known more than he was letting on...

Anyhow, that was my black panther sighting. I've included a couple of little maps to show the area...I reported it sometime later, I think to The British Big Cats Society, but they never responded to me.

All the best,
Andy"

Following page: The farm Andy visited with his father and a rough map indicating the location of his panther sighting.

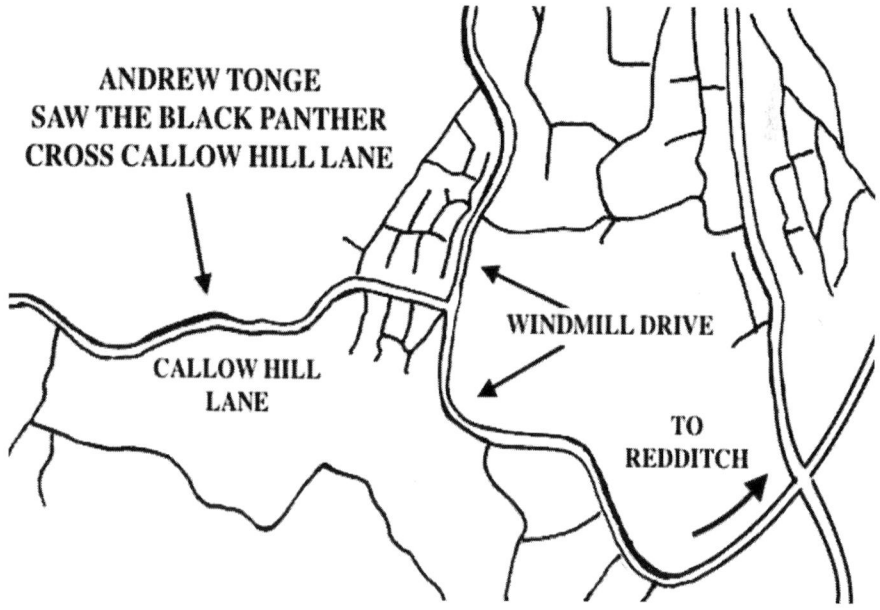

ANDREW TONGE
SAW THE BLACK PANTHER
CROSS CALLOW HILL LANE

CALLOW HILL
LANE

WINDMILL DRIVE

TO
REDDITCH

BACK TO BEMPTON

It is ironic that I had been spending many nights out on the cliff-tops at Bempton and Speeton, sometimes alone, and at other times in the company of my friends Steve Ashbridge, Andi Ramsden or Bob Brown. Ironic because the place we usually set up our cameras and tripods is close to the areas where the unknown something is killing.

From the edge of the cliffs it is impossible to see the surrounding sheep fields because the land rises up on a gradual slope, but it is the location where much unexplained phenomena seem to originate. So many things have been reported in close proximity to this area, and I will not the reveal the exact locations out of respect for the people involved, but it is very close to where David Ellis saw the glowing blue light on the cliff tops, and the dirt path where the 'man in black' suddenly appeared one hot summers afternoon - much to the surprise of a couple out walking. Both stories are in *Truth Proof 2*, along with many more.

When unusual things happen around the East Yorkshire coastline this particular area always seems to get a mention. Is that just coincidence? I suspect it is close to the centre of the strangeness, a magnet drawing in and throwing out the surreal. I first became interested in the area because of the lightforms. I have seen them myself, and trawlermen and rock anglers confirm that they have been seen for as long as anyone could remember. After searching newspaper archives I realised the lightforms were just one part of so much more.

Most of it goes unreported, unless something truly amazing is reported, then it makes the local papers. Interestingly it is usually people from outside of the area who contact the papers. Looking back through old newspapers reveals other random events of strangeness that often happen around the same time, but they are never connected, and become lost and diluted into insignificance. However, the same 'active zones' are mentioned time and time again. All I can do is observe and document, but I feel the strangeness must have intelligence. How else could it remain so elusive and always remain one-step ahead of any plans to capture it on film? I wonder if it is a single phenomena that adapts to fit all situations – something pure and all-knowing that exists and evolves around our thoughts and emotions.

TERROR-FIRMA

On February 19th 2018 I contacted the owner of a remote farmhouse close to the affected area. I wanted to gain his permission to park on his land. From there I could easily access the nearby fields where the mutilated animals were being found. I told him I had been working with John, the farmer who had found thirty of his sheep trapped in the corralled area the previous year, and a few other people who knew what was happening. He knew some of these people and since it was not the first time I had visited his farm, he agreed and suggested that I park close to his farmhouse. This would save me walking the long distance from the main road to the affected fields. I was grateful and assured him I would close all gates and respect the land.

It was an awful day when I arrived, with fog rolling in from the sea, which made visibility less than eighty feet. This did not deter me and after putting on my wellington boots I set off into the fields. I wanted to start by walking the boundary fencing. These areas are used by game animals and predators, such as fox and badger. They run along the fence line until they find a low point in the land or some other weak spot that allows them to access the adjoining field. It was a wet day and these animal footprints were clearly visible in the wet ground. I have to admit that I was actually looking for something else; large dog prints or even evidence of a big cat. I saw neither or anything to suggest such animals had ever been in or around these fields.

The area is huge and split into many parts. It is fenced by five-inch square-link fencing, which has a single strand of barbed wire running along the top. It is four feet high and appeared to be in excellent condition. Two roe deer stood watching me from a distance; they had no intention of letting me get any closer and they jumped the fence, disappearing into the woods.

I took great care when walking the fields looking for any possible clues, but I found nothing in the first half of my walk. I eventually reached the boundary of Danes Dyke and decided to walk its entire length, only stopping when I came to the back road that runs from Flamborough to Bempton. In all the years I have lived in the area, this is the only part of the Dyke that I had never walked. It was an eerie place to walk as fog rolled in around the trees. No one had ever reported being attacked by an animal in the Dyke and, as far as I was aware, only sheep and deer had ever been found dead there. After recalling the extent of the injuries inflicted on the mutilated sheep, I was becoming more and more wary. I need to point out that I never expected to find anything; I just wanted to get a feel for the place. I have been brought up around farms and livestock all my life and I was sure I would find clues, if they were still present. But apart from the two roe deer and a few pigeons I saw nothing of interest that morning.

An hour and a half later the fog had not lifted, but I still had plenty of daylight, and I wanted to cover the rest of the area before going home. I had not been walking long when I found a few fragments of jawbone. I picked them up and placed them into a plastic bag. As I approached the fence-line that separates the fields, I could see a sheep skull sitting in the grass on the other side of the fence, amongst other bits of fragmented bone. When I found more areas like this, with skulls and jawbones, it convinced me these were definitely the places where the sheep had been attacked. I assume the bones were picked clean by fox and badger.

After studying the remains of bones and some wool, and considering the locations I found them, it became apparent to me that whatever killed them would have used great stealth. It might have instinctively thought about the best place to kill its prey, and also where to remain hidden. The majority of the carcasses were closer to the cliffs, out of sight of the farmhouse, at the opposite side of the field to Danes Dyke. Most of these killings also appeared to have taken place at night.

To me this meant two things; either the sheep were wary of something lurking in the Dyke and chose to keep well clear after dark, or the killer came up from the cliffs and killed the sheep that were closest to the cliffs. A predator will always choose the path of least resistance. As I write this, I find myself falling into the trap of thinking this is a killer that we are somehow familiar with. It is not.

In TP2 I reported my own encounter with a large animal that suddenly appeared over the cliff edge and ran into the darkness. At the time we knew nothing about the sheep deaths, but it is fact they were occurring when this unidentified animal appeared. I wrote that it was light brown in colour and that I did not think it was a deer. I could not understand how it suddenly sprang up from the cliff edge and move with such speed. Could this have been the sheep killer?

With the light fading and the weather closing in, visibility was becoming poor, so I decided to make my way back to the car. I was changing my footwear and preparing to leave the area, when I noticed another car pull up further down the lane. I had permission to be there so I did not need to be concerned. Two men got out of the car, followed by four large dogs: three German shepherds and a fourth that I cannot recall - it was just big. At first the dogs were running about on a ploughed field until they saw me, then they began running towards my car, barking and growling. I had to stop the car to avoid running them over, then I lowered my window half way down, gesturing a smile and a wave to the two men, who were now approaching me.

One of them,wearing blue overalls and a yellow high-visibility jacket, walked towards the car. His dogs were snapping and snarling in my direction.

Hi-Viz:
"Don't let 'em jump up at your door."

These were *his* dogs, so how the hell could I stop them jumping up at the door and get them under control? A few words bounced around inside my mouth, but I bit my tongue. I estimated him to have been around 55 to 60 years old. He looked quite stocky and wore a cap, silver rimmed glasses and had white to grey hair.
For some reason he did not look very happy.

Hi-Viz:
"Have you been for a little walk?"

He spoke very slowly and sarcastically and I took an instant dislike to him. His mate, who was a bit younger, was standing behind my car with three of the dogs, who seemed to have lost interest. I always speak to people with respect and expect the same, but this stranger was talking down to me, as though he was addressing a small child.

Paul:
"A little walk? No not really. I have been for a walk though, all the way through the Dyke and around the fields."

Hi-Viz:
"Why?"

Paul:
"Why not? It's not a crime to have a walk is it?"

Hi-Viz:
"Why have you been walking round here?"

Paul:
"I'm interested in a few things that have been happening. Quite a few sheep were killed last year."

Hi-Viz:
"Badgers. Badgers killed 'em, an' note else."

I could see this conversation was going to be pointless and I would have put the car window back up and driven away if his dog had not been standing in front of the car.

Paul:
"Ok."

Hi-Viz:
"Some might think different, but arr know it wer' badgers."

I glanced down at my side mirror. The second man and the other dogs had moved away, so I let my window down fully. This man was really annoying.

Paul:
"How do you know its badgers?"

His face flexed into a frown, probably because I had dared to question his superior knowledge, then he put his hand on the car roof and moved a bit closer to the window.

Hi-Viz:
"It's badgers thats killing 'em; sneaking up on 'em when they are asleep and biting 'em around the throat. That's how I know, and yer canny tell folk who know."

I appeared to have angered him with just a few words. The sad thing is, although his opinion was as valid as anyone's, it was the way he chose to deliver his opinion that annoyed me. If he had not been such a self-opinionated know-all, I would have told him my views on the killings. I would have also made a point of saying that I could be wrong; because at this moment in time, we simply do not know what is responsible.

Mr Hi-Viz began telling me why he knew it was a badger, by explaining how he once knocked one down with his car. Apparently, he jumped out of the car and tried to move the animal with his foot. I was then told the injured badger lunged at his boot, showing him a mouth full of razor-sharp teeth designed for killing sheep. That's how this man knew it was badgers. I saw no point in telling him that I had been brought up around farms all my life and had never heard of a badger systematically killing fully-grown ewes for fun.

All of the killings occurred under the cover of darkness or during the very early hours, and the sheep that were found the following day had not been killed for food. Apart from having their throats ripped out, eyes and ears removed and faces skinned, they were relatively untouched. That is until the badgers, foxes and crows found them the following day and began to pick the remains clean. It was clear to me that this one-way conversation with Mr Hi-Viz was going nowhere. He did not want to hear anything except his own voice.

Hi-Viz:
"I know what's killing 'em. It's a badger and its killing 'em all in exactly the same way. That's how I know it's a badger. Yer can't tell folk that know."

Of course, his last sentence was absolutely spot on - no one *could* possibly tell him anything. He obviously knew everything. So I slowly raised the car window and drove off. The best part of that encounter was watching him slip away into the distance through my mirror.

COUNTING SHEEP

On Wednesday April 18th 2018, exactly four months from the day they were removed, John's sheep were reintroduced into the fields. I asked him if I could monitor the area over the coming months and assured him that I would not be taking anyone with me on my early morning visits, not even my little dog Wolfy.

I received his approval and on April 20th I was up extra-early. My little dog Wolfy ran excitedly around my feet, anticipating a long walk. He was going to be disappointed. My bag, containing two cameras, was packed and ready and I was wearing my GoPro body camera, so I felt well prepared to capture anything that might come my way.

It was a bright clear morning and the sun was already up when I arrived. The time was 5.55am and the land was already alive with birdsong. I quickly took a few pictures of the farm entrance then walked towards the fields. I could see sheep with new-born lambs grazing in the distance and when I glanced towards the nearby trees I wondered if the killer was still around. Maybe it could even have been right next to me? That might sound like a crazy thought, but I believe there is something real and unknown residing in Danes Dyke.

I will never forget the feeling when I was pulled backwards in Danes Dyke by an invisible force. It was a real experience, but I don't think I will ever understand it. I had just arrived in the area and was lifting my camera to take a photograph. Suddenly I felt a sensation, that I can only describe as somehow magnetic, that caught a hold of me. It was enough to stop me in my tracks. So I know from first-hand experience that there is something with unknown capabilities residing in the area of Danes Dyke.

The sheep seemed unfazed as I walked along the edge of the field. I counted fifteen ewes - a far cry from the year before when three to four hundred sheep grazed the land. The grass was wet underfoot. I had put a pair of wellington boots in the car, but decided to keep my walking boots on. Not one of my best ideas, as I soon discovered. The thick grass combined with the morning dew soaked my feet, but I was not about to turn back.

All of the sheep were in the top fields, closest to the farmhouse, which was a wise precaution in view of what had happened in the past. In the weeks and months to come they would have to be put into the fields lower down towards the cliffs. This was where most of the killings took place and it must have been a major concern for John, having to leave livestock unattended in that area.

I walked slowly down the field looking for anything out of the ordinary, anything different. In truth, I didn't have a clue what I was actually looking for.

There had been nothing to see, other than sheep and grass, as I left the fields and stepped onto the cliff path. To my left I could see RAF Bempton in the distance, and on my right was the Flamborough peninsula jutting out into the sea. It was still very early and I wanted to fit as much into the morning as possible, so I decided to walk towards Flamborough. After walking for about twenty-five minutes, I stopped at Danes Dyke. It is interesting that the Dyke runs parallel to many of the areas affected by unexplained phenomena, and as its name suggests, it was used as a defensive entrenchment by the ancient Danes. It cuts across the land for two and a half miles, finishing at the edge of the Bempton and Flamborough cliffs - effectively dividing the five-mile area of land known as Flamborough Head, from the rest of East Yorkshire.

The Dyke was created in the Bronze Age at a similar time to many of the earthworks found on the Yorkshire Wolds. We know this because of archaeological digs that took place in 1879, where over 800 flint tools were found; the same types of tools found in and around the ancient tumuli and earthworks on the Yorkshire Wolds. I have always thought that these early people knew what they were doing when they constructed their huge burial mounds. It cannot be chance that they are found in areas of high strangeness; places where magical things once happened and still do.

I had been taking pictures during my walk and thought it would be a good idea to walk along the top of Danes Dyke to take some photos of the surrounding land. It is a great vantage point and one that I might revisit in the future.

I estimate that Danes Dyke is about forty feet deep in places and up to forty feet wide in others. It would be easy for an animal to use if it wanted to avoid detection. The surrounding bracken was just beginning to show signs of life after wintering under the earth and would be close to four feet tall in a few months time. The woodland on the Flamborough and Bempton side of Danes Dyke is old and rarely used, and the paths that I could see had not been walked on for a long time. If an animal wanted to find somewhere to lie low this would be a perfect hiding place.

I saw an old sign nailed to a tree with the words *Private Property - Keep Out*. I don't think anyone had been around to enforce that for a long time. As I continued to walk along my mind jumped back and forth between the notion of a living, breathing big cat being responsible for the sheep deaths and the idea it could have been some form of unexplained phenomena at work. It really was a puzzle that I could not solve.

After walking for about half a mile and seeing nothing more interesting than a barn owl on a hunt, I noticed a long strip of white on the ground at the opposite side of the Dyke. Even at a distance I suspected it was wool and a few minutes later my suspicions were confirmed. I had found the remains of at least one sheep. The wool and bones were dispersed over an area of around twenty feet by six feet, and had been there for quite some time by the looks of things. I took pictures of the skull and spine then paused to study the surroundings in more detail. Judging by the amount of wool present I think the sheep must have been taken there whole. The fleece was almost intact, as though the animal had been skinned right where I stood.

There was a badger set quite close by, and it had been suggested by some people I spoke with that badgers were responsible for the killings. The man who I nicknamed High-Viz seemed quite sure this was the case, when he had spoken to me weeks before.

Looking down from the top of the Danes Dyke entrenchment that day I could see problems with his theory. Between the sheep that graze on the fields is a 100-metre wide area of rough woodland. This is separated by a four-foot high fence with single-strand barbed wire running along the top. After that there is another field with more fencing that separates the woodland from the fields where livestock graze. The fences are well maintained and the wire is five-inch square-link so nothing can get through, except small animals like rabbits.

The skull I found was from a fully grown adult sheep, which must have weighed 70 to 80 kilos. So what could lift it, dead or alive, up and over two four foot fences - and then pull it up a steep 40-feet incline and back down the other side? An adult badger is no taller than 12 inches at the shoulder and weighs around 13 kilograms. As far as I am aware they are incapable of jumping four-foot high fences while carrying an 80 kilo sheep in their jaws.

I could see the fencing in both fields for hundreds of yards in each direction and there was no sign of wool anywhere on the barbed wire. So how had the sheep got here?

Where ancient woodland meets farmland: image from the top of Danes Dyke

Above: My own silhouette can be seen in the shadow of Danes Dyke ridge.

LIGHTS ABOVE, EYES BELOW

I had been visiting the cliffs of Bempton and the surrounding area at least four times per week for over two years in the hope of catching sight of the lightforms. The lightforms are detached from all we understand, but engage the minds of all who see them. They offer no clue about where they come from or where they go. They just appear and disappear.

One night in early June 2017, the lights presented themselves to Bob and me, but we never saw them again until the evening of Monday November 5th. It might have been Guy Fawkes night in the UK, but these sparkling orbs shone brighter than any man-made fireworks.

Lightforms
Monday, November 5th 2017

I was with Bob Brown, the host of *Beacon of Light Radio*. We arrived at the RSPB car park at about 6.45pm. It was a bright moonlit night, but a cold wind blowing off the North Sea made standing on the cliff tops an uncomfortable experience. After changing our footwear we made our way down towards the cliff edge. We don't have to walk very far to find a good vantage point and there is never anyone around at that time.

After a walk of about three quarters of a mile we stopped and I began setting up my cameras on their tripods. The main problem out on the cliff tops is the cold damp air. The equipment has to be covered at all times because it soon gets saturated in moisture. This in turn makes it virtually impossible to be ready at an instant if the lights appear.

At around 7.10pm Bob yelled out, *"LOOK!"*
He was pointing to an area of sky just out from Flamborough Head. A bright orange sphere had suddenly appeared, closely followed by a second one, that appeared to 'switch on' below it. In the time it took me to uncover my camcorder and switch it on, the lights had vanished. They had not flown away or drifted with the wind, they had simply switched off. It was a bright clear night, so we would definitely have seen them if they flew away.

Below: Some of the many lightforms I have photographed over the years.

I placed a heavy towel over my camera and decided to leave it switched on. Fifteen minutes passed with nothing happening and I was about to switch it off to save the batteries when, without warning, another lightform suddenly appeared in the sky. It only lasted a few seconds, but it was closely followed by a second light, appearing further up the coast towards Filey. The second light immediately became two intense globes of orange, that for some amazing reason did *not* illuminate any part of the sky around them.

I did manage to capture them on film and over the next one and a half hours the lights presented themselves thirteen times in various places over the sea. We heard no aircraft and saw nothing to indicate that these spheres were flares, because there was no smoke or the sound of a discharge. More importantly, they did not come *from* anywhere; they just appeared and disappeared. I managed to film them five times out of the thirteen occasions they presented themselves. One of these short clips is quite revealing; it shows a single orange orb that becomes two, then a red pulsing light appears to come from the left hand side of it. The two orange orbs vanish instantly, but the pulsing red light can still be seen moving away.

I used this unique footage as part of my presentation for the *Outer Limits* UFO conference in 2018. It has since been featured in the documentary I made with Chris Turner called *Bringing Down the Light*.

Nights like this make the months and years of standing in cold remote areas worthwhile. We have seen many other things of interest, but it is the chance of seeing the lightforms that always draws us to the clifftops.

Eyes In The Darkness

In the months between 2016 and seeing the lightforms on November 5th 2017, Bob Brown and I began observing something that left us feeling very unsettled every time we visited Bempton Cliffs.

On the distant hillside below the fields, there was something in the darkness, watching us. The eyes were always the first thing we looked for after setting up our equipment. It was a fact that at some point during the night when we directed a torch onto the hillside, they would always be glaring back at us from the darkness. These yellow eyes puzzled us every time our torch beams connected with them. We had no idea what kind of animal it was, but judging the size of the eyes and the gap between them, it was not small. I don't think we felt fear - at least I didn't - but they *were* intriguing. Had we known what was happening to nearby livestock at the time we might not have been so relaxed.

From time to time we would turn around and scan the darkness with our torches. Call it paranoia or just plain curiosity, we just could not shake off the feeling that we were being watched. And we were right. The eyes were always in the same place on the hillside every time we were on the cliff-tops. So many strange things were happening around this time that I suppose the eyes were of secondary importance, because we were in close proximity to what I have called the 'killing zone' - an area where many farm animals were being mutilated.

Was it coincidence that US military trucks had been parked close to the same hillside during the summer of 2017? At the time, we assumed they were monitoring something in the sky; perhaps nothing more than a standard military exercise. Although, as the information seeped out, I think it is possible they were also looking for something in the sky, on the ground or beneath the waves. I don't know if they were aware of the animal that I saw with Bob, but we never saw a military truck and the eyes at the same time.

The trucks were very interesting. We could see them clearly and I assume they could see us, but the eyes were different. Whatever they belonged to wanted to remain hidden. They were the eyes of a wild animal; an animal of quite some size, considering how big they looked at a distance. They were bright yellow in colour, and what we found most interesting was, that as soon as our torch beam hit them, they seemed to duck down or look away. We would leave it for a minute or so and then look again, and they would be glaring back in our direction. What kind of animal would just sit on a hillside observing two men with cameras?

This was not just a one-off occurrence; we saw them many times after dark. They unnerved Bob more than me. I don't say that in any macho way, but I figured that if it wanted to get closer to us, it would have done. My opinion on this mystery animal changed when I discovered what was happening to nearby animals and livestock. I wondered if the yellow eyes belonged to the animal responsible for the mutilations. Perhaps we were not as safe as we thought we were. Did the people in the military trucks know what was happening?

On one occasion I decided to walk in the direction of the eyes, hoping I could aim a torch and take a picture at the same time. We estimated they were about 500 metres away, but the contours of the land are quite deceptive at night. At one point I found myself gradually descending into a hollow in the field and out of sight, much to Bob's alarm. He began calling me back, saying I was making him feel nervous. I turned back; I couldn't see the eyeshine anymore, even though I had cut the distance between it and me in half.

It has always puzzled me that we cannot see any discernible shape behind or around those eyes. Using the long grass to gauge its height, we could tell that whatever this was, stood between four and six feet off the ground. I realise that my attempts to get closer to whatever was observing us was not one of my best decisions - especially because of what was happening around those fields throughout 2017. But if the opportunity presented itself, I would probably do it again. At this moment in time I am no closer to discovering what was killing all the animals, but I don't think it was any predator we are familiar with.

BODY IN THE COVE

On Tuesday November 7th 2017 I received a phone call from my friend from Buckton, Ian Wilson. There was urgency in his voice and I immediately suspected that he had seen something on one of his early morning walks.

Ian:
"Paul, have you heard anything about the body that was found in Selwicks Bay yesterday?"

This was news to me and despite it being a genuine tragedy, I was not at all surprised to hear that another body had been found.

The timing was interesting, because two nights before this, Bob Brown and I had seen the lightforms off Flamborough Head. I have no reason to connect the two incidents, except they appear to have occurred around the same date and were in very close proximity to one another. It was later confirmed on local radio that the body was found during the daytime on the morning of the 6th. Ian couldn't tell me much more, other than he thought the deceased was male, but I wanted to find out more. So I decided to jump into the car and head towards Flamborough to see what I could learn about the tragedy. I had no expectations of finding anything, I just wanted to gather as much information as possible.

After talking with locals, the first thing I discovered that morning was that the body had not actually been found in Selwicks Bay. I suspect someone had reported the location incorrectly, or they had said it was Selwicks Bay because this was the closest place with a name to where the body was found. The area looked quite deserted and there was police tape and restrictions in place. From the little I could gather, it appeared that the body had been found somewhere below the lighthouse. I suspected at this stage that the cause of death was most likely to be suicide.

I spoke with a couple who were walking along the cliff-tops. They told me that a group of schoolchildren had discovered the body in a sea cave on the previous day. That would have been November 6th, which probably meant that the tragedy occurred on the 5th. The next morning I travelled back to Flamborough. The first thing that came into my mind while driving down towards the lighthouse was how normal everything looked. No one would have ever known that just a few days earlier the area had been the location of so much activity.

I stood on the cliff-top looking down onto the beach, 200 feet below. If someone fell anywhere along these cliffs they would not survive. Maybe that is what happened. It was ironic that, just a week before, I had looked down onto the same cove from the top of the coastguard lookout tower. The former coastguard station had closed in 2010 and was going to be sold at auction; I was there because I was interested in buying it.

The activity I saw on the beach the day before was directly below the former coastguard station, in an area that is quite inaccessible. Assuming the man had slipped and fallen, it would not have been possible for him to reach the edge of the cliff with ease, because of all the hawthorn and gorse. I was intrigued to find out more surrounding the circumstances of the death.

I was considering my next move, when I noticed a lady with a small dog coming out of a bungalow opposite the lookout station. She began walking in my direction, so, assuming that she must have lived there, I thought it might be worth asking if she knew anything about the events of the past few days. When I said good morning she immediately asked if I was a reporter. This was an easy mistake to make, because I stood there with a camera and notebook. I quickly assured her that I was not a reporter and explained that I lived in Bridlington.

Dog walker:
"Well the news reports said he was found in Selwicks Bay, but he wasn't. They found him down there, in a sea cave."

Following photographs: Selwicks Bay viewed from the coastguard lookout.
Selwicks Bay from the cliff-tops.
The lighthouse and cliffs as seen from the beach.
One of the many sea-caves found in the cliffs.

Selwicks Bay (seen from Flamborough coastguard lookout)

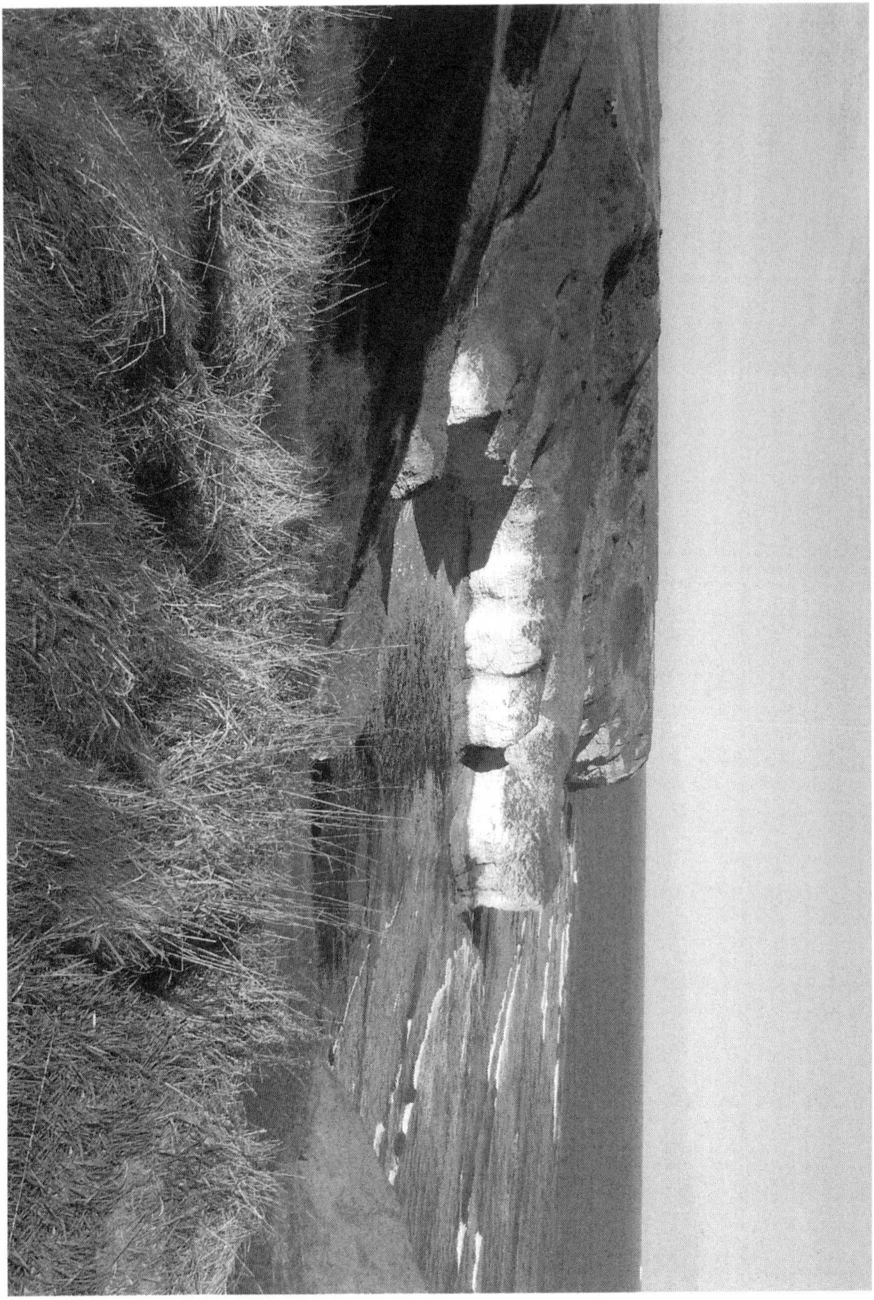

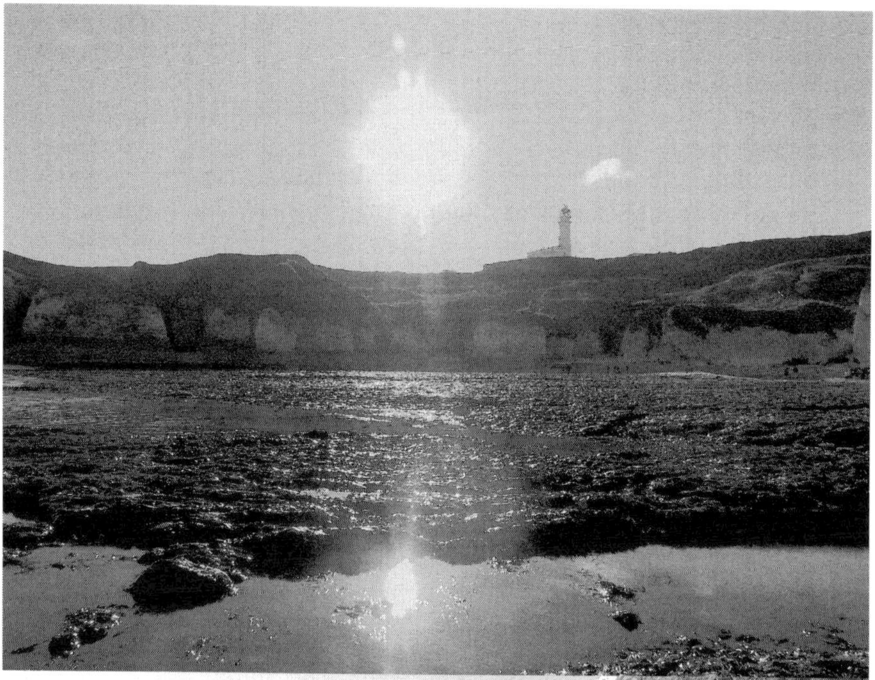

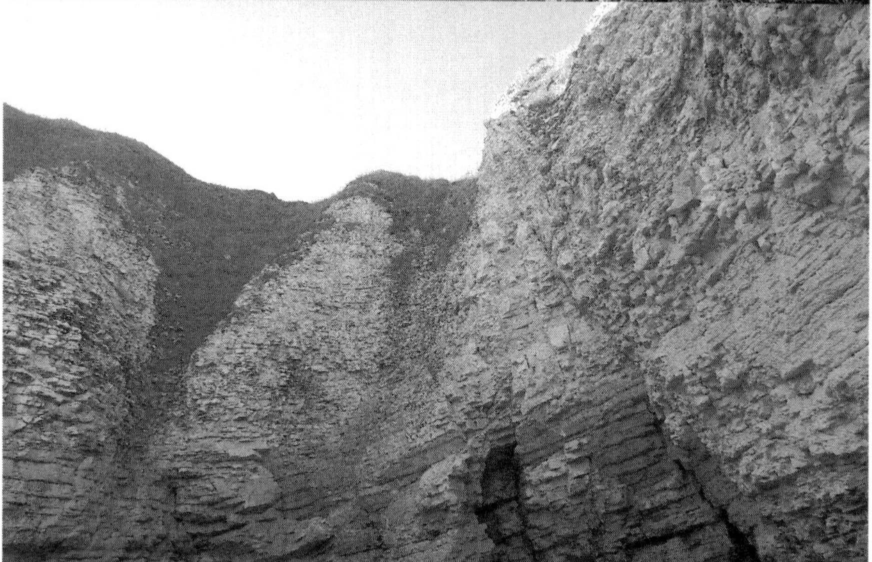

I was pleased we spoke because this woman seemed to know exactly where the body had been found, and 'surprise, surprise' it was *not* Selwicks Bay.

Dog walker:
"A group of geography students from Dundee had discovered the body yesterday morning. From what I understand, the cave he was found in was well above the high water mark. Even the big spring tides don't reach inside that cave."

Paul:
"So from what you are saying, it does not sound like he drowned and was then carried into the cove by the sea?"

Dog walker:
"I suppose he could have drowned, but that doesn't explain how he came to be in the cave. And he couldn't have jumped into the cave. I don't know anything else really. The authorities did not talk to us or ask us any questions. I was with my friend who has the shop on the cliff-top by the lighthouse, so we saw most of what was happening throughout the day."

This was an interesting conversation and if what the lady said was correct, it could possibly rule out the idea the man had committed suicide by jumping off the cliffs or died by drowning. Of course, at this point I had no idea how long he had been inside the cave and there was every possibility he could have died of natural causes. The lady pointed down to a gap between the rocks, that lead into an even smaller cove.

Dog walker:
"That's where he was found; down there in that little cove."

I have been to this cove many times over the years, with my wife Mary and our girls when they were younger. It has six small caves, with two that are open to the sea. The other four are higher up the beach. I know that it becomes inaccessible as the tide comes in, so there is every possibility that this unfortunate man could have found himself cut off, and in the freezing November conditions, he might have died from hyperthermia.

Looking down into the cove you would never have guessed that days before it had been teeming with emergency services. The lady told me she had seen the police, the coastguard, crime scene investigators, and the underwater marine search and rescue - as well as the ambulance service, who, in her words, did something that surprised her.

She told me that before descending the 150 steps down to the beach below, the paramedics unloaded an array of lifesaving equipment, including a defibrillator. I could only presume this is standard procedure because they have to be prepared for any eventuality. Alternatively, perhaps they were unsure at that point whether the man was alive? This suggests to me that, alive or dead, the man could not have been in the cove or in the water for a long period of time.

As I stood talking with the dog walker, I could see four or five different groups of schoolchildren and older students. They were all clambering around on the beach below with clipboards. They all wore yellow high visibility vests and hard hats. I smiled to myself; this was health and safety gone mad. It looked more like a scene from a construction site, rather than a school field trip - an example of just how crazy we are as human beings. Ironically, on warm sunny days, the same beach sees families with young children, who run around in bare feet and bathing costumes. Such school trips are a regular occurrence and another reason why I do not think the man's body could have remained undiscovered in the sea cave for very long.

Dog walker:
"I stood with my friend at the shop near the lighthouse, and we watched it all happening. They taped off the area and would not let anyone down into the cove. Its all very strange that no one was told a thing and no one was asked any questions. The paramedics went down there with all their equipment and were bringing it all back a short time later."

It wasn't until I saw the local newspapers the following week that I learned the name of the dead man. He was 59-year-old Alan Timms from Bridlington.

The article below is the only information I have found relating to the body in the cove. It was published on Thursday November 9th 2017 in the *Bridlington Free Press* newspaper:

"*Humberside Police have now identified the man, who died on the beach near Flamborough, as Alan Timms. The 59-year-old has lived in Bridlington since 2010. Geography students from the High School of Dundee were on a trip to Selwicks Bay when they spotted the body on the beach on Monday November 6th. A spokesperson for Humberside Police said: 'We currently do not believe the circumstances of his death are suspicious. However, we are asking for help from the public. Please call us if you saw or spoke with Alan in the past two weeks or have any information that could help us to piece together his movements prior to being found.'*
Mr Timms body was discovered by a group of schoolchildren on a trip from Scotland on Monday. The students, from the High School of Dundee, were on their annual trip to the Yorkshire Coast when they made the shocking discovery at Selwicks Bay.
Humberside Police say they do not believe that the circumstances of his death are suspicious. Police are keen to hear from anyone who saw or spoke with Alan in the past two weeks or have any information that could help them to piece together his movements prior to being found."

Nothing more has surfaced about this tragedy since then, but I refuse to let it slip away without further research, because I feel sure there is something more to discover.

FLARES OR INTELLIGENT LIGHTFORMS?

On the evening of Wednesday February 7th 2018 my friend Andi Ramsden called my landline to tell me he had purchased an expensive telescope the previous weekend. He seem quite excited about setting it up to view the night sky. Andi was at his back door having a cigarette as we spoke, when suddenly, his voice became louder and he began giving me a description of something he could see in the sky.

Andi claimed that a bright orange sphere had suddenly appeared, then vanished seconds later. He said the light was high in the heavens and appeared to narrow like the pupil of a cat's eye, before disappearing. During our conversation my mobile phone rang. It was Steve Ashbridge. I told him I would call him back as soon as I had finished my call with Andi. Ten minutes later I returned Steve's call and unbelievably, he had seen the same thing as Andi - and this was the only reason he was phoning me. Steve and Andi only live about 5 miles apart, but what are the chances of them both looking up into the sky, at the *same* time, and both seeing the same thing, which only lasted a few seconds?

Pyrotechnics

The next day Steve phoned me again to inform me that the light he saw the previous night had been explained.

Steve:
"It was a coastguard exercise Paul. They were showing new recruits how to use pyrotechnic flares."

This seemed like a perfectly reasonable explanation to me, although I hadn't seen them myself. The only part that didn't seem to fit was that Andi had told me the light he saw was way up in the heavens. I called Andi to tell him what Steve had said and that the sighting of the orange sphere had been solved - but he was having none of it. Andi insisted that the light was far too high in the sky to be a flare and I wasn't about to argue, mainly because I was just passing on the information Steve had given me. Not satisfied with the explanation of coastguard flares, Andi decided to do some research of his own about the light in the sky. He called me later that day.

Andi:
"Hi Paul, I have found out from a member of Hornsea coastguard that there was a military exercise last night, so Steve was right. But what he told me next was interesting. The flares used in the exercise were white phosphorus, which only reach a height of 1000 feet. They burn bright, give off smoke and travel with the wind. I told the coastguard what I saw and he said it couldn't have been anything to do with their exercise."

This information further strengthens my theory that the lights I saw with Bob Brown on November 5th were nothing to do with fireworks. We had seen orange spheres up and down the coast, and as Andi had said, any flares used in a search and rescue exercise would be glowing white.

If Andi was right, this also ruled out the light that he and Steve saw from being a flare; they had described it as a bright orange sphere, just like the ones I saw with Bob. I suppose it is possible that a military exercise was also taking place off Flamborough Head in November 2017 on the night I saw the lightforms with Bob. The statement that a military exercise is taking place seems to be the standard explanation whenever the orange spheres are seen. I have lost count of the number of times the lightforms have appeared in complete silence, to be followed by the arrival of military jets ten or fifteen minutes later.

On Thursday February 8th I decided to spend the day around Flamborough and Bempton. Reports of the lightforms were still in the forefront of my mind and the sheep deaths were starting to interest me a great deal; I just knew there was so much more to these killings than random dog attacks. I also wanted to see if I could learn more about the body that was found in the cove below Flamborough Lighthouse in November 2017.

These were three separate incidents, all in close proximity to each other; two of them ending in death and all of them a complete mystery. There was nothing obvious that could connect one to the other, and I don't think anyone had ever looked for a connection before me. These events do not operate on any level that we can understand, and I think that until we begin looking outside of what is considered normal, we never will.

I decided to drive up to the lighthouse first; I wanted to speak with the lady who owned the gift shop in the lighthouse car park. I suspected that she might have heard something about the body in the cove in the three months that had passed.

The shop was closed when I arrived, so that was one line of enquiry I could not follow up. However, I was not about to give up, so I parked my car and considered my next move. Looking around I could see sheep in the distant fields that ran down to the cliffs, so I decided to have a walk around the area to see if I could pick up any clues. The landscape is rough grass, gorse, brambles and hawthorns; all shaped by fierce winds blown off the North Sea, that constantly batter the land. Every living thing, from the cliff face to the car park, leans inland.

As I walked back to the car park with my dog Wolfy, I saw a woman in the driveway of one of the twelve small bungalows opposite the lighthouse. I put my dog in the car and decided to ask the woman if she knew anything about the body in the cove. The bungalows are only a few hundred metres away from where the emergency services had set up camp in November, so there was a chance she may have heard or seen something. Perhaps it is an odd thing to ask a complete stranger about the discovery of a body, but if I didn't ask, I would not be able to move any further with my research.

After introducing myself and explaining what I was looking into, the lady asked me if I was a reporter. I assured her that I was not and gave her a little background about the *Truth Proof* books. She told me she knew very little about the body in the cove, adding that no one had said a word - which I thought was unusual. She pointed to another bungalow five doors down and told me that the lady who lived there might be able to help, so I thanked her and walked towards the property.

Before I could knock on the door it was opened. I was greeted by a slim lady in her mid-40s, who probably thought I was trying to sell her something. It was another of those moments when people say they cannot help and the door shuts. I assured her that I wasn't a reporter and repeated a similar introduction to the one I had given five minutes before. She looked at me for a few moments before speaking; I suppose the last thing she expected to hear was a complete stranger enquiring about the body in the cove.

Slim lady:
"I'm not sure what happened and we haven't heard anything. We usually find out something. I think the body was taken away by the coroner and that was the last we heard. Did he jump?"

She seemed to know less than I did. I told her the body was discovered in a sea cave above the high water mark, but that was all I knew - and I cannot even be sure that was correct.

Slim lady:
"I wish I could help you. I'm ex-coastguard, but they never tell us anything. Once a body has been taken away that's our job done."

She could not tell me a great deal, and it seemed pointless pressing her for more information that might or might not be related. Everything connected to this tragedy seemed locked down. What I needed were facts and, so far, all I had was nothing more than hearsay. However, as soon as she told me about being ex-coastguard I thought it was worth asking about the lights that had been seen off the coast. I felt sure she must have been involved in call-outs involving the red and orange spheres, so I told her about a few of the things from the *Truth Proof* books; including the chapter on the flares that never were.

Paul:
"So, during your time working for the coastguard, did you get many reports of flares out at sea that were unresolved."

Slim lady:
"All of the time. In most instances, distress flares are the only way we can locate people who are in difficulty at sea."

I realised I should have rephrased my question.

Paul:
"Sorry. What I should have said was: over the years I have searched newspaper archives in East and North Yorkshire and found coastguard call-outs to reports of red and orange flares. On many occasions,

lifeboats from all areas have searched the sea for hours and found nothing. Were you ever on duty or did you ever hear about these type of call-outs over the years?"

No One Knows

Slim lady:
"Oh yes, I know about the lights you are talking about. We have had reports of them, but we could never get to the bottom of what they were. I have been here all my life - I'm a true Flamborian - and I have seen them myself more than once, but I don't know what they are."

This was developing into an interesting conversation. For the first time, I had a coastguard telling me they were aware of the lightforms, even though she had no idea what they were. She was at all times respectful of her former job as a coastguard and was careful not to give away any confidential information.

Slim lady:
"The difficult thing with these lights that keep on being reported, is that they don't act anything like flares. There was an incident some years back, when a boat lost power and was in danger of getting washed towards the rocks. The whole area over the cliffs and out at sea was lit up by flares. We could see the smoke and everything was lit up around them. I know which lights you mean, they are different. When we have had binoculars on them, it is impossible to gauge how far away they are. We just cannot tell if they are miles away or in close. Another thing; they are very bright, but they don't illuminate anything around them. They are odd, but no one knows what they are."

Her observations were echoing my own findings. This conversation alone was worth my trip to Flamborough.

Cliff Lane - Christmas Day 2018

Cliff Lane is a lonely place to be walking at any hour of the day, but this was exactly where my friend Ian Wilson decided to go for a walk on Christmas morning at 6am. He told me he had been restless all night and thought an early morning walk would do him good, so he set off from his home in Buckton around 5.30am. Nothing stirred on land or sky at that hour, and he loved the open air and silence.

The roads and pavements were slippery and as he turned the corner onto Cliff Lane, he could see the narrow single-track road was bristling with ice. Ian walked carefully up the lane to the sound of his own footsteps crunching on the icy road. As he passed Bempton caravan park something caught his eye over the field that runs parallel to the site.

Ian:
"I couldn't believe what I was seeing Paul. How many times have me and you walked this lane in the early mornings and never seen a thing. I stood at the entrance of that pea field, where that triangle of earth appeared in the summer. Two lights were over the field Paul, very low in the sky. It was about six o'clock. I just stood watching them, they were close but I couldn't hear anything, I couldn't believe what I was seeing to be honest."

I asked him about the colour and size of the lights.

Ian:
"One of the lights was red, the other orange and they were sort of pulsing. Not switching from one to the other, just slowly pulsing. But they were very close together. I watched them for a few minutes then they moved really fast to another part of the field and stopped instantly. I mean they just stopped. They did this all over the field, like they were mapping something. I think the best way I can describe their movement is to say they moved like a printer - if that doesn't sound too daft? After about ten minutes, maybe a bit longer, they moved across the road to the fields at the back of the pig farm. I decided I had walked far enough and turned back. I don't know what it was, but I had seen enough. I felt a bit scared."

Ian's sighting sounded amazing, I wish I could have seen it. The only thing I could think of that can fly from point A to point B then stop instantly, would be a drone. But even drones make a noise and at that hour he would have heard it. Ian assures me that no one was around and that the lights were completely silent. I would not have even considered a drone as a possible explanation had it not been Christmas day, but what child or adult would be flying one at 6am on such a cold morning? Ian also assured me that the only footprints on that icy road were his.

I asked him again if he was sure it wasn't a drone - I couldn't help myself.

Ian:
"Are you kidding me Paul? It was six o'clock in the morning, freezing cold and dark. No, it wasn't a drone."

This sighting, like most of the things seen and reported, remains unsolved. I wonder how much activity actually takes place when no one is around. Most of the phenomena appears to be happening under the cover of darkness, or at a time of day when very few people are around. I think there can be no doubt that we are dealing with something that has incredible intelligence.

BRINGING DOWN THE LIGHT:
The Bempton Missing Time

On December 18th 2017 I was invited to talk on the *The Unexplained With Howard Hughes* radio show. I always feel privileged to be asked onto Howard's shows because he has such a great following. Howard wanted to talk to me about the latest research I was involved in - which happened to be the Cliff Lane story.

Whilst on air Howard told me he had received several emails and texts from someone claiming to have had a very strange experience on the cliff-tops at Bempton on December 14th. This really surprised me. I couldn't help wondering what were the chances of my being on the show on the 18th and a witness from my own area contacting Howard on the 14th? After Howard had explained, I discovered that this new information was very relevant, because it placed three new witnesses directly into the Cliff Lane story.

I have changed the contact's name to Stephen, to protect his identity. The following email was read out on air by Howard Hughes and it outlines what the witness says happened to him and two friends, while they were out walking the cliff-tops at Bempton on December 14th.

Stephen:
"Having left the Bempton RSPB car park at around 7pm we walked down to the cliff path and on towards the lighthouse. Our entire walk normally takes us an hour and ten minutes. At approximately 7.30pm we saw a brilliant flash of white light that turned everything daylight for a split second. It puzzled us but we thought nothing more about it until we reached the car. Expecting it to be 8.10pm, we were perplexed when we looked at our watches and realised that it was in fact 10.15pm."

I though this new information was quite amazing. If true, these three walkers had somehow lost over two hours of time. Howard gave me Stephen's contact details, with his permission, and we have now been exchanging emails. Stephen and his friends are still very confused about what happened to them in that period of missing time. And, for the moment at least, they have stopped visiting the cliff-tops at Bempton.

After reading some of the emails, it was clear that some of the incidents that Bob and I had experienced at Bempton during 2017, had also been witnessed by Stephen and his walking companions. He told me they had even seen military trucks dotted around the cliff-tops. An additional piece of the puzzle that surprised me, was that he said the military personnel they saw were armed.

Here is one part of an email sent to me by Stephen:

Stephen:
"My friend (who was with me the night in question) has been looking at properties for sale in the area - Speeton in particular. We saw the military trucks ourselves, we even saw men armed with rifles, as if they were looking for someone - although in fairness, it could have just been a military exercise."

If he was telling me the truth, and I have no reason to doubt him, it would appear that more than one truck was seen around Bempton cliff-tops in July 2017. The fact they also saw military personnel armed with rifles makes me wonder what circumstance would have made that permissible? My mind switched briefly to the mutilated sheep found in the area. I wondered if the military were looking for whatever was responsible for killing livestock? Stephen's final thought; that it could all have been a military exercise, could be correct, but nothing had appeared in the local newspapers advising civilians to avoid certain areas. The trucks were around for a number of weeks, not days, so surely the public should have received some kind of warning? Is it standard practice for military personnel to walk around public areas with rifles?

Stephen:
"We haven't been back to Bempton for a few weeks, but we have been spending a lot of time at Speeton Cliffs. There has been a few odd occurrences which, on the whole, I think could be explained away. But there has been one more flash of light, in a similar fashion as last time, which I doubt was weather related. Without checking, I think that happened two Fridays ago. However, I don't believe there was missing time in this instance. We have spoken to several locals, to ask about the area my friend plans to live in. At the same time I let it slip into

conversation what had happened at Bempton. Around half were aware of the events and one elderly man claimed to have had a similar experience. However, that was in 2010."

I had briefly mentioned the sheep killings to Stephen in a previous email, although I had not gone into any detail. At that point, I had sent him three emails without receiving a reply and had just about given up on the idea of being contacted again. Thankfully, he did get in touch.

It was clear from the replies that I *had* received, including the one below, that Stephen was very much of the opinion that whatever we were dealing with, had an earthly explanation. Unless that's what he wanted to believe? Perhaps at the very back of his mind he felt that something unexplainable had happened - something that is hard to accept if you believe that science has all the answers. I will always respect the views and opinions of others, but I know that strange things do happen; things that really should not, in a world where day follows night. But we should never dismiss something, just because it goes against everything we believe is possible.

I think my emails to Stephen challenged some of the phenomena that he previously believed impossible. It was clear that he had thought long and hard about what might have happened in the two hour period after they saw the flash of light. I don't think any of the scenarios I had suggested felt right to him, but who could blame him for feeling that way? Something happened and that two hours of missing time he and his friends experienced must have been a terrible thing to deal with.

Stephen:
"I'll be frank. I don't believe any of this to be alien abduction (though I have noticed a foreign scar close to my appendix scar). If anything it's tests being undertaken by the military or something totally different we could never fathom."

These were interesting comments because I had never once mentioned alien abduction. The fact that UFOs are frequently reported in the area may have brought him to that conclusion, but these were his words, not mine. The appearance of a foreign scar is interesting and suggests that something must have taken place during his period of missing time. But

I wonder what made him think of alien abduction? I think the fact that the military were around at the time, could mean they had some part to play - but were they observers or players? I personally believe they were observers - observers who were fully aware that the phenomena was in the area and active.

I wondered what Stephen meant by *"something totally different that we could never fathom."* Could it be that he was confronting a truth that a total sceptic would rather not face? This is, after all, a sweeping statement that covers lots of ground. But it might help someone avoid admitting to themselves that something exists that they do not want to believe. I have to be honest, I think that if the things Stephen and his friends experienced had happened to someone else, he would not have believed them. After I had told him about some of the events that were happening in the area, things that could not be denied, his replies to me offered explanations that fitted his own belief system. It occurred to me that after his missing time experiences, Steven had started to question his own beliefs.

Stephen:
"I will be honest Paul, I believe that sheep mutilation in general is carried out by regular people who lust after creating a hoax, just to get people like us talking about it - similar to the people who went out of their way to create crop circles. I'm not saying all crop circles or sheep mutilation are the result of mischievous involvement though. Missing time and strange lights after all cannot be hoaxed."

I agree 100% with Stephen when he says that many of the crop circles and animal mutilations reported are being created by people. I cannot agree that they are regular people, however, because in the case of the animal mutilations, calling them 'sick individuals' would be a better description.

I also cannot accept that sheep were being killed just to create a story for people with an interest in the unexplained. The places these animals were being found are so remote, and I am sure the farmers never intended anyone finding out that it was actually happening. I believe they would have preferred to have kept it quiet. So for that reason alone, Stephen's explanation falls short. For one thing, I did not learn about the sheep until 2018. By that time almost a year had passed and in all that time, livestock were being killed and no one, except the farmers who were directly involved, knew anything about what was happening.

I am very grateful for Stephen's emails, not least because I believe he has researched every avenue to find a rational explanation for what he experienced in December 2017. I am sure that if he had found one, he would have told me. Whatever happened to him on those cliff-tops has affected him in such a way, that he is now questioning himself and wondering what is possible and what is impossible.

It is interesting that he had begun slipping details of his experiences into conversations with strangers, then formed opinions that offer a more earthly explanation – but still leaving the door slightly open to the possibility that something extraordinary happened. These are indicators to me that he found the event deeply disturbing. I know this because I have wrestled with these problems for most of my life and although I accept that his experience is different, I cannot un-see what I saw as a child and invent a rational story. I am currently writing about my own personal experiences, which will be published in the near future.

Even if we disregard Stephen and friend's missing time event, it does not make all the other strange events I have reported so far go away: the triangle of bare earth in the pea-field, the black triangle seen moving below Speeton Cliffs, the lights I saw under the sea. Together with the rectangle of red light I saw on the cliff-face and military trucks with armed soldiers seen monitoring the area, this makes quite a list - but it does not end there. What were the men in white overalls doing on the old RAF base? And was it just coincidence that the deer found with the hole in its side was discovered on the same day as the thirty sheep packed tightly into the corralled area near Cliff Lane?

It Never Stopped, It Just Waited
May 18th 2018

The Cliff Lane story does not seem to be going away anytime soon.

The farmer who suffered all the sheep losses throughout 2017 moved some sheep back to Bempton the following April and he promised to let me know if anything happened. When something did happen, as usual I had to find out for myself. I don't for one second think what happened was deliberate, but I wish I had been informed as soon as he discovered the first animal death of 2018.

On Saturday May 12th I woke up very early, after a restless night and found myself standing in the kitchen at 4.45am waiting for the kettle to boil. For some reason I felt like I had to visit Bempton to check on the sheep. I don't think it was a premonition or anything. I just had the urge to go. I quickly made myself a cup of tea, gathered a camera and a few other things and was soon heading out of Bridlington towards Bempton. It was a dull and miserable morning and the sky gave no hint about how the day ahead would be, so I put on a pullover and jacket.

This time I decided to take Wolfy along with me. I would keep him on his lead at all times around the livestock; although he is so good-natured that he would not bother them anyway. We arrived at the farm at about 5.15am and after putting on my wellington boots, we set off towards the open fields. The last time I was there the farmer had returned just fifteen of his sheep to the field. Now their numbers had swelled and I estimated there was about 200 sheep grazing in the top field, all within sight of the farmhouse.

Everything looked so peaceful; the day was warming up, steam was rising from the dew-soaked grass, and I was beginning to wish I had not put on my jacket. It was hard to imagine that months earlier, parts of the field had been littered with slaughtered lambs. A frightening thought to dwell on, because they were proof that something deadly and elusive had been present throughout 2017.

A lone roe deer buck stood in the middle of the field, like a nervous guard looking at me as I approached. Oddly enough, he didn't seem keen to run away into the relative safety of Danes Dyke woods, which I didn't give much thought to at the time. As I got closer, he simply moved further back preferring to keep me at a safe distance. Most of the sheep had now given birth, and lambs of varying ages and their mothers stared cautiously at me and Wolfy as we passed. There was nothing of interest to see in the field, so I decided to walk along the cliff-tops towards Danes Dyke.

I had been there on the previous Wednesday night with Steve Ashbridge. The top of the Dyke is amazing and gives full 360-degree views. It is the perfect place to sit and observe everything; from lightforms, to the sheep in the fields below. I remember that night had been quite uneventful; I had seen a golden light appear out at sea, but that was inconclusive. Then at about 9.30pm, Steve also saw a golden light appear on the cliff-tops. He said it was a little further inland and appeared to be moving. It puzzled him, because he only saw it for a few seconds. With such amazing views it would have been easy to see someone carrying a light, but once it had gone, he never saw it again.

I thought about this as I walked along the field with Wolfy that morning. Steve is not the kind of man who would say he had seen something if he had not actually seen it. I suppose the light he saw could have been one of many perfectly explainable things, but no matter how hard we tried, neither of us could not think of one.

When I reached the area roughly where Steve had seen the moving light on Wednesday night, I stopped walking for a moment. I was midway between Danes Dyke and the RSPB nature reserve - you might call it the middle of nowhere. The North Sea was to the right and there was open farmland to the left. It made no sense to me how the light that Steve had seen could simply appear and disappear in such an open place. But this was Bempton, and not everything a person sees and experiences in this area make sense.

I carried on towards Danes Dyke. Its grass and bracken-covered banks rise steeply from the cliff-tops to over ten metres above sea-level at their highest point. However, it is worth the climb and a few minutes later I was standing on the ridge taking in the amazing views. I looked down at the grazing sheep and saw the roe deer again. He seemed perfectly at home surrounded by them, but I still could not understand why he chose to stay in the open field and not hide in the woods.

When I was there with Steve on Wednesday night we noted, at about 10pm, that all of the sheep became very restless and began making noise. It was too dark for us to see what was disturbing them, but the commotion only lasted for a few minutes. I think it's time I invested in some thermal imaging equipment for such situations.

I walked along the ridge of the Dyke to where the open fields meet the woodland. The Neolithic earthwork is an amazing example of human determination to build something against all odds. Built with primitive flint tools thousands of years earlier, it is as impressive today as it ever has been. I carefully climbed down the bank of the Dyke and into the woods below, I could almost feel the age and history of the land beneath my feet. It was about 6.15am when I slowly made my way through the trees. The woodland was alive with birdsong; they were all high on life after surviving another winter on the edge of the North Sea.

It soon became apparent that someone else was also interested in the wildlife inhabiting the wood, because I saw two trail cameras set about two feet off the ground, sort of hidden in plain sight. I wonder what the owner of the cameras thought when he reviewed his images and saw the mighty little Wolfy in a few of them.

Danes Dyke really is a spooky place; perhaps partly due to some of the things I have been told, and partly because of some of my experiences whilst walking through here. Being pulled backwards by an invisible force was one of the strangest, but on this morning I felt as though I was being watched, for some peculiar reason. I saw nothing to indicate that I was, but I could not shake off the feeling that there were eyes on me.

I decided not to walk along the top of the Dyke on my return to the farm. I had already covered that part of the walk earlier and found nothing unusual. So I made the decision to leave the woods behind and cut across the middle of the fields. I could see a stile about twenty metres away, which would be as good a place as any to climb over the fence.

As I walked along the edge of the wood I happened to glance towards an overhanging hawthorn tree. Its thick bow must have fallen over many years before and there was a six foot round hollow beneath. A large canopy of branches had grown from the broken trunk creating a natural shelter below.

Deer In The Hawthorn

When I looked more closely I was shocked to see the carcass of a young roe buck lying dead on its side in the hollow. I studied it for a while and looked at the surroundings, trying to make sense of what I was seeing. The animal had not been there for very long, because its eyes looked sharp and clear. It looked so out of place beneath the hawthorn tree, as if it had been gently placed there.

The deer had a very large hole in its side and I could see its internal organs. They looked undamaged, which was odd, considering the extent of the wound, midway between its underside and ribs. Four or five ribs were missing, although I could not tell if they had been bitten off or removed in some other way. It looked just like the wound had exploded from the inside out.

I had no explanation for what I was seeing, but I took a few pictures of the carcass and the surroundings before getting closer. I had suspected the deer had not been dead for very long and my suspicions were confirmed when I placed the back of my hand onto its neck. It was still warm. Looking much more closely I could see that something had been removed; something had taken half of its liver. I say 'removed' because I could not see any signs of claw or bite marks. It was a very peculiar sight, and I still had this unshakable feeling of being watched.

I pushed a stick into the ground and tied Wolfy to it with his lead - if I lost him Mary would never forgive me. I took some more pictures, then I got another stick and began to carefully run it through the fur around the deer's neck. I was looking for any signs of bite or claw marks, but I found nothing. I repeated the same procedure on every exposed part of the animal's body. I could not see any signs of trauma anywhere, apart from the huge hole in its side.

Another odd thing I noticed, there was no sign of blood anywhere on the ground or on the fur. Whatever did this had no problem going through part of the ribcage to gain entry to the liver, so how could that be possible? I grabbed the animal by its antlers and turned it over. The deer was perfect on the other side, there was not a mark on it anywhere.

After gathering as much information as I could, I set off across the field back to the car. It was sad to see such a magnificent animal mutilated in such a way. I might have continued looking for answers, but I decided to leave. My head was already full of unanswered questions.

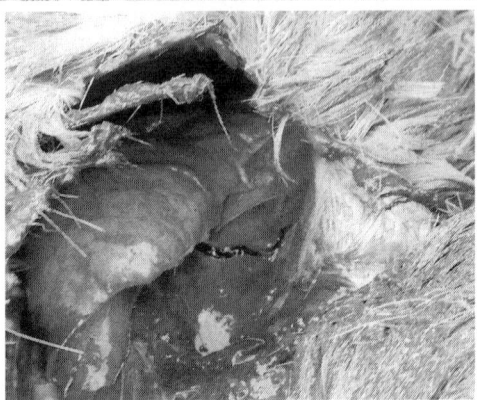

The deer carcass exactly as I found it beneath the hawthorn branch

Close-up showing deer's exposed ribs and the remains of its liver

I had found the deer less than twenty feet away from the field where the sheep had been killed throughout 2017 - but could it really be the same killer? In many instances the sheep had their throats torn out, the skin stripped from their faces but they had not been eaten. Something had already taken part of this deer, and just like the sheep, there was absolutely no sign of a struggle.

As I approached the other side of the field, I saw a farmer driving a quad bike up and down the hedge side. We had never actually met but I recognised him and knew he was already aware of the sheep deaths. I waved and called out to say hello. For some reason he just glared at me and carried on up and down the hedgerow on his quad bike, I'm not sure why people behave in this way. I can understand some being wary of strange faces, especially when so much livestock was being killed, but I was not the enemy.

I walked towards my car and could see the farmhouse and John, the farmer, who was in the driveway with his wife. His two old Labrador dogs came running towards me, so I picked up Wolfy and put him under my arm. It was plain to see they were good-natured dogs and were just doing what all dogs do. They were letting us know this was their territory. When I had contacted John in 2017 he gave me permission to park next to his farmhouse; which saved me a long walk. It also gave me the chance to speak with him and keep up to date with anything unusual that might have happened.

John:
"Hello Paul. Did you find anything interesting on your walk."

I nodded and handed him my camera while I put Wolfy in the car. I didn't say anything until I had shown him the pictures of the deer. He raised his eyebrows and looked more than a little surprised.

John:
"Whereabouts did you find this Paul?"

Paul:
"It was on the edge of the wood under a tree. Whatever killed it must

have still been around because it hadn't been dead that long. I put my hand on it, it felt warm and it wasn't laying in sunlight."

John looked down at my camera as I slowly flicked through the images. He said that he would tell Tom, adding that he would be interested. He was referring to the man I had just seen out on the quad bike, who I already knew was very keen to find out what was killing the sheep. I also suspected he did not like the idea of my presence around the fields. You cannot please everyone, not even when you are actually trying to help.

John:
"Another lamb was killed last week Paul, the same as the others killed last year. But this was a very young lamb, so we are not sure if it's the same killer. In a way I hope it's not. We don't want a repeat of what happened last year."

I didn't bother to comment. My gut feeling was, that whatever was responsible, has never gone away. The only reason it stopped was because the sheep were taken out of the area.

Paul:
"What day did you find the lamb John? Because we were up on the ridge of Danes Dyke last Wednesday until quite late, and the sheep began making a lot of noise at around 10pm."

John:
"It was Thursday morning, the 10th."

Is it possible that me and Steve had actually been up on the ridge of Danes Dyke the night before, at the time John's lamb was killed? I think it is. Perhaps May 9th was the start of the next wave of killings?

The lamb was found with similar injuries to the sheep that had been killed throughout 2017. Just a few days later I had discovered a freshly killed deer in very close proximity to the same field. A gambler might say the odds of these two deaths not being connected were slim - and I'm not a betting man, but I would have to agree. One thing that puzzles me - the injuries inflicted on the roe deer were nothing like the wounds on the sheep. So although I believe they are all connected, there are still factors that set them apart.

Before I left, John asked me about something that I found interesting. It was something he must have forgotten to mention back in 2017.

John:
"Was the deer you found frothing at the mouth like the sheep?"

That was a surprise, because I was not aware the mutilated sheep had shown any signs of frothing at the mouth. I wish I had known this bit information when I had spoken with the livestock auctioneers and local vets last year. It may be of no significance, but I think it has to mean something. Any piece of information, no matter how unimportant it may seem, is always worth having.

Further Investigations

Early the next day, Sunday May 13th, I decided to go back for a second look at the deer carcass. I wanted to see how much predation had taken place overnight. I phoned my good friend Chris Wright and told him what I had found. Chris had become very interested in my research and was more than happy to make the journey from his home in Scarborough to accompany me to Bempton. We had discussed my work many times but this was the first time Chris and I had ventured out onto the fields together.

We arrived at John's farm at 8.30am and entered the affected area. We saw the lone roe buck, which was still out in the field grazing among the sheep. I wondered if he knew there was something in the woods that was capable of catching and killing him? He didn't leave that field for weeks. This in itself is unusual, because wild deer always make a fast getaway at the first sight of people. The sheep had been moved into the lower part of the fields, down towards the cliffs. Even the farmer remarked how strange it was that the roe buck did not want to leave the field. For some reason it must have feared the woods more than us.

When I left the deer carcass the day before, all of its internal organs looked to be in place, except its liver. I had examined the animal myself. When I looked carefully at the photos I had taken, I could see the liver appeared to have been sliced clean in half and it showed no signs of teeth marks. I have a high quality Nikon P900 camera and its 16-

megapixels allows me to zoom in very closely, but I saw no signs of teeth marks anywhere on the inside or the outside of the animal. Someone suggested to me that it might have been shot. In my opinion that was definitely not the case. What I saw inside the deer's open wound, were perfectly unmarked internal organs, (well, apart from the liver) and a gunshot wound would not have been so selective. If this were the case, I should have seen blood, but I didn't find one spot of blood anywhere on the carcass or on the ground.

As we approached the edge of the field I pointed out to Chris the area where I found the carcass. I remember telling him how it was pure chance that I had even found it at all. When we arrived at the hawthorn tree, the deer had gone. We looked all around; by the side of the field and in amongst the bracken and brambles, but it was not there. Then Chris pointed out that the grass was flattened at the back of the hawthorn tree. Then he noticed that the flattened grass went even further, forming a half metre wide path, that stretched all the way through to the other side of the woods.

It was difficult to understand how an unknown something had managed to drag the deer out from the point behind the hawthorn tree. It obviously had done, but branches and thick vegetation would have made it very difficult to get beneath the canopy of the tree. So whatever it was, must have had some strength. Chris and I followed the flattened grass to where it ended and there we found the remains of a half-eaten carcass. Its right hind leg and entire right side were missing and, on closer inspection, we could see that all of its internal organs had gone, except the heart.

I initially thought the deer weighed about one hundred and twenty pounds. Chris and I estimated that about fifty pounds in body weight was left. If I am correct, then something in the region of seventy pounds of meat had been consumed during the night. Of course, there could have been more than one animal feeding on the remains. There is no shortage of foxes and badgers in these woods so either one of these opportunist carnivores could have found the carcass during the night.

Even though the animal had suffered massive trauma, the lack of blood still puzzled me. Whatever had killed it, literally smashed through its ribs, so we should have expected to see blood. With that in mind, we searched the surrounding area looking for blood spots on the grass or leaves or anywhere, but we found nothing. I was beginning to wonder if the deer had actually been killed somewhere else, then placed under the hawthorn tree afterwards.

I took some more photos then Chris helped me to lift what was left of the carcass and put it high into a large sycamore tree. If the predator was a big cat, then only a cat would be able to climb the tree to get at the meat. We made sure it was wedged tight by fixing its head and antlers between branches. We then spent the rest of the morning searching the Dyke for any kind of clues, but found nothing.

What Predator?

The next day I decided to go back to Danes Dyke. I just could not get the image of the deer out of my head. If this was not enough proof that some kind of large predator was active in the area, nothing would be. The million-dollar question was, *what type of predator was it?* I initially thought it could only be a big cat, but where were the bite marks and the claw marks to back up the theory?

It was mid-afternoon when I arrived and the sun was high in the sky. As I walked across the fields I could see the roe buck again, grazing among the sheep. He kept a safe distance, never taking his eyes off me, as I headed down towards the cliffs. I still could not understand why he seemed so reluctant to leave the field. I didn't want to hang around on the cliff-tops, I just wanted check the carcass and go home.

The small strip of woodland by the edge of the field was lush and seemed idyllic in the afternoon sun – quite the opposite of what I saw two days before. I found myself stopping every now and then to check the surroundings. It was hard not to feel a little wary after seeing the horrific and fatal wounds inflicted on these poor animals. I passed the hawthorn tree where I first discovered the deer, then headed towards the large sycamore, where we had placed its remains the day before. Even at distance, I could see that it was not there.

The carcass was now on the ground, about six feet away from the tree. I do not think it could have fallen because I had wedged its head and antlers firmly between the branches. Pulling out my camera from its bag, I began to take more pictures. I did not intend staying around it for very long, because the exposed flesh was now attracting lots of flies. It was also clear that more of the carcass had been consumed.

I discovered later that day that two more deer carcasses had been found, close to a farm at Speeton. I had already been told I had very little chance of seeing their remains, and after several failed attempts to speak with people at the farm, I gave up. Once again, all I am able to do is give my opinion based on the things that have been happening. I think it is fair to say, there is a strong possibility that the Speeton deer-kills are linked to the others. The distances involved are minimal and dead roe deer are not found that often, so to learn about three carcasses being found around the same time, all within a mile of each other, suggests to me that they are connected.

Thinking back, I wondered if the gold lights that Steve and I saw on Wednesday night were in any way connected. Should I even be saying such a thing without proof? The lightforms are a real phenomenon with unknown capabilities, so I would suggest that anything is possible. People have asked me to produce proof of their existence, and aside from video footage, I cannot. But no one should take only my word that they are real. There are thousands of people from all walks of life, all over the world, who have seen them. Although I very much doubt they will have anything more to offer than an account of what they have witnessed.

This does not mean the lightforms are any less real, and we should not dismiss them because they cannot be understood. This phenomenon goes over the head of established science and has nothing to do with tricks of the light, Chinese lanterns, meteorites or some other naturally occurring phenomena. I believe they are something else entirely, perhaps an, as yet, undiscovered lifeform.

ROAD KILL OR SATANIC SACRIFICE?

Many theories have been put forward to explain why so many animals are being killed. It has been suggested that the killings might be ritualistic, a form of occult practice, or even some deranged lunatic who takes pleasure from inflicting pain. It was even suggested that the deer had probably been hit by a car. It seems everyone had an opinion and no one had a clue.

I cannot even consider the suggestion of the killings being ritualistic, the locations are simply too remote. I am fully aware that such practices would have to be performed in secret, and the old RAF base does have a history of such things, but to kill so many sheep and deer under the cover of darkness, to my mind, is close to impossible. Could all of the deer have simply died of natural causes and then been scavenged by foxes and badgers? I suppose that theory could be put forward as an explanation by some. But does that explain why only half of the deer's liver was removed, or why heads were even missing on some of the animals found?

Whatever the cause, the absence of blood puzzles me the most. You would think, with such wounds, there would have been massive blood loss. The ribs on the roe buck, that I found in May 2017, looked as though they had been blasted with a shotgun, from the inside out.

The sheep mutilations are just as hard to fathom. They cannot be the work of any known predator. The fact that ears and eyes are removed and their faces are stripped of skin, screams out that something very unusual is happening. No barrier exists that can stop or detect this phenomenon, which moves between land - and also sea - since I was soon to discover that injuries inflicted on harbour porpoises gave me proof of this.

There is simply nothing to explain what is happening. The deaths appear to be so random and unplanned. I wonder if the killer sees in advance of everything we do? Something is enabling it to carry out these things without making mistakes or leaving any clues behind. This disjointed chaos requires intelligence and seems to operate outside of our vision and understanding. One day science will accept the reality of these things. For now, however, they are part of an over-science that cannot be touched or understood. All I can do is wait for more of the story to unfold; but as I write this, at 7.20pm on May 17th 2018, I don't think things are going to stop anytime soon.

June 2018

I continued to visit the affected area throughout May and into June. Then on the morning of June 1st John phoned to tell me he had found another dead sheep. He said its throat had been torn out and he didn't think it had been dead for long.

I went up to the farm later that day to look at the carcass and the area it have been found. The animal's eyes had been removed and part of its left ear. Nothing else appeared to have been touched and I could not find any trace of blood in the field. On June 11th John discovered a third sheep in similar condition. I told him I didn't think this was going to stop until the sheep were moved out of the area all together. I wish I knew what was responsible, but even now, I don't have a clue. I think it is highly likely that the same thing, whatever that 'thing' may be, is responsible for all of the deaths - but because the origins of the killer are still unknown, makes things even more complicated.

At 5am on Tuesday June 12th, I found myself back in the affected area. The first thing I noticed was that the roe buck was missing. He had finally left the field. I searched the woods and surrounding fields for three hours and found nothing of interest. The highlight of the morning was reaching round for my GoPro camera, which was attached to my bag, to find it had gone. Lost in the long grass, it was a £300 casualty I could have done without losing.

At times I wonder if the phenomena is actually playing with me. It is almost as though the animals are only being killed when I am not around to find them. I say this because on the evening of Wednesday June 13th, John called me to say he had found a fourth dead sheep earlier that day. I paid him a visit and was able to obtain photos of this 80-kilo ewe. The animal's throat had been completely torn out, its entire face had been stripped of skin and both its eyes and an ear had been removed. Nothing else on the carcass had been touched. It was almost a year to the day when I had first begun researching this particular mystery. Who would have thought that a triangle of earth in a pea-crop would have opened so many doors to the unexplained?

I began visiting the same fields between 5.00 and 5.30am almost every morning throughout the year, in the hope that I would find some clues. If, as some people have suggested, a big cat was responsible for the deaths, it would have been easy for it to take the sheep. By June, the grass is so long that anything could move about virtually unseen. Talk of a genuine big cat roaming the fields and woodlands of East Yorkshire is nothing new; if it could be proved that such an animal was responsible, it would be extraordinary. But the evidence points to something far more advanced.

Reports of a large black cat in the area only confused matters, because no one thinks anything other than such a creature, could be responsible for the Bempton killings. Years ago, people would laugh when someone said they had seen one, because it was 'not possible'. Now, because no one has any real idea about what could be responsible, a big cat is being considered as the explanation.

No Ordinary Cat

In August 2017 I sold a copy of *Truth Proof 1* to an elderly couple who owned a holiday home in Bridlington. After reading my book they contacted me to say they had a story they wanted to share.

The couple visited Flamborough Lighthouse on June 6th 2017; something they did several times a week during their holiday. They loved looking at the wildlife and watching the boats out at sea. However, on this particular day they saw something different, something so out of place that it that it shocked them both.

They were sitting in their car overlooking the fields that lead down to the cliffs; beyond which is nothing but open sea. They could see a few sheep grazing in the field close to where they were parked, then suddenly, a large black cat appeared. It ran from the cover of some gorse bushes, across the open field and into a hedgerow. There was no mistaking what they saw.

Visitor Lady:
"We were just sat looking out to sea. It was getting towards dusk, the light was fading, but we could still see everything very clearly. I saw it first and asked my husband what he thought it was.

He instantly said it was a cat, but it was definitely not a domestic cat. It was a genuine big cat, in the truest sense of the word. It broke cover and ran with its belly low to the ground until it reached the hedgerow, then it began to slink along the treeline. It was in the field with the sheep and I don't think they even noticed it. We had binoculars and a camera on the back seat, but we were so shocked by what we were looking at, that we did not even think about using them. Its fur was jet black and very shiny; I would say it was about as tall as a Labrador dog. But it was much longer.

I realise what I am going to say next might sound odd; after all, I have never seen a big cat before in my life - but I remember thinking it looked a bit too long. I don't know why. It was much bigger than any domestic cat and seemed longer than it should have been for its height. Its hard to explain, but we both saw it and we both thought the same."

This big cat sighting was very interesting and it highlights how strange the area is - but this was June 2017, and as yet, I still knew nothing of the mysterious deaths of livestock around Bempton and Flamborough. When I did eventually find out, I wanted to connect the big cat to the animal deaths. However, that notion changed very quickly when I saw the damage to the animal carcasses.

From the description the couple gave, a cat this size would have no problem killing livestock, such as sheep and deer - except there was no evidence that the animals were being eaten. So could this creature really be the sheep killer? It was doubtful; unless it was capable of selecting certain body parts, stripping the skin from its victims faces and just leaving the rest behind. Sightings of big cats are just another anomaly thrown into the mix, or perhaps they are 'pulled into' this land of high strangeness? I say this because I dare to think the unthinkable and often wonder if something else is stepping into and out of our reality.

A Clean Cut

On Tuesday July 3rd John called me at 7am to say he had found another dead sheep. He told me he had found it the night before, but didn't bother to call me because it was a late hour. I am not sure when this one was killed, because I had searched the fields the day before and found nothing out of the ordinary. John thought this particular animal had been dead for a number of days before he discovered it, but it does not add up. I had already covered every part of those fields on July 2nd and I am certain I saw no dead sheep at the time.

John:
"Good morning Paul. I've just inspected the sheep and found another one dead. I think you should come up here and look at this one. It's had its face stripped like the others, but something has cut half of its ear off. I cannot work out what killed it. The skin seems to have been cut away around its neck in a sort of V-shape. It looks very strange."

I paused, and mentally began retracing my movements from the day before.

Paul:
Well I was there yesterday John and I walked all around the fields. I didn't see anything out of the ordinary.

John:
Are you sure you came up here yesterday morning? I only ask because I am sure the sheep has been dead for two or three days; it's beginning to smell a bit ripe."

I arrived at the farm a short time after John's call. He was right, something *had* removed half of the sheep's ear and the cut was very clean and precise. Apart from having the skin removed from its face, the rest of the carcass looked perfect. All of the sheep had been sheared a few days before, so it would have been easy to see any bite marks or scratches. John was also right when he said the animal looked like it had been dead for two or three days; the smell was horrendous, its stomach was swollen and it was beginning to decompose. All I can say is that it definitely was not in the field the day before.

INCIDENTAL UFOS

UFO Bigger than a Battleship

Amazing stories seem to come my way when I least expect them. I learned about this one on May 18th 2019, during an out of the blue conversation with some strangers that Bob Brown and I met while we were up at Bempton cliffs.

We had set off for the cliff-tops around 7pm and were there a short time later. The sun was settling behind some thick grey cloud, making the early evening sky look dull and overcast, but it was surprisingly warm. We parked up at the RSPB nature reserve and saw a few cars and motorhomes still there; with men and women keen to photograph the seabirds that come to nest along the cliffs at this time of year.

As Bob and I walked from the carpark to the cliffs I could see two men with cameras walking up the path towards us. Like all of the people, apart from us, their day on the clifftops was over. As we got closer we nodded and said hello, and the two men did the same. Then one of them looked at me and said, *"Are you the UFO guy?"* I stopped instantly and said, *"Yes. Do I know you?"* I have to confess to not recognising them, but they obviously knew me. I assumed they knew about me from the *Truth Proof* books. Since the release of the books I have met quite a few people who come to the area hoping to see or experience some of the phenomena I've researched.

Both men looked to be in their mid-60s. The one who spoke to me was about 5ft 8 tall with thinning silver hair. He told me his name was Andrew and that he used to live in Scarborough. His friend, who had not spoken at that point, introduced himself as Martin, he was over 6ft tall and of medium build.

Martin said that he had met Bob and me the previous year and we had spoken about the lightforms, but for the life of me, I could not remember the conversation, and neither could Bob. He told us they had hoped they might bump into us. Then Andrew began to tell us that he had seen a UFO and asked if we wanted to hear about it. I said yes and was glad to hear his story.

Andrew:
"I've not really spoken about it to many people. It's not the kind of thing I would normally talk about, but I'm willing to tell you because I know you investigate these things. I doubt anyone else would believe me. I was in Scarborough with my daughter at the time; she's thirty now and was only seven when we saw it, so this is going back twenty-three years.

It was incredible really. I remember that I had taken my daughter to the arcades on the sea front to let her play on the slots. It was something I did maybe once a week. After that I would take her to Scarborough Spa where I would have a beer and she would have a glass of pop and some crisps. I think it was September, although I am not certain, but I know it was the time of year when the nights began to draw in. We were looking out to sea over towards Bempton and Flamborough, because I remember seeing the cliffs silhouetted against the sky and the sweeping beam of the lighthouse. But I could also see something else.

There was a big globe of white light about half-way up the cliff-face. It looked very bright. Then others began to appear, one after another, until there was a line of five round white lights that stood out from the cliff face. I saw a red light above them as well. I remember thinking they were all exactly the same shape and size, and evenly spaced out. I am convinced they belonged to one solid object. Whatever it was, it must have been massive.

Paul:
"Did anyone else see them or was it just you and your daughter?"

Andrew:
"No, there was a man at the next table to us who saw them too, and he was quite interested. He said 'Well that's a first, never seen anything like that before.' I don't think we could believe what we were seeing."

I asked Andrew if he could be sure that what he saw was not just something ordinary; such as a helicopter or even lights from some boats on the water.

Andrew:
"Well, I'm used to seeing all sorts of things out at sea off this coast. In

the winter we ring seabirds (guillemots) around Filey Brigg. You see all sorts of weird stuff; strange lights and things, but I have never seen anything like that before. It was the sheer size of it all for a start; the lights were big and they were evenly spaced out. The gaps between each one was massive."

Paul:
"How big would you estimate this to have been then - compared to a car or large boat?"

Andrew:
"I can only tell you what I saw, but those lights actually came out a long way over the sea, away from the cliff-face. From where we are right now, I think they would have stretched as far as the RSPB centre, at least."

Paul:
"Are you telling me that this row of lights was so big, it would have covered that distance?"

Andrew:
"Probably more. I'm not kidding you, it would have been even longer. I think it would have stretched from the centre over there, past the cliffs behind us. I didn't see anything in between each light except an even gap. But I am sure it was one solid object."

I asked him why he felt so sure that it was one object and not just a string of unexplained lights.

Andrew:
"Because it moved as though it were one piece. The lights came out from the cliff-face and began to move in a slow circular motion away from the cliffs. They moved as one. It sort of circled around and then went back to the same position. Then after a minute or so, the lights went back into the cliff-face, one by one."

Above: an artists impression of how Andrew saw the red & white lights.

Paul:
"They came out from the cliffs? Didn't they just come from around the cliffs? And did the lights flash at all?"

Andrew:
"They were big, bright and constant, with no flashing. The red light above was a little bit bigger. And no, they didn't travel backwards or forwards from around the corner. I know the coastline very well and whatever we saw that night definitely came out of the cliff, out of the rock itself."

Andrew's story sounded incredible, but accounts like this are the reason why I keep coming back to Bempton. I often tell people who want to visit the area, that the chances of being in the right place at the right time are slim. The only difference with locations like Bempton are that the odds are a little better. Sightings like this prove to me that the incredible can and does appear at any time, usually when we least expect it.

After Martin and Andrew had left us, I counted how many paces it took Bob and me to walk from where we were, to reach the RSPB visitor centre. It was 413 paces - which equates to well over 1000 feet. And Andrew had said that he thought the lights would have stretched further still, perhaps extending out over the cliffs. I remember the mainstream news at the time had reported sightings of a UFO the size of a battleship. Andrew's object appeared to be larger than that.

He told us that his daughter was seven years old at the time and was now thirty, which dates his sighting to August 1998. A few months before Andrew talked to us, I was told of another UFO encounter. Incredibly, the three men who witnessed it said the object actually landed, less than eight miles away from Bempton on the outskirts of Hunmanby village. This was also in August 1998 - but it does not end there. Earlier in 2019 myself and Bob Brown interviewed a rock angler who was out fishing on the cliff-tops. He told us about the night he was taking part in a fishing competition, when a 'spaceship' landed in a nearby field. He said that everyone who was there on Bempton cliff-tops that night had seen it. This was in November 1998.

The witnesses to all three of these incidents have no connection to each other and none of their accounts had ever been published or spoken about before I began researching. I find it incredible that so many witnesses had similar experiences in 1998. They can't all be misidentification.

No doubt these three accounts from 1998 will form a large part of another book. I was certainly pleased that Bob and I had met Andrew and Martin at Bempton that night.

UFOs at Christmas

When we think about the most amazing UFO sightings we automatically think of Roswell, the Rendlesham Forest Incident or the Ariel School Sighting in Zimbabwe. These historic sightings are so prominent and interest in them snowballs over time. Whenever UFOs are mentioned, these cases are revived and thrust into the public eye once more. We must acknowledge that they were unique, but they do not stand alone.

There are other sightings that are just as incredible, and those reported in East Yorkshire in the UK are no exception. This small corner of the country continues to surprise me with the vast array of unexplained phenomena that it exhibits. Over land and sea, along this wonderful coastline, there have been literally thousands of reports that go back many decades. My own research uncovered an incredible encounter from 2009, where multiple witnesses saw a group of UFOs over the sea at Wilsthorpe, just a few miles up the coast from my home in Bridlington. The military arrived less than a day after the boomerang-shaped objects were seen over the sea, and the sightings continued to be reported, all the way through 2009.

The Wilsthorpe Incident has all the ingredients to make it one of the greatest UFO encounters in the world. The details I uncovered all help to build a case for the sighting being a genuine UFO-related event - which proves my point, that the incredible is seen all over the world, but very few sightings ever gain public attention. So I was not surprised when I received an email on January 1st 2019 detailing a UFO that was seen a week earlier, on Christmas Eve. I may not have been surprised, but I was amazed after reading what the witnesses claim to have seen.

The account was nothing short of sensational. The email was sent to me by a man named Alan who told me that his wife and son saw the UFO at 8.50pm on December 24th 2018. As soon as I read it, I knew that I had to find out more. I had been receiving reports of unexplained objects seen along the entire coastline of East and North Yorkshire throughout December. This latest report though, was more detailed.

Later that day I spoke at length with Alan and his son Tom. Alan works as a taxi driver in Hull, and had it not been for him working the busy Christmas period, he would have been with his family at the time. He admitted feeling disappointed that he never saw the UFO himself, but he gave me an outline of what happened, before putting me in touch with his son Tom.

Tom:
"I was taking my Mum to work for a night shift. Because it was Christmas I need to say that we were stone cold sober, so in no way did alcohol influence what we saw. But the thing is Paul, what we saw is stuck with me forever now. I just cannot think of anything else it could have been. It is a bit frightening really. I can still see it in my mind as clear as anything. It was monolithic.

We'd left home and were driving along Stoneferry Road. We got as far as the bridge that leads onto Clough Road and that's when I saw it. Even now it really is unfathomable trying to understand just how big the thing was."

I asked Tom to try and describe it. I also asked how it made him feel.

Tom:
"It was an upside-down triangle with two lights at the top and one light at the bottom. The lights were deep, deep red; not like a normal signal red, they were more claret coloured. It just stuck out like a sore thumb. Me and my Dad went back the next day and took pictures, and I was able to work out its huge size due to a nearby chimney. I reckon what I saw was about 400ft top to bottom, but the span of this thing was massive - I would say 800ft.

I'm still amazed by what we saw. If you can imagine seeing a huge ship *slowly coming out of the fog, and I'm talking huge - like the Titanic. That's what it was like. It's so hard to explain but it was almost like everything was getting drawn into it. That's the feeling I got watching it emerge; that it was absorbing everything. I reckon that even if someone had aimed the most powerful spotlight at it, it would have sucked in the light. I know how mad that must sound, but you had to be there. I saw it first; I was in shock for a moment, then I said to my Mum, 'What the hell is that?' She replied saying, 'Oh my god.'*

I asked Tom if its lights were illuminating anything else around it:

Tom:
"The lights didn't really give us any clue. I mean they were bright, but they didn't show this thing in any detail. It was so deep and absorbing. I don't know, I can't explain it really. It was blacker than anything I had ever seen, but the lights on each corner didn't penetrate the blackness. I remember saying to my Mum, 'I'm going to turn left into Bank Side Road'. That took us about thirty seconds. I planned on taking a photo once I was on the road, but in that time it had completely vanished."

I asked Tom if it could have flown away.

Tom:
"I don't think it flew away, not something that size. I think it just vanished, like it somehow became invisible. It freaked us both out completely, but we just carried on with our journey. Then as we reached Air Street we saw a single red object moving towards where we had just seen the huge one."

Tom explained that because it was late on Christmas Eve, they didn't see any other cars on the road. He said that after dropping his mother off at work he drove the same route back home and, although he saw nothing else, he never took his eyes off the sky all the way back. I asked him if he felt the huge triangle, or the intelligence within it, was aware that it had been seen. Tom couldn't tell, but he knew how it made him feel.

Tom:
"As soon as I think about it, I can see it. It's kind of terrifying knowing that something so big could just be there. It's imprinted in my mind now and I will never forget it for as long as I live."

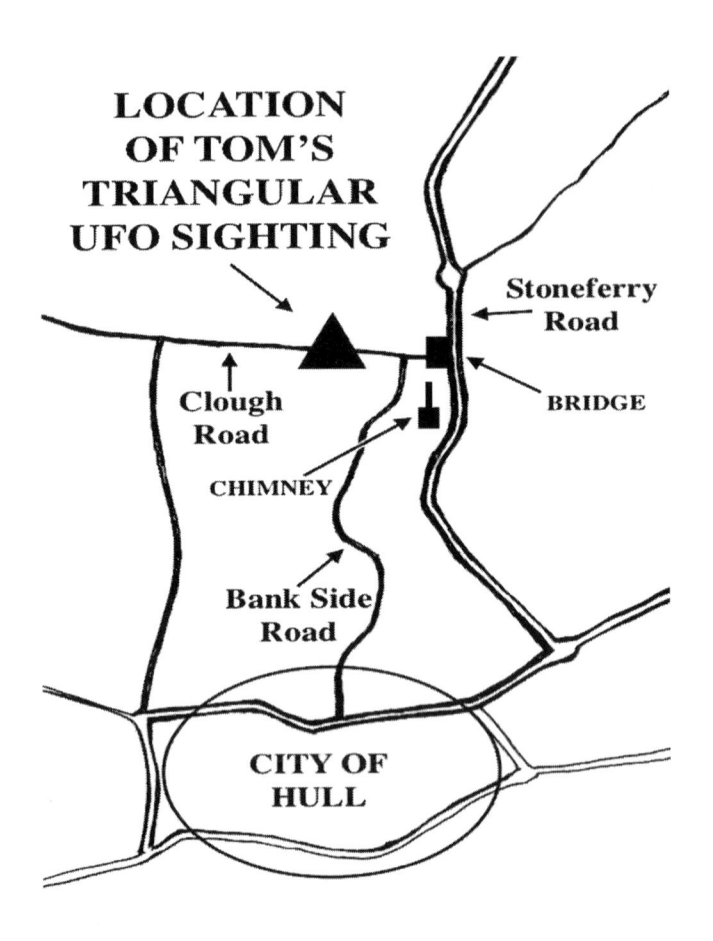

LOCATION OF TOM'S TRIANGULAR UFO SIGHTING

Stoneferry Road

Clough Road

CHIMNEY

BRIDGE

Bank Side Road

CITY OF HULL

I couldn't offer any advice to Tom or his mother to help them understand or come to terms with what they saw. It was something so 'off the scale' of normal that I would have needed to be there myself. True phenomena triggers a visceral reaction, affecting us deep within. It rarely provides us with a deeper understanding.

Later, I told Tom about my own sighting of a large silver object I saw over Hull on December 14th, ten days before his experience on Christmas Eve.

I had thought it would be worth spending some time observing the skies over Hull, due to the volume of reports I had received that month. I was with my friend Bob Brown at the time and we had travelled to Fraisthorpe, which gave us great views of Hull and the surrounding villages. At around 8.30pm we saw a large object suddenly appear in the sky. It was silver in colour and oval-shaped and looked as though it was hovering directly over the city. I recorded a few seconds of our sighting on my camcorder before the object disappeared.

All of these sightings coincided with an article in the *Hull Daily Mail*, which claimed that fighter jets had been scrambled to intercept another unidentified object seen flying over Preston Road. This was just three miles east of where Tom and his mother had their sighting. The object chased by the jets was described as having a short body, with no nose or tail, but huge wings. It was seen hovering silently and motionless in the sky at around 4.30pm on December 13th. On December 17th *Sky News* also reported that RAF Typhoon jets were scrambled in response to an unidentified object.

In subsequent news reports the explanation was that a Cessna light aircraft, flying directly over Hull, was responsible for the sighting. I suppose this would have been perfectly plausible if Cessnas were huge and had the ability to hover in the sky.

With A Little Help From Social Media

The world of social media does have its place within my research. My name had been tagged in a *Facebook* post about a UFO that was seen over the sea on Monday July 2nd 2018.

When a young woman named Julie posted a message to ask if anyone else had seen a strange object out over the sea, she received the usual barrage of sarcastic remarks for telling the truth. Is it any wonder people are so reluctant to talk about seeing anything unusual?

Because I was tagged into the post, it was brought to my attention, so I sent her a private message. I explained that I was interested in what she had seen and asked if she would consider giving me a few more details. Here are the messages we exchanged on July 2nd:

Paul:
"Hi Julie, hope you don't mind me messaging you, but I would love to know a little bit more about what you saw in the sky today. It is a genuine message: I write books about this kind of thing and would love to hear more. My books are called Truth Proof. Regards Paul."

Julie:
"Hiya, there isn't really much to say. But I'm happy to help however I can."

Paul:
"Nice one, thanks. I only mention the books I write so you can see I am genuine. What colour was the object and how high in the sky do you think it was Julie? And did you hear any sound?
Also, if you were to take a guess, how big would it have been, if you were close to it?"

Julie:
"Ok, so, I have no idea about anything to do with distances/scale/ratios or anything. I really couldn't say. I was looking in a north easterly direction from Bridlington old town. At first, it appeared to be completely stationary, then it slowly started moving, but it was hard to tell in what direction. It eventually dropped below the roofline of the houses behind me - but I don't know if it got further away, or lower, as it appeared to be shrinking too, but by the time I had got upstairs to look out of the window, it had disappeared."

Paul:
"Could you do me a rough sketch of its shape please? It does not have to be anything brilliant, just the shape of what you saw."

Julie:
As crazy as it seems, this is something like the shape I saw. It was a definite solid shape. Not a cloud, not vapour. It had defined edges.

Julie's own sketch, showing the shape of the object she saw.

Paul:
Hi Julie, thanks for sending me all that info, it truly helps. If you were to take a guess, where would it have been in the sky, roughly? I mean, if you were directly below it, where do you think it would have been? In addition, how big do you think it would have been if you were close to it.

Julie:
"It was out at sea, over Bridlington Bay, possibly near the wind-farm out there. It was a clear morning and there was nothing else in the sky to offer any sort of scale/comparison."

Julie's observations of the UFO were interesting, although it is impossible to say whether her sighting was connected to any other phenomena happening at Bempton at the time. Although I think it is important to include it here as part of my research for *Truth Proof 3*.

THE PHENOMENON IS ELUSIVE

The cryptozoologist and documentary film-maker Christopher Turner is interested in my research, and on Saturday July 7th 2018 he came to stay at our home for a few days. We planned on doing a few all night stake-outs in the affected areas, so I contacted the farmer and various other people to obtain permission to be on the land. The last thing I wanted to do was end up explaining to police officers why we were there at three in the morning.

Chris was in the process of making a documentary called *Elusive;* about the accounts of a 'cryptid' that we refer to as the Flixton Werewolf. And part of the reason Chris came to stay was so he could interview a few first-hand witnesses who had seen and heard unusual things around East and North Yorkshire.

Some of these witnesses were still genuinely traumatised by what they had experienced, but these people had spoken to me when I was researching the first *Truth Proof* book and now they offered to tell Chris what they saw and experienced. I wanted him to make the best use of his time, so I arranged interviews for him with four first-hand witnesses while he was here. Although each of them had experienced something that defied explanation, I need to stress that I am not suggesting such an animal is responsible for the animal mutilations at Bempton. I have no proof of that.

At around 8pm on the first day we loaded the car and set off towards Bempton. By 8.30pm, weighed down with cameras, lights, food and other accessories, we were walking towards the affected area. It was a wonderful night and the conditions were perfect; the air was warm and the sky was relatively clear. I know the phenomena does not perform to order, but if anything were to happen, we would have been in a prime position to observe it.

About four hundred nervous looking sheep were grazing the lush grass as we set up camp. I suppose our reasons for being there were macabre. After all, we were hoping to catch a glimpse of whatever was responsible for the killings and perhaps the end result would have been the death of an animal - but how else would we find out?

Although the entire night was uneventful, we had a good opportunity to share opinions and ideas. Chris Turner's approach to this work is not that far away from my own. We both know something very real is out there, but at this moment in time, it is impossible to put a label on this 'unknown something.'

I have noticed that the phenomenon appears to be changing and evolving, because just when I think I might have found a clue, something happens that opens my mind to other possibilities. One such incident comes to mind here, but it is so bizarre that I was unsure whether to have even bothered writing about it at all.

When I arrived back home early morning on May 12th, after finding the mutilated roe buck, my wife Mary told me about something she experienced at 3.40am that same morning, while I had been sleeping.

She said that she woke up to find everything was blurry. Her first thought was that she had another eye infection; something she has suffered with for a number of years. Then she told me she blinked and rubbed her eyes and suddenly saw lots of colour. By now Mary knew she was awake and blinked again, trying to understand what it was. That's when she saw a colourful image projected high on the wall beside her – but it was an image of the animated characters from the Scooby Doo cartoon.

I wish I knew what to say or whether this had any meaning, but Mary told me they extended up onto the ceiling, and did not bend where the ceiling met the wall. It was hard for her to explain, but she said they all looked so real and exactly like the cartoon. The whole thing lasted about four minutes and in that time she blinked and rubbed her eyes at least four times.

Because we have experienced so much unusual phenomena around the house, I installed a CCTV camera system, which includes the bedroom. So I immediately switched on the TV and grabbed the remote control to open up the CCTV screen menu. For some reason the system had stopped recording days before. I'm not suggesting that some unexplained phenomena was responsible, because it could be down to human error, but I don't think the CCTV would have captured anything.

Whatever Mary saw, I think it was being projected through her mind. But why did it happen? It is so far-fetched and so detached from any of the events happening at Bempton. Whatever really happened lasted only minutes but remains a complete mystery.

Chris Turner and I passed our time at Bempton that first night, with nothing more interesting to report than the sheep becoming restless at about 11pm. In the early hours, the gaps in our conversation left a silence that was, in fact, quite deafening. I quickly realised that if anything were to have happened out there, no one would have heard or seen a thing. It was good to spend time with Chris. He told me things that were very helpful; information that I had never heard before. I hope at some point, before *Truth Proof 3* is completed, we will meet up again and attempt to solve the puzzle.

An Average Day
July 15th 2018

Do any of us have average days? What is average in a person's life? Today, like all others, will never come again. Surely for that reason alone it is not average. I'm not sure such a day exists. We can never get them back. Every day that has passed has gone forever and our lifespan contracts with each and every one. I guess what I am saying is that nothing is average and every moment is unique.

On June 15th 2018 at approximately 5am, I parked my car and began walking across the fields towards the affected area. My plan was to walk the field in sections, covering the area as quickly as possible, without missing anything. The grass was now showing signs of age and starting to fade and fall back. Having between three and four hundred sheep constantly chewing at it does not help the life expectancy of grass.

People say that animals are more sensitive than us and can detect areas and situations that do not feel right. Something was definitely happening in this field which made me think the theory could have some truth attached to it. At least as far as these sheep were concerned.

They never stop eating and a large number of animals can soon reduce long grass to nothing more than stubble. But what I found interesting was, they had started to eat the grass furthest away from the woods. I thought about this each time I visited the affected area. They were eating their way towards the woods like slow fire. I noticed what was happening, because I was still looking for my missing GoPro camera. I was hoping, by some slim chance, that they would eventually eat their way towards it. One part of me clung to the idea that it was still waiting to be found, as the sheep advanced across the field. But they were so reluctant to move into that area, that there had to be a reason.

Could they sense a weird change in the atmosphere as they got closer to Danes Dyke woods? Did they know, somehow, that the killer - the unknown *something* - resided there? Or could they even detect a subtle change in the fabric of our reality among the trees in this location?

I had found three deer carcasses the day before, at the opposite side of Danes Dyke. They were close to the road, but in a private part of the woods. It was impossible to say what had killed them, because they were in such an advanced stage of decomposition. Finding all three in one place rang alarm bells in my head, but it was clear, even from the sunken remains, that nothing of what could have been considered 'prime cuts of meat', had been removed. And I did not intend to disturb the carcasses, because the hot weather had made for near-perfect conditions for flies.

In some dark way, after discovering the roe deer the day before, I half expected to find a mutilated sheep. I spent over two hours looking for clues in the fields that morning, but I found nothing - not even my GoPro camera. If I had walked around with my eyes closed, I might have had a better chance. I sometimes get the feeling that I am only seeing what the phenomena allows me to see, as though it plays tricks on my mind, constantly switching and evolving with every opportunity.

On that average day I was back home just before 8am. Mary was up and about and Wolfy sounded his usual volley of barks when I walked by the kitchen window. It was now time to sit down and write up a few notes; which didn't take long because nothing had actually happened. Nevertheless, every day needs documenting, no matter how uneventful that day might have been.

From Terra Firma To Terror Below The Waves

When John first spoke to me about the loss of his livestock, he was of the opinion that the suspect responsible for killing his sheep was a phenomena: his words not mine. I continued to call it the *unknown something*. I had not seen or heard anything to convince me of what exactly was responsible, but that changed when I found out about mutilated porpoises that were being discovered along the coastline.

When I learned about the dead marine mammals, and saw the photographic evidence, I immediately recognised similarities to the sheep and deer deaths. At that moment John's choice of words, describing this unknown something as a *phenomena*, seemed to fit perfectly. Could it be possible that the unknown something, responsible for so many unexplainable animal deaths, had also found its way beneath the waves? And should I really be considering this?

The very idea is frightening, especially when there is no evidence to explain what is happening. The unknown itself is creating the fear, but may be creating fear is part of its agenda. I now wonder if the lights beneath the sea off Bempton, that I saw with Bob Brown on July the 25th, had a more sinister element attached to them. I had never considered all of these things until seeing the porpoise images.

In February 2018 a picture of a porpoise was sent to me by phone messenger by a lady named Steph, who lives in Bridlington.

She told me how she had discovered the carcass whilst walking on the beach between Sewerby and Danes Dyke. Before I saw the photograph, Steph's description of the porpoise and the location she found it, made me wonder if, somehow, it could have been another victim of the sheep killing phenomena. I have to admit that this was something I had never considered before - until Steph told me the porpoise looked in perfect condition, except for a large circular hole in the side of its jaw. Her words triggered a memory of reports of other dead harbour porpoises found around Sewerby and Flamborough during 2017. So with these thoughts in mind, I decided to try and trace anyone who had found these dead sea mammals along the shoreline in that time.

Steph's photo of the young porpoise she discovered in February 2018

I did not know for sure how, or even if, this part of the puzzle was connected with the other animal mutilations - but it was another mammal which appeared to have fallen victim to an unusual killer. And since all the mutilations were in such close proximity to each other, none of them could be discounted. I also had to acknowledge the fact that it would be highly unlikely there were different unknown killers, all operating at the same time.

Much of what occurred around Cliff Lane in 2017 didn't come to my attention until 2018. I honestly believe that if I had known about the sheep mutilations earlier in my investigations, I might have linked them to the deaths of the harbour porpoises. The injuries present on all of the animals were highly unusual, and all of the carcasses were found within the same geographical footprint. For that reason alone, I think there is a strong possibility that whatever killed one of them, killed all of them.

Steph's observations of the dead sea mammals are interesting, although she never came to me thinking anything paranormal had happened. She just thought the injuries were strange at the time. Then after we had arranged to meet in town, she told me about the pictures she had taken with her phone. This is what Steph had to say about what she found:

Steph:
"I was walking along the beach with my daughter; from Sewerby towards Danes Dyke. It was low tide and we just stumbled upon it. I don't think it had been there long. It looked in perfect condition, apart from a very deep hole in the side of its jaw. At first I thought we had found a child's inflatable toy. We just couldn't understand it. There wasn't any blood and it was high up the beach amongst the rocks; it looked like it had just been placed there. Oh, and it was well above where the waterline would have been at high tide."

Steph's recall put my mind into overdrive, then I remembered speaking with a man called David who works for a local undertakers in the town. David told me he had seen several dead porpoises below the cliff-top foghorn station at Flamborough Head in 2017. I needed to know if they had suffered similar injuries to the one found by Steph and her daughter - so when I spoke with David, several days later, he confirmed that the porpoises he had discovered did indeed have unusual wounds.

Porpoises Found

I contacted my friend Andy Barmby, a sea angler from Bridlington, who is regularly out along the cliff-tops and rocky outcrops fishing for sea bass. I remember Andy telling me he had also come across a few dead porpoises in 2017. We speak quite regularly and I consider him genuine and reliable.
Andy has been lucky enough to observe the lightforms on more than one occasion, and his account of their sudden appearance in Thornwick Bay, while he was night fishing, is documented in *Truth Proof 2*.

When he originally told me about finding the dead porpoises, he had never actually said anything about finding any marks on them; it was more of a passing comment than anything else. Like many of the people I speak to, Andy does not have the same enthusiasm than I do for the unexplained. Andy gets a thrill from sea fishing. I personally cannot see the attraction, although I am sure he would say the same about my own fascination with the unexplained.

I was pleased when Andy told me that he had taken a few photos of the dead porpoises he found. When I saw his photographs for myself, it was clear there were similarities to the sheep carcasses that were being found at Bempton. It may seem an odd thing; to compare a sheep and a porpoise - if that is even possible? But I would say, in this case, that it is, because the wounds were equally horrific and death must have been instant. On both animals the area below the jaw had been targeted and the end result was devastating.

Two of Andy Barmby's photos of the porpoises he found at South Landing.

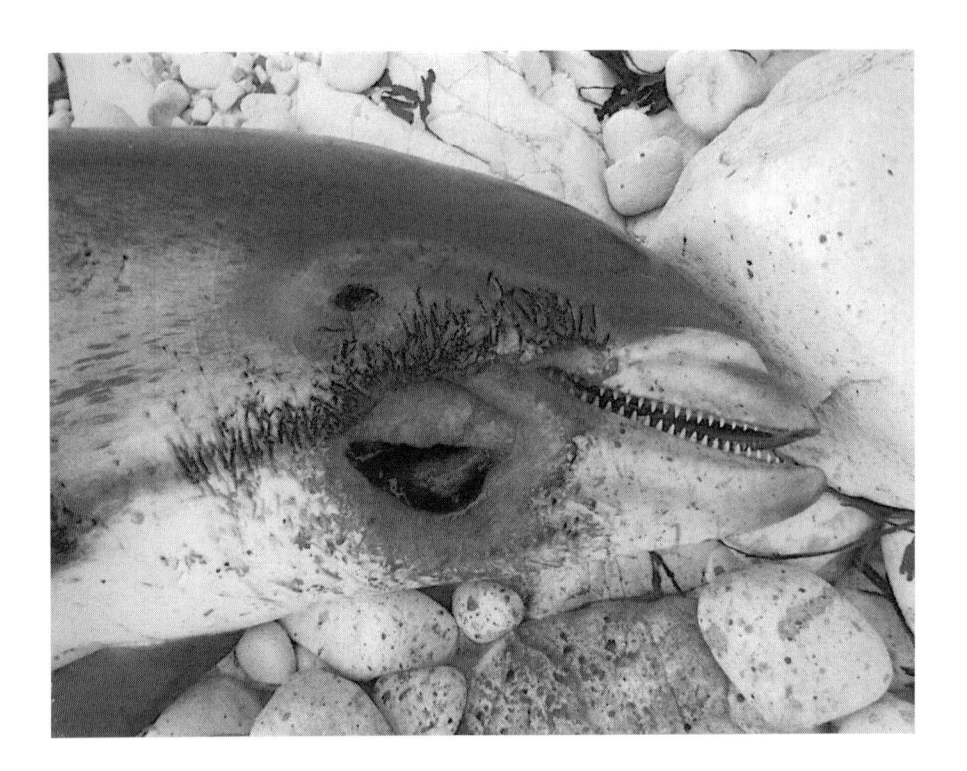

So is it a coincidence or is it the same phenomena? I think there is a strong possibility that it is the same, for a number of reasons: the unusual nature of the killings, the close proximity of them all to one another - and the fact that they are happening in an area which has repeatedly displayed unexplained phenomena throughout its documented history.

Andy Barmby told me that he found the first porpoise in early June 2017 - which was an amazing coincidence, since the sheep deaths appeared to have begun in the same month. The deer with the 3-inch hole in its side was found on June 28th on Cliff Lane, and on the same day, less than one mile away, the thirty sheep were discovered, crammed into the tiny enclosure on John's farm. The first porpoise Andy found was discovered high above the water line on the beach at Flamborough's South Landing. He found the others all around Flamborough and Danes Dyke. In all cases, their injuries were very similar.

I believe I have only touched the tip of the iceberg with the porpoise deaths. I also suspect that dead porpoises could have been found below Bempton Cliffs, if it was not for the risk of witnesses being cut off by the deadly tides, because no one ever goes there. We might never know the true number that have been killed, and up to this point, I doubt anyone, anywhere in the world, has connected the deaths of marine mammals with the deaths of sheep and other land-based animals - but I honestly believe there is a connection.

Many places around the East Yorkshire coastline are inaccessible, due the risk of people being cut off by crashing waves and rising tides. The rocks below Bempton Cliffs are no exception and can be extremely dangerous. I am sure this is the only reason more mutilated porpoises have never been found in the area.

Writing about the incidents around Cliff Lane continues to gather momentum and it is impossible to say when it will stop. The vast majority of people in the area are totally oblivious to what is happening. Nothing I have been researching has been published in the local newspapers and I suspect that staff at the RSPB nature reserve are unaware of the local animal deaths. I would have expected that an organisation which is committed to animal and bird conservation would have spotted the signs. I have even spoken to various members of staff at the RSPB reserve over the years about the lightforms, and asked if anyone had ever reported any UFO activity. I was told yes *and* no - officially and unofficially. Meaning, members of the public *have* told staff about unusual things they have seen, but they are not publicised. I actually have a report from a former staff member, who observed a sphere of red light entering the sea off Flamborough Head.

I think, before I finish this book, I will have even more to add. I am not sure I will have any answers, but I think I already have enough information to suggest that most parts of the Cliff Lane story are connected. I just don't know how.

THE COUNTRY PARK DEATHS

A few years ago I began researching a strange series of wallaby killings at Sewerby Country Park, just two miles up the coast from Bridlington. It was an amazing story that began in late June 2011 and involved the discovery of the decapitated bodies of wallabies from the park zoo.

The deaths revealed a pattern of similar killings all over the UK and even stretched to the other side of the world in Australia. The deaths also appeared to have been carried out by an unknown something.

During my investigations, I contacted Professor Robin Allaby at the University of Warwick. His name had appeared in a few newspaper articles in association with animals that had been found dead in unusual circumstances. These animal mutilations were from 2011 and in different parts of the UK, but it was clear that the professor wanted to discover what was responsible.

An Expert Opinion

When I told him about the Sewerby Park wallabies he was of the opinion that a fox was the most likely candidate. He told me that, in his opinion, foxes are highly underrated predators. I could not disagree with the professor's expert opinion, because a fox is an amazing predator. However, I do not think a fox could be responsible for the deaths of the wallabies at Sewerby Park. I was keen to gauge the professor's opinion on the Cliff Lane sheep mutilations, and sent him some images that I had obtained of the animals found between 2017 and 2018.

Below is an email I sent to the professor in May 2018.

"Dear Professor Allaby,
you may remember that we emailed last year regarding the decapitated wallabies discovered by park keepers at Sewerby Hall zoo in 2011.

I have recently discovered that throughout 2017, sheep were being found with their throats ripped out at a place called Bempton, which is local to where I live in East Yorkshire. I have spoken at length with the farmer who owned the sheep and he is at a loss as to what kind of animal would kill an 80-kilo sheep, but not eat it. Evidence has shown that the killer is known to come back over the next 3 to 4 nights and kill more sheep in the same manner. Then nothing more happens for weeks, until the process begins again. This was the pattern of events until the sheep were removed from the affected area on December 18th last year.

From what I am told, and from looking at the images, the sheep appear to have bled out on the spot. As though they were hit by a fast and ultra-efficient killer, that does not seem interested in consuming the meat.

The farmers have tried everything; including leaving carcasses in the field, in the hope that the killer comes back to feed - but it ignores the carcass and simply kills another in the same field. The fields where the livestock graze are in a very remote location and it is hard to imagine what is responsible. The surrounding farms are aware of what has been happening and have been extra vigilant, but no one seems to have clue what is to blame.

You may not have time to offer opinion and I respect that; I just wonder if you have heard of anything similar to this type of attack.
Regards Paul Sinclair."

I only gave the professor a brief outline of what had been happening. I did not want to waste his time, or my own, by going into detail, until I was sure he could give an informed opinion.

When we had exchanged emails about the wallaby killings in 2017, the professor said he believed a fox was the most likely culprit. Whilst I respected his opinion, it was not one that I fully agreed with, since it appeared that the wallabies heads had been removed by using a very sharp blade - and foxes don't carry knives!

I received the professor's reply on May 18th 2018. It is based on the limited information I supplied him with in my first email.

Reply from Professor Allaby - May 18th 2018:

"Hi Paul,
in cases like these we have still only found foxes at the scene - in terms of DNA traces - which is obviously open to interpretation. Personally, I think it's possible that a fox could have done this.

I know people are generally incredulous on this point, but the evidence points to where the evidence points. I suspect foxes are under-rated in their predatory capabilities, and certainly they have historically been implicated in bringing down red deer calves in Scotland in the past century. Probably we are not talking about your normal cat-sized foxes here, but perhaps some of the more elusive and rather large dog-foxes.

As to the identity of the predators, I have been completely, and remain, open-minded. I will not be super-surprised if we pull up big cat DNA one day, but so far, it's been fox, after fox, after fox leaving traces and never a cat. From the evidence we produce, it's hard to conclude cat so far..."

It was wonderful to receive a reply from the professor, that did not dismiss the possibility that genuine big cats could be present in the United Kingdom. As crazy as it sounds, I do not actually think we are dealing with something that is explained as easily as a big cat - although I am very grateful for the professor's views. His knowledge and scientific background have my full respect.

In my second email I went into more detail about the circumstances in which the animals were being found. It was clear from the outset that Professor Allaby has a fair and honest approach, and he only looks for clear-cut factual evidence. Unfortunately, the type of things I have seen and been told about, do not leave factual hard evidence. Perhaps this is part of the reason that mainstream science refuses to look at these types of cases, because this is an 'exotic science' and no amount of logical thinking seems to work.

My second email to Professor Allaby - May 18th 2018:

"Thank you Robin,
I wish you were closer, because I would love to get a DNA sample to you from the sheep or the deer kills - or even the porpoises; which have been found around the same time as the land mammals.

I will not keep sending endless emails, but I should also have told you that I very carefully checked the deer found at Bempton, and could not find any other marks on its body; no scratches or bites or puncture wounds. I would have expected to see bite marks on the deer's liver, as it appears to have been cut in half. I would have also expected to see blood - unless the animal was already dead when the fox, badger or cat had discovered it.

I have attached an image of one of the sheep carcasses for you; they are always found like this and no meat is ever taken.

Thank you for taking the time to reply.
Regards Paul."

I never made a reference to the *Truth Proof* books in my emails. I just wanted the opinion of a respected academic who wasn't about to judge me as a tinfoil-hat wearing lunatic.

Reply from Professor Allaby - May 18th 2018:

"*Curious Paul. This doesn't sound like a predator at all when you put it like that. Dare I suggest that humans might be involved? It reminds me of the wallabies that kept on turning up decapitated, but all the meat left.
Robin.*"

Professor Allaby's brief reply was similar to how I imagine many people would think about this subject. He was correct that the circumstances of the killings do not sound anything like the behaviour of any known predator. I don't actually think we are dealing with something that science can understand, because this is an *over-science* and we are in a place where traditional scientific thought does not work.

I was pleased he remembered the wallaby decapitations of 2011 - even if he had forgotten that it was me who told him about them. I say that with respect, because, although we may be looking at these strange occurrences with differing opinions, we do have one thing in common - the desire to find out what is responsible.

Email extract: my next email to Professor Allaby - May 18th 2018:

"...*One farmer has lost close to 50 sheep, and he says it is not an animal doing the killing, it's a phenomena. Those are his exact words, not mine, so I will not rule out anything Robin. I am meeting up with him this weekend and have already decided to ask if he thinks anyone dislikes him enough to kill his livestock...*

I'm not sure if you remember, but when I first contacted you a few years ago, it was about the wallaby decapitations. I don't think I ever told you all the details, but at the same time the wallabies were being found decapitated here in the UK, the same thing was happening 10,000 miles away in New South Wales. It happened in many animal parks all over the UK, and in Australia - decapitated wallabies were found all the way up the coast. I don't know how that works or what the odds of such a strange combination of deaths would be.
Regards Paul"

Reply from Professor Allaby - May 18th 2018:

"Aha! It was you who mentioned the wallabies to me. Yes, I remember. It made an impression. That sounds like a social media spread phenomenon then – have you investigated Facebook? Probably would need MI6 level clearance to find the evidence, I suppose.

Perhaps this farmer should invest in some wildlife cameras, to see if he can catch the culprits. Is this an area with big cat folklore in it? Exploring possible motives here.
Robin."

At this point I had not thought about using social media as an investigation tool. In all honestly, I cannot believe this is how the idea of the mutilations could have become so widespread. I could tell the professor had given these animal deaths a great deal of thought, but for me personally, too many things stand in the way of that theory. This might be a plausible, if not unlikely explanation, but because it is possible, it diverts us from daring to think the unthinkable. Is it possible that groups of people, using social media, could actually organise themselves, in different parts of the world, to catch and kill wallabies, deer and porpoises?

Email to Professor Allaby - May 18th 2018:

"Yes Robin, it was me who told you about the wallabies. No I have not tried researching with social media, but I did contact various animal

parks in the UK. They told me first-hand, but said they had no idea that other parks were affected. I also contacted parks in New South Wales, Australia. They told me about the wallaby killings and said that, in many instances, a fox was blamed - but the park rangers were of the opinion that it could not have been a fox, due to the clean cut.

One more thing, these were Bennett's wallabies; the big ones. And the park rangers in New South Wales said they are too big and strong for an ordinary fox to take on. They also said it would have to be able to use a sword, due to the clean cut!

When the farmer here in the UK first got the police involved, they came with night scopes and watched a field. The next day another sheep had been killed, but they saw nothing. They have trail cameras set up as I type this, but so far they have not revealed any clues.

I have been investigating sightings of a big cat in this area for a few years now; lots of people claim to have seen it. The problem I have; linking a cat to the sheep killings, is that no meat is ever taken. The roe deer I found showed no signs of marks, and it is the same with the sheep, apart from their throats being removed...

Regards Paul."

Reply from Professor Allaby - May 18th 2018:

"Dear Paul,
I actually meant perpetrators could be spreading the practice through social media, and possibly, there may be some evidence there about shared practice. Very interesting that your sheep killing area is also reputed for big cats. This leaves me very suspicious.

The samples I have been sent...had been eviscerated, so your report would seem to contrast there – a left cut liver seems very unlikely. Amazing that scavengers hadn't taken it, but I suppose they probably did not have time before it was discovered.
Robin."

Email reply to Professor Allaby - May 18th 2018:

"Robin,
I do not know what is responsible for the killings, but for me, so many factors rule out humans for the deer kills. The locations I am looking at are very remote, and how would they actually catch a wild deer? Sheep yes, but a deer? I would have to say the same about the wallabies. As for the porpoises, I am even more in the dark.

Would you mind if I say that you believe a fox could have done this, when I write about the killings? I would not put your views/opinions over in a bad light, I just think it is good to get the opinions of other people; including local vets, you and the farmers directly involved. It makes for a more balanced view and I hope it shows I am not being biased.
Regards Paul."

Final reply from Professor Allaby - May 18th 2018:

"No, I don't mind Paul.
Best,
Robin."

I am very grateful to Professor Allaby for taking the time to share his views, based on the information I supplied him with. The professor's opinions are more grounded than my own, in that, he is looking for something that can be proven, something that is known to exist and something that is capable of killing the animals - or creating possibilities for such things to happen. Whereas I believe that whatever is responsible is a genuine unknown, with abilities that our science has not even begun to consider, let alone think about.

WHAT IN THIS WORLD IS GOING ON?

In my last book I wrote about my research into the lights seen over the sea and the flares that never were. Since then more information has come my way which adds weight to my theory that these lights really are *Intelligent Light Forms*. This was a term I created back in 2002 to describe the unexplained spheres of light seen all around the East and North Yorkshire Wolds and coastline.

My first website was called *'ILF-UFO'*, which I published in 2002 to share reports of these strange lights and other phenomena. In recent years I have seen the term 'Intelligent Lightforms' become more mainstream and it is now used by several other researchers, which I think is perfectly acceptable. It just bothers me when I read about people who claim they came up with the term 'Intelligent Lightforms', when they didn't come up with it at all.

Historic UFO Sighting Off Bempton

In early 2018 I was given an envelope containing many first-hand accounts of unexplained phenomena. It was given to me by a highly experienced trawlerman, now retired, who travelled to Bridlington from Hull to meet me. (One of the accounts of phenomena is so sensitive that I dare not even write about it at this point in time.) The trawlerman's career spanned many decades, and he worked all over the world and in some of the most dangerous seas imaginable. He was highly respected by those who worked alongside him over the years.

On Monday April 23rd 1973 the trawlerman was working as a crew member on board a supply vessel delivering parts, food and fuel to some new off-shore gas rigs. Their plotted course saw them pass Flamborough Head and move up the coast. Visibility was good and the sea was calm.

The sketch below was drawn after his sighting and is taken from notes and observations he kept in a personal logbook. No one on board the ship, including the trawlerman, could explain what they saw on the cliff-tops of Bempton that night. And although this may be an historic account, I think it is significant enough to include in this chapter because of its unusual nature and the location.

Mon 23rd 4th 1973 = 00:11

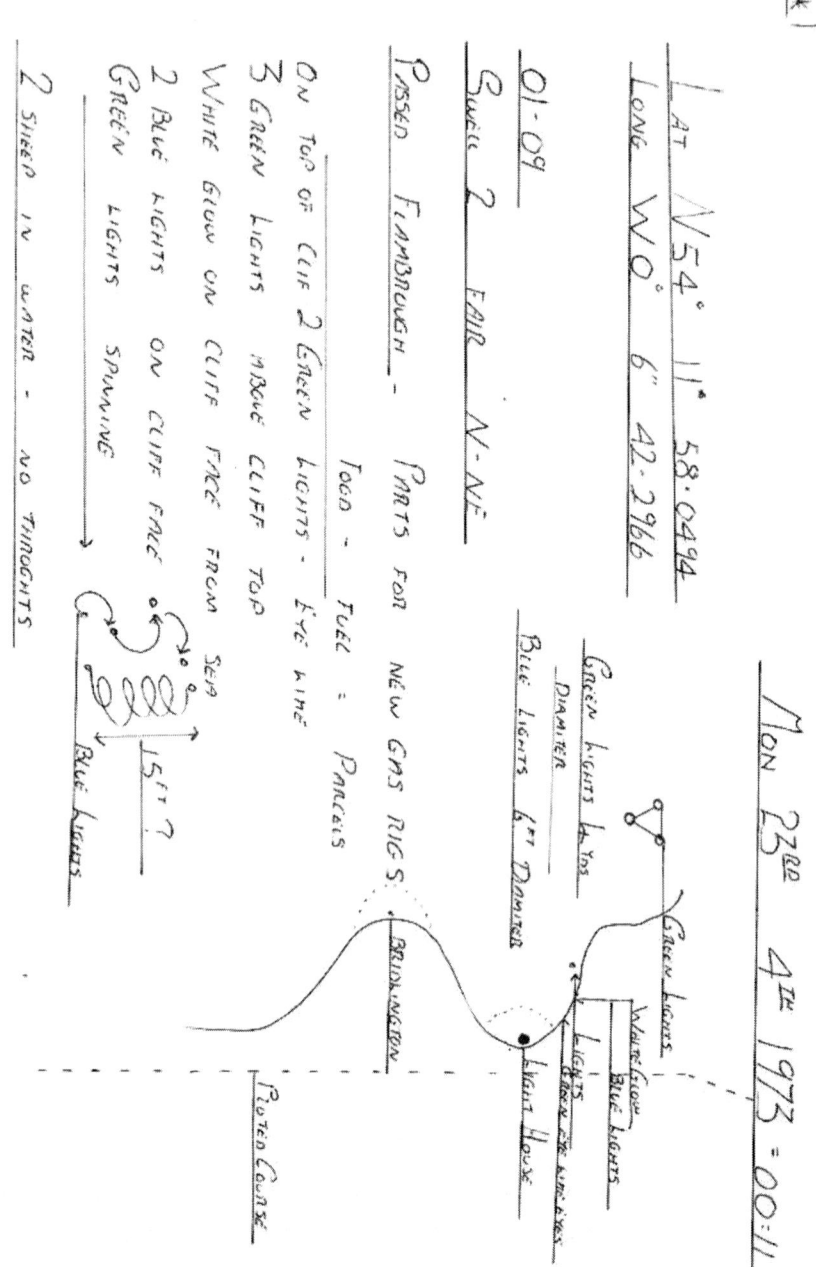

LAT N 54° 11' 58.0494
LONG W 0° 6' 42.2966

01-09
SWELL 2   FAIR   N-NE

PASSED FLAMBROUGH - PARTS FOR NEW GAS RIG S
                    FOOD - FUEL - PARCELS

ON TOP OF CLIFF 2 GREEN LIGHTS - EYE LINE
3 GREEN LIGHTS ABOVE CLIFF TOP
WHITE GLOW ON CLIFF FACE FROM SEA
2 BLUE LIGHTS ON CLIFF FACE
GREEN LIGHTS SPINNING

2 SHEEP IN WATER - NO THROUGHTS

Six Miles Off Bempton
April 23rd 1973

A few days after receiving the drawing and details of the account I went to Bridlington Lifeboat Station to see if I could gain more information about the sighting. I wanted some help to get an accurate position for the supply ship, using the latitude and longitude given to me by the trawlerman.

Chris works at the lifeboat station as the only permanent member of staff. He is always helpful to me and I have got to know him over the years. After reading the information I shared with him, he was able to tell me the position of the ship when the crew observed the UFOs. Chris estimated that they were about six miles off the coast of Speeton and Bempton, which places them four and a half miles north of Flamborough Head. And it looks as though they witnessed three or four different things, all apparently happening at the same time.

The trawlerman had told me, that from the supply boat, they could see the cliff-face was glowing white. He said it looked as though the glow was coming from the sea. They also saw two blue lights on the cliff face, but at first they noticed two green lights on top of the cliffs. For some reason he described the green lights as looking like a pair of eyes and I got a shiver looking at his drawing, because this was the same area I have spent many years observing the land, sea and sky. Lots of the accounts from TP1 and TP2 come from this location.

I find it quite amazing that this incredible sighting had remained in a note book, unreported for the past forty-four years. It is another example of the ability of this area to produce unexplained phenomena over many, many decades. The coordinates match very closely to where a military jet had vanished from radar two years earlier. RAF Lightning XS894 disappeared out at sea, six miles off Flamborough Head, on September 8th 1970. This is an area of the sea where trawlermen often report magnetic anomalies that affect their on-board compasses.

Of course, nothing we can see or detect proves that one event is directly connected to the other. But when a concentration of strangeness continues to present itself over many years, I think we have to at least consider that they could be linked - even if we cannot understand how.

The full list of reports from this area is long and full of every exotic phenomena imaginable; including sightings of big cats, the ghost of big railings and the lightforms that appear out over the sea. Then there is a much darker side, where people have actually vanished without a trace and others report experiences of missing time. The phenomena extends a short distance inland, where, in recent times, mutilated animals continue to be found - which I am sure is not a new development.

People living in and around the affected area are very secretive about everything that happens; only breaking that silence if it becomes a necessity. I researched for many years before finding the true extent of what was happening. An example being: I once asked a former Flamborough lifeboat man if he was one of the men who observed a huge and silent black triangle over Bridlington Links Golf Course in the 1990s. I already knew he had been there because another witness had given me a detailed account, but the former lifeboat man denied any knowledge of the sighting. However, years later, when we met under different circumstances, he told me all about it.

Land Lights

Of course, I cannot deny what my *own* eyes have seen. In late 2017, while I was out on the cliff-tops during an observation, I saw a section of land light up, at the back of The Leys fields. I remember standing there in the darkness wondering what could have made this happen. I saw nothing in the sky at the time, but a section of the field *did* light up for a split second with a rectangular white light, which seemed to illuminate the surface of the land.

With everything that had happened, past and present, I had been feeling increasingly nervous about going onto the cliff-tops alone – and seeing the land suddenly light up, for no apparent reason, did not help matters. I remember hanging around for a few minutes at the time, to see if it repeated, and when it didn't, I just left the area. But I have not been up there alone during the night since that happened.

The amazing thing about Bempton, and locations like it, is the fact that strange things happen and no one breathes a word - or in the case of the missing men, they seem to be soon forgotten.

The trawlerman's account from 1973, describing the glowing cliff-face and coloured lights, must have been an incredible sight. From the drawing and data he provided, it was clear to me that the activity appeared in the same place where phenomena are happening today.

A Highly Unusual Night

The landscape in 1973 was the same as it is now. The cliffs are vertical making it impossible to access them on foot and no boats would attempt to get close either, due to the treacherous rocks that litter the seabed around this area of the coast. It would be a foolish thing to do, even in daylight - so what *did* the crew of the supply boat observe?

The trawlerman's description of the lights is interesting; two blue lights, each one, he notes, were about 'six feet' in diameter, and two green lights, he described as being 'four yards' in diameter. The blue lights move in a pendulum motion, one above the other, then the lowest one appeared to swing upwards to replace the highest. Seconds later a new lower light repeated the swinging motion and moved above as before. This sequence of events continued throughout the observation. And all the time the two green lights were spinning up and down like a corkscrew.

A little further up the coast the crew also observed a triangle of stationary green lights above the cliff tops. I doubt if anyone on land saw any of this, because there is usually no one around the area that late at night. It was past midnight after all. After studying the trawlerman's drawing and notes I read a line of writing at the bottom left, which is even more chilling: *"Two sheep in water, no throats."* Could this suggest that something truly sinister was taking place that night?

I'm not exactly sure where, along the ship's course, they observed these two dead sheep in the water, but I cannot help drawing a comparison to the sheep mutilations reported in 2017 and 2018. The manner in which this information suggests they were killed, sounds remarkably similar to how sheep are being found mutilated today. I think it is a strong possibility that the same phenomena around today was responsible for the deaths of these two sheep in 1973.

There is little more I can add to this account. I even checked the tide times for March 22nd and 23rd 1973, from archive newspapers of the day - just in case they revealed something unusual, but they did not. This only highlights the kind of difficulties researchers face. Usually a search of the archives can reveal a slow build-up of other phenomena, occurring before the main event, but I found nothing before, or after, the events of that highly unusual night - even though windows of unexplained phenomena are constantly opening and closing in this location.

MORE FLARES THAT NEVER WERE

The *Maritime and Coastguard Agency* Logs

In early 2018 I was fortunate to obtain a few logbooks from the old Flamborough coastguard station. All identifying names and incident numbers had been removed from the logs and I cannot disclose who handed them to me. However, they are real and the incidents documented inside them were, for the most part, reported in the same areas of high strangeness that I research. No surprises there.
It is also worth mentioning that the lifeboat call-outs documented inside these logbooks are just a few of the many, many incidents recorded over the years.

The lightforms are real and incidents recorded inside the logbooks from the Flamborough Maritime and Coastguard Agency are just one piece of a much bigger puzzle. If I were given access to study more of the logs, as a long-term project, I am sure a great deal could be learned from them. It is unfortunate that this information is not readily accessible to the public; who are never supposed to see the logbooks. But what I have seen and read, I cannot un-see - and this includes lifeboat call-outs to investigate suspicious lights over the sea around Bempton and Flamborough.

Nothing in the reports has been covered up, but they have been worded in such a way that the true extent of call-outs to unknowns is disguised. I have already been informed by a member of the MCA that I will never find terms like 'UFO' used in any logbook reports, but I think it is clear that the coastguard have, at times, been called out to investigate sightings of unidentified aerial objects - and they are at a loss to explain them.

The number of unresolved lifeboat searches over the years, for the unexplained lights, must tell even the most hardened sceptic that something unusual is happening. Just because we cannot explain or understand it, does not mean we have to ignore the fact. And the formal explanations for what people have seen, are in some instances, ridiculous - bordering on stupid.

If we accept that something out at sea is deemed important enough to initiate a search and rescue attempt, then that 'something' has to be real. That argument becomes even stronger when we realise that this has been repeated over many years, without explanation.

Not every observation of lights over the sea is UFO related, but many are genuine unknowns and if we could see the full extent of this we would have an argument that Intelligent Lightforms are presenting and raising sufficient concern as to launch life boats and other emergency services.

The following images are from genuine lifeboat and coastguard logs. They are just a few of the many authentic incidents of emergency call-outs that span decades, from along the North and East Yorkshire coast.

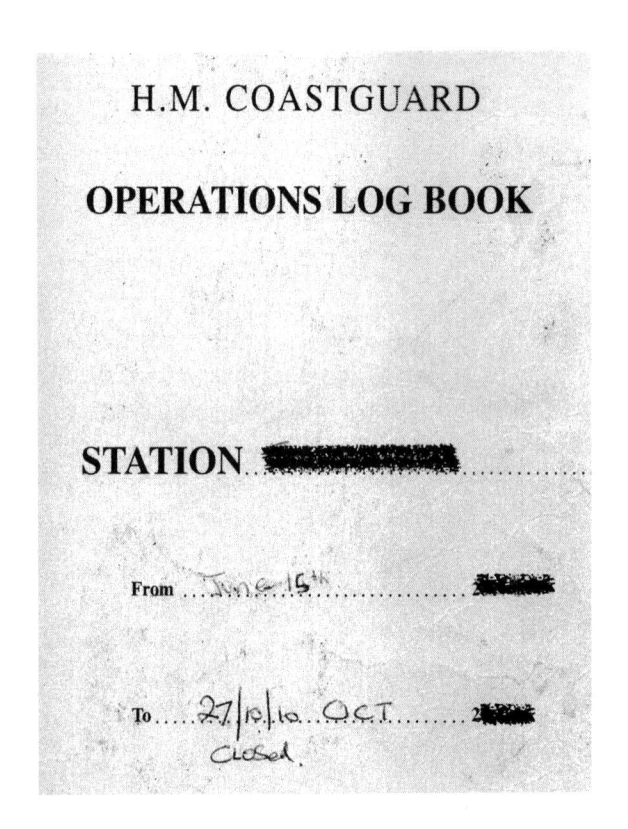

H.M. COASTGUARD

OPERATIONS LOG BOOK

STATION ▬▬▬▬▬

From June 15th

To 27/10/10 OCT
Closed.

Aug — Call out required to investigate sighting of flare in vicinity of South Landing

"AUG: CALL OUT REQUIRED TO INVESTIGATE SIGHTING
OF FLARE IN VICINITY OF
SOUTH LANDING"

From	Events and Occurrences - Remarks - Text of Message
20 46	Paged to investigate red flare. Met with first informant. Details passed to Humber. Further reports indicate flare was a Chinese Lantern.

"20:46 PAGED TO INVESTIGATE RED FLARE
MET WITH FIRST INFORMANT. DETAILS PASSED
TO HUMBER. FURTHER REPORTS INDICATE
FLARE WAS A CHINESE LANTERN"

ROYAL NATIONAL LIFE-BOAT INSTITUTION

RETURNS OF SERVICE BOOK

STATION ▇▇▇▇▇

30th June ▇▇ to 20th June ▇▇

> At about 21.30 on 24 8 76 I received a call from the
> Humber CGHQ that a red flare had been seen off Hornsea. This
> was for information only, and not an anticipatory but I informed
> the coxswain. About half an hour I was asked to launch and
> did so and the lifeboat made for the area between Skipsea and
> Hornsea where the flares had been seen. The informant was
> ------------, of the coble ▓▓▓, a member of the Flamborough
> crew and quite reliable. Shipping in the vicinity assisted and
> also cobles Undine and Northwind. Nothing was found after a
> thorough search and it was called off about 02.00 and the
> lifeboat returned to station.

"At about 21.30 on 24 8 76 I received a call from the Humber GCHQ that a red flare had been seen off Hornsea. This was for information only, and not an anticipatory but I informed the coxswain. About half an hour I was asked to launch and did so and the lifeboat made for the area between Skipsea and Hornsea where the flares had been seen. The informant was -----, of the coble -----, a member of the Flamborough crew and quite reliable. Shipping in the vicinity assisted and also cobles Undine and Northwind. Nothing was found after a thorough search and it was called off about 02.00 and the lifeboat returned to station."

> Report of flares NE FH HD soon by
> MRCC too cliff top investigation +
> on the bottom Silex Beach FH L/B
> Tasked para flares put up nothing
> untoward standing down

"REPORT OF FLARE NE FH HD SOON BY
MRCC TOO CLIFF TOP INVESTIGATION &
ON THE BOTTOM OF SIL*? BEACH FH L/B
TASKED PARA FLARES PUT UP NOTHING
UNTOWARD STANDING DOWN"

> 22.12 Called to investigate object on east corner of Thornwick Bay. Met with first informant, searched all area. Along with FL LB. Nothing found.

"CALLED TO INVESTIGATE OBJECT ON EAST
CORNER OF THORNWICK BAY. MET WITH FIRST
INFORMANT. SEARCHED ALL AREA. ALONG
WITH FL LB. NOTHING FOUND"

I was particularly intrigued by this final log. Just what were the coastguard called out to search for on the east corner of Thornwick Bay?

A Visit To Flamborough Lifeboat Station
July 15th 2018

I had no expectations of finding any useful information as I drove towards the lifeboat station at Flamborough's South Landing beach.

A few days earlier I had been informed that the Flamborough lifeboat crew had an exercise planned for 9.30 on the morning of Sunday July 15th 2018. I was told that if I visited the station and asked nicely, they might allow me to look at some of the old emergency call-out logs.

Visiting Flamborough lifeboat station had been on my 'to do' list for a few years. My reasons for not visiting earlier were based on my previous experience of Flamborough folk and their reluctance to share information. I have spoken to quite a few Flamborough people over the years and had success, but it was never easy. This visit would involve me standing in a room full of seasoned lifeboat men and hoping to get a favourable response. I didn't feel that confident.

When I arrived at the station, I was surprised to see it so busy. There were dog walkers, kayakers and people in wetsuits milling about on the shoreline, and watching the lifeboat as it slowly moved down the slipway towards the sea. There were old men sitting on wooden benches around the station: former lifeboat crew who were reliving old times. I recognised one of them as Les Robson; a former mechanic and coxswain of the lifeboat during the 1980s. He didn't know me, but I had read about his heroic exploits in the Bridlington library archive. Their eyes fixed on me as I walked towards them. All I wanted to do was look though a few old lifeboat logs, surely it could not be that difficult.

Paul:
"Hello. Could you tell me who is in charge please?"

Les Robson:
"David Freeman is the man you want, he's upstairs. What do you want to know?"

I explained that I was writing a book about unusual events in the area and that I was interested in lifeboat callouts to investigate unexplained lights. Les didn't seem surprised when I mentioned the lights.

Les:
"If you go up those stairs and ask him, I'm sure he'll help you if he can."

A few minutes later I found myself standing inside the lifeboat station control room. Five sets of eyes fixed onto me as I walked through the door and I asked if I could speak to David Freeman.

I always find these initial meetings hard work. It would not be half as difficult if I were asking about something that was classed as normal.

When one of the men identified himself as David, I took a step closer and I explained to him that I was doing research for a book. I told him that I had already been to the Bridlington station and seen a few of their call-out logs.

David:
"If you don't mind waiting a few minutes, I will see if I can find anything of interest for you."

It came as a surprise to me that no one in the station raised an eyebrow when they heard I was interested in call-outs to lights over the sea. One of the men even asked if I would like a cup of tea, while I waited for David to find the logbooks.

My visit to the station did not turn out to be as rewarding as I had hoped - as far as information about unexplained lights was concerned. But I found the men very helpful and they were interested in what I had to say, which surprised me a little. When David returned, he handed me a logbook containing lifeboat call-outs for 1995 and 1996. He told me I was welcome to come back again, and said he was not sure where the older books had gone, but said he would try and find them for me.

I sat there for a while and drank my tea while I studied the reports. I discovered there was nothing of any significance, because 1995 and 1996 proved uneventful, as far as unexplained lights over the sea were concerned. But the day had been more than just average, because I learned from the old guys out on the benches, that a few of the crew were still around who had been involved in the search and rescue for crashed RAF Lightning XS894 in 1970.

For that reason alone, my visit was worthwhile - I may write more on this at some point in the future.

IAN RICHARDS' PREDATOR

Just when you think you have heard it all, another story surfaces that pushes the curve of the surreal even further outside of normal.

I first spoke with Ian Richards about two years ago when he contacted me to discuss something he saw on Moor Lane at Carnaby. Ian told me about a huge black dog he had seen running across the fields, and his account supported a similar story I was told by two security guards, who were on night shift at Carnaby, around the same time.

But a chance meeting with Ian, on March 14th 2018, unlocked another strange story that happened close to Bridlington town centre. It was a story I never expected to hear that day.

I came out of the post office on Quay Road in Bridlington to find Ian waiting for me outside. We had seen each other and spoken briefly before I had gone inside to post some books, and I was pleased to see him waiting. We had not spoken for a while and it was good to have the opportunity to speak with him again. After interviewing as many people as I have over the years, you get a feel for the ones who are keeping as close to the truth as possible. I sensed an honesty about Ian's words the very first time we had spoken and I valued the information he gave me.

Christ Church Bridlington is just across the road from the post office and it was something that happened behind that church in 2007 that Ian wanted to talk to me about.

In 2007 Ian Richards was a joinery contractor working on the new Christ Church community training and resource centre, known as the Key Centre. The £1.2 million centre was built on land at the back of the church. It is a large and bold blue and white building, which stands out in stark contrast to the church's dull brown sandstone.

As Ian and I talked, he began telling me about seeing something, as he worked at the centre one afternoon, that unnerved him to the point of feeling scared. We stood outside the post office looking over towards the church. It is a big impressive building from 1841, built by an architect by the name of Gilbert Scott.

Ian:
"I saw something weird behind that church Paul, something I will never be able to explain. We had just about completed all the work on the new centre, and I remember standing out in the car park. I suppose I was feeling satisfied with the finished project."

We continued to talk as we walked en route towards Ian's van, which was parked close to the church.

Ian:
"I can show you exactly where it happened, if you have the time Paul?"

This was great! I had only come into town to post a few books, but now I found myself speaking with a first-hand witness to a strange incident. Even better; we were standing less than 100 meters from where he'd had his encounter. I still had no idea what Ian had seen, but I was not about to turn the offer down, and a few minutes later we were standing in the car park beside the Key Centre.

Ian:
"I was stood about here Paul, and it was over there when I first saw it."

Ian pointed to a two metre high steel fence that runs along the boundary of the church grounds, less than fifteen metres away from where we stood. On the other side of the fence is a narrow footpath that runs along the back of a row of old terraced houses on Victoria Road and comes out at Wellington Road.

Ian:
"It was there Paul."

Ian was indicating to an area of the fence with the branch of a tree growing through it.

Paul:
"You mean roughly where that car is parked?"

Ian:
"Yes, about there. I was just standing back and admiring our finished job on the Key Centre and something caught my eye. I looked, but

couldn't really see anything at first. I was sure I had seen movement; you know, when you see something from the corner of your eye? But something just looked wrong. It's hard to explain.
About half-way up the fence there was an area that was sort of shimmering. You know the effect you get when you see something in the distance on a very hot day? But this was close and the day wasn't that hot."

Paul:
"Was it shaped like anything Ian; I mean did it look like anything you could relate it to?"

Ian:
"No, it was just a strange shimmering shape; it was like translucent jelly. I could see the fencing through it, but it rippled and shimmered. It was weird. I thought to myself, 'What the hell is that?' Then I saw it begin to slowly move along the top of the fence-line. I looked around to see if anyone else was about, but I was on my own. The thing was fairly large and the biggest part of it seemed to be about six feet off the ground covering the top half of the fence.

I wish I could describe it better Paul, but the truth is; I have never seen anything like it. Have you seen that film Predator – where that invisible alien is hunting Arnold Schwarzenegger in the jungle? Well that's the kind of effect I could see - not the shape of a man - just a shimmering shape moving along the top half of the fence. I remember watching it until it just seemed to fade away."

I don't think I will ever understand how one strange happening can connect to another or even if they do, but this next account occurred in the same place as Ian Richard's sighting.

The Christ Church Ghost

On Sunday March 18th 2018, a friend of many years called to see us at our home. I have changed his name to John for this short account.

John works in town and has recently moved house from Wellington Road to Quay Road, just around the corner. He told me that on some days, after work, he visits an elderly friend on Wellington Road before going home. His friend, called JR, used to be his nearest neighbour before he moved. John told me that, to save time, he uses the footpath between Christ Church and the old terraced houses on Victoria Road.

This is where his story gets interesting. I had not told him anything about Ian Richard's account of the strange translucent shape, but John suddenly told me that he had seen something strange himself on two occasions, very close to where Ian saw the shape, while visiting his old neighbour. I still find it amazing that I was told of both of these accounts within four days of each other, even though they occurred years apart - and neither men knew each other. I only made the connection due to their respective stories. Although I cannot stress enough, that John's account contains recent events, it is probably not directly connected to Ian Richard's experience.

I made John a cup of tea and asked about his new home and how he was settling in. His main reason for calling was to look at a reclining chair that my wife and I said he could have. We asked him if he wanted to stay with us for a meal, but he said no. He told us that he was calling to check on his friend JR, before going home. That's when he told me about what he saw.

John:
"I knew I had something else to tell you Paul - wait till you hear this! When I go to see JR I usually save time by using that path that runs by the side of Christ Church."

I kind of knew John was going to tell me that something strange had happened. At the same time I could not quite believe it, because he was talking about the very place I had visited with Ian Richards just four days earlier.

John:
"I have seen a man walk across that path from the church grounds and go into a wall. I thought I was seeing things the first time, but I have seen him two times now."

Well this was different; a man vanishing into a wall? I never expected to hear that. The back of those terrace houses has a two and a half metre wall that runs the full length of the footpath opposite the fence. There are no streetlights on the footpath, and without the wall, the properties would be a prime target for burglars.

Paul:
"What do you mean John? Are you saying you have seen a ghost, is that what you're saying?"

John:
"I don't know what I saw Paul. He was wearing a black suit and a hat and he just walked across the path and vanished. I have seen him two times now and in the same place at around 2.30pm each time."

I am just astounded by the synchronicity of these two amazing accounts. John had obviously not witnessed the same thing that Ian had seen years earlier, but it was still a highly unusual story from the same location. For me to be told about it within days of hearing Ian's account is also an amazing coincidence. The two men do not know each other, but I have since told Ian Richards about John's experience. I now wonder if another window of high strangeness has been discovered?

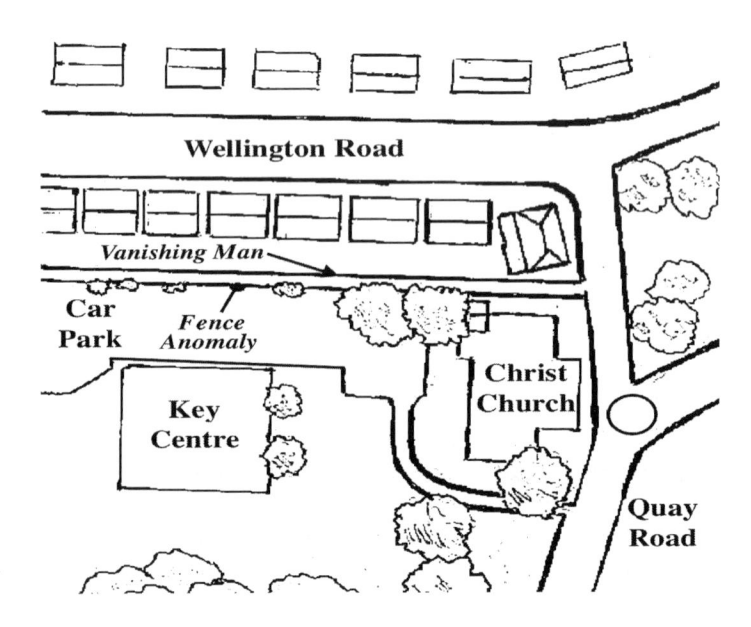

Myself in the car park by the steel fence, where Ian saw the shimmering anomaly

Footpath behind Christ Church where John saw the vanishing man

SIGHTING OF THE CAYTON PANTHER

On March 16th 2018 I received a phone call from a lady named Christine. She wanted to tell me about something strange she had seen two days earlier, close to the village of Cayton.

Cayton, Flixton, and a number of other small villages, sit on the edge of an area of ancient land in the Vale of Pickering, known as Star Carr. Eleven thousand years ago this flat area of land was the site of an extensive lake. It is now the most important archaeological site in North Yorkshire. The artefacts that have been found in its rich, fertile earth are like nothing found anywhere else in the world and archaeologists working at 'the Carrs' have even uncovered evidence of sacrifice and shamanic practice. I love all the unusual stories that come out of this area and Christine's is just one of many. I think the similarities they often share make them more than misidentification or coincidence.

Christine keeps horses on the Carrs, on a farm close to Cayton, and spends many hours around the area with her dog and tending to the horses. On Wednesday March 14th 2018 she decided to take her dog in the car and go for a walk; something she does most days of the week. After a short drive she parked at Cayton Cricket Club and began to walk with her dog through the grounds. Christine crossed over Carr Lane and began walking along a road called West Garth, where some new houses have been built on the left hand side.

Christine told me that as she walked her dog, she looked across the fields between the new houses and noticed a big black animal low to the ground. It appeared to have broken cover from some nearby trees on the edge of the far field and she actually saw it crawl across the open field on its belly. At first Christine thought it was a big black Labrador dog, but soon realised, by the way it was moving, that it was no dog. She was certain that it was a cat, in fact she called it a panther of some kind.

Christine:
"It was just coming out of the long grass and was looking around to see what was what. I wondered if anybody in the new houses had seen anything. I know that one farmer puts his sheep in the field behind those houses, where the land rises up."

Christine's panther was seen emerging from the hedgerow into this field between houses on West Garth

Myself at the location where Christine saw the big cat crossing the field.

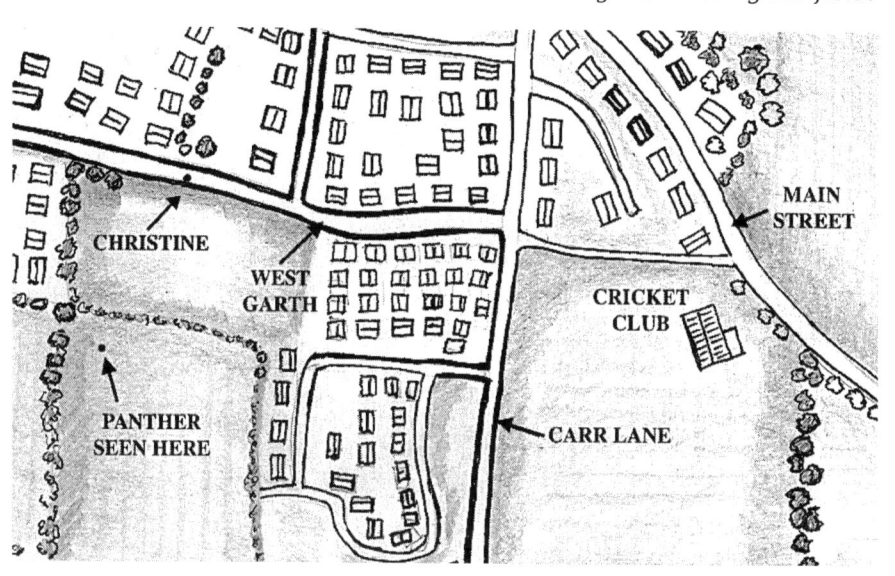

Paul:
"So would you say it was bigger than a Labrador?"

Christine:
"I would have said it was 'longer'...definitely. More than four feet long. And it was crouching, so the tail was down. But when it moved it seemed to be considering whether to come out or not. I could see it was thinking whether to go or not... Then I thought there must be somebody in those bushes nearby, so it must be their Labrador. But it certainly didn't look like a domestic dog. I could see the gleam on it, like a sheen on the coat.
Then I watched it move about a quarter of the way over the field and then it stopped. It looked as though it was going to head back, as if it had seen or heard something. Then, all of a sudden, it went over to a cluster of trees, but was still crouching low to the ground. I looked all around to see if there was anyone about, but there was no one."

Christine told me she had never seen anything like it before, and as a respected member of the local community she had no intention of telling anyone in case she was ridiculed. But a friend, with an interest in the unexplained, told her about my books, so she decided to talk to me about her sighting. I believe Christine to be an excellent witness and have no doubt that she saw a large black cat of some kind.

I have also come to realise that the strangeness in these areas does not just end after one unusual event.

The Filey Lightforms

I do not know if there is a connection between reports of big cats and UFOs, but on the same day that Christine saw the panther at the Carrs, my daughter Sarah, who lives in Cayton, phoned me to report a sighting of twin lights in the sky.

Sarah was with her husband in the car, on their way from Cayton to *Tesco* supermarket in Filey, when they were shocked to observe orange spheres of light in the sky. The distance between the panther sighting and where they saw the lights is less than three miles, so I cannot imagine how the two are connected. There is nothing to link them, other than both incidents occurred on the same day and in close proximity. Is this pure coincidence or should we always look for other events of high strangeness when something happens? I think we should at least consider it - especially since my research has highlighted many clusters of different phenomena over the years, all occurring around the same time. I think the lightforms sighting and the panther sighting earlier that day *are* unrelated to each other, but they emanate from the same 'bubble of strangeness' that appears to open and close in this area from time to time. The Filey UFOs were seen just before 7pm on Wednesday evening March 14th. I received Sarah's phone call just seconds after their sighting.

Sarah:
"We both saw them at the same time, it was really odd. A large circle of bright orange light just appeared in the sky. It shocked us really, because it was so low and quite close. Then another one appeared at the side if it, and they just stayed there in the same place for about ten seconds. Then one of them went out, and the other one switched off a second or two after that. We didn't even think about taking a picture of them, it all happened so fast."

Paul:
"You said they were bright - did they light up a large area of the sky around them?"

Sarah:
"No. They were bright, but they didn't seem to light up the sky like a flare would do; if that's what you mean?"

Paul:
"Yes, that's exactly what I mean. So did you see smoke or anything else around them?"

Sarah:
"Well another thing that could rule out flares, was that it was quite windy and these lights didn't move. And they were deep orange - I thought flares were red or white? That was the first thing we talked about when we saw them."

Below: an impression of Sarah's twin lightform sighting over Filey.

I love the fact that Sarah was with her husband at the time, because he is usually so dismissive of all things UFO-related, but he had no explanation for what he saw with his own eyes. So now I had two reports, by different witnesses, of sightings of things that should not belong. I wondered if we were about to experience another outpouring of unexplained phenomena like the 2009 Wilsthorpe Incident?

Perhaps these things never stop? The Cliff Lane mysteries began in early 2017, but who is to say that things were not happening before that. Most of the locations where these things happen are so far away from the public eye, that many may go unnoticed. The sad thing for me as a researcher is that I believe I am only getting a tiny percentage of what could be an enormous picture. Christine's panther sighting was on the same land where so many other people have reported seeing the creature known as the Flixton Werewolf, as described in my first two books.

I wish I knew how the big cats and UFOs fitted into these situations; the cats appear to be real flesh and blood animals to the people who observe them. Yet where is the evidence that they are preying on livestock?

I have recently discovered that more sheep are being killed in mysterious circumstances twenty-two miles away at Ravenscar. Like Bempton, Ravenscar sits on the edge of the North Sea. So is this killer using the cliffs and a network of inaccessible caves to evade detection? Or perhaps we are dealing with something else - a complete unknown that comes from beneath the sea; something alien to all that we know and understand.

Something has to be responsible for the lights beneath the sea off Bempton, that I saw with Bob Brown in 2017 - and something is responsible for killing sheep in the fields that run along the clifftops. The farmers I have spoken with do not believe it is a dog or a big cat. One of them calls the killer 'a phenomena' and like me, he cannot understand why, after finding a dead animal, nothing is eaten.

So far I have not heard anyone from the farming community talking about livestock deaths around Star Carr, especially if a panther-type animal is active in the area at the moment. It is March 17th 2018 as I type this, so I am sure things could change, but if I do discover livestock on the Carrs being killed and not eaten, can we really blame it on a big cat? If the deaths follow a similar pattern to the sheep killed around Bempton and Speeton I would have to say no.

A Visit to Star Carr

On March 23rd 2018 I decided to spend the day around Star Carr. I had initially arranged to meet Christine at Cayton Cricket Club, then walk with her to where she observed the panther, but her farrier called to say he had a cancellation, so she needed to attend to her horses. This meant our meeting was postponed, but I had no intention of letting that spoil the day. I parked my car close to the cricket ground and set off on foot towards the Carrs. It was a cold bright day and because the ground was still waterlogged from rain and snow in the previous week, I hoped I might get lucky and find footprints.

There was no one else was around as I walked Carr Lane; the road that runs between Cayton and Folkton. It was amazing to be walking on ground that carries so much history. I know the Carrs hold much more of the past than any of us will ever discover and it is a location you could spend a lifetime researching. There is no other place like it in the world. As I walked on this ancient earth, I have to admit that it gave me a thrill to think of all of the things I had been told, and the things that had been seen and experienced on and around the Carrs.

At various intervals I saw deep drainage ditches that cut across the fertile land and it was easy to see how wildlife might move undetected on these open fields. In the past I have stood on top of Staxton Wold looking down onto the vast open space that is the Carrs, and wondered how so many unexplained things could come from one location - and if it was real where did it hide?

From such an angle, looking down onto six-metre-deep drainage ditches that crisscross the land, I soon realised that hiding would not be such an impossible task for an animal. So avoiding detection would certainly not be that difficult for a panther-like cat. That is, if you subscribe to the theory that they are actually a living breathing mammal.

To call them drainage ditches does not really do them justice. They are actually streams in their own right, and are over two metres wide in places and quite deep. Until that point I had misjudged the amount of wildlife these hidden water systems could contain.

I spent about four hours walking the area, taking pictures and looking for anything unusual, but found nothing to suggest a big cat had ever been there. Of course, I only scratched the surface that day of an incredibly large land mass that would take months to cover in detail. Even then I would only be touching on a small percentage, due to the land that is privately owned and farmed by different people; who I suspect would not take kindly to strangers walking about on their land.

At about 2pm I decided to make my way back to the car. I had made the mistake of wearing rigger boots instead of Wellington boots and my feet were beginning to ache from walking through the muddy fields. Cayton village came into view as I reached the railway crossing, then from a few remote houses on the very edge of the Carrs, suburbia slowly emerged. The cricket club was to my right and to the left was the newly built housing estate. I tried to imagine why a big cat had been seen so close to a populated area and, like Christine, I wondered if anyone else had seen it.

More Big Cat Clues

Asking complete strangers if they have seen anything unusual is no easy task, and more often than not I come away wishing I had kept my mouth shut. So far I had not spoken to anyone all day, but when I saw a man on the front driveway of a house, quite close to the cricket ground, I thought I would ask if he had seen or heard about the black panther.

Paul:
"Excuse me, I am sorry to bother you...is it possible I could ask you something?"

He looked at me for a moment as I approached; maybe he thought I was trying to sell double glazing or push my religious views.

Paul:
"I'm doing a bit of research for a few farmers in East and North

Yorkshire. They have suffered considerable livestock loss and have no idea what is killing them. I was contacted last week by a lady who lives in Cayton who says she saw a big black cat close to the cricket ground over there."

The man smiled and seemed to know what I was talking about.

Man:
"I haven't seen it, but the man who lives in that house says he has."

He was pointing to a large white-painted house a few doors away. I asked if he minded whether I say who told me to ask about the cat sighting.

Man:
"Tell him Frank told you. I'm sure he won't mind telling you about it. He swears he saw it."

I thanked Frank and said goodbye, then went to knock at the door of the nearby white house. I wasn't quite sure what to expect, but at least I knew that whoever lived there had seen the panther.

When the door opened I was greeted by a large man in his mid-60s. I quickly explained that I had just been talking to his neighbour a few doors away, and that I was investigating reports of a black panther that was seen the previous week.

White house:
"Well I can tell you with certainty that it is real. I have seen it, but it was about two years ago. It gave me quite a fright I don't mind saying."

I asked if he was sure about what he saw.

White house:
"Oh yes, 100% sure. I know exactly what I saw. It was in our back garden, so I got a real good look at it. I remember going into the garden with our dog, we have a Staffy, and he suddenly went charging down the garden. When I looked I thought, 'oh there's another dog. What's that doing there?'

Next thing, our dog stops dead in his tracks. He didn't move, he just stood there staring. Well, by then I could see why. It was a bloody black panther. I got a real good look at it. There's no mistaking what I saw. It was definitely a black panther. It looked at the dog and let out an almighty screaming growl, then it leapt into the air. I'm not kidding, I have not seen anything move as fast. It must have leapt fourteen feet. It cleared the hedge and was gone. I saw it a few times after that. I know the postman has seen it as well."

I could not believe what the man was telling me. I knew the cat was real and now my investigations were finding more meat around the bones of the story. Before our conversation ended, the man's wife came to the door and asked if I would like to call back the following week to discuss the matter some more. Then she told her husband to tell me about the snake.

Location in the garden where the black panther was seen

White house:
"Oh yes. For a few years, in the summertime, we have seen a big snake. It comes into the garden from the dyke."

I assumed that he meant a common grass snake, which is the largest of the three native snake species we have in the UK.

White house:
"We have no idea what it is. It's about ten feet long and it's orange and yellow. Scared me to death the first time I saw it. All the grass was moving, sort of swaying in a curving motion, so I went to look. And then I saw why. It was a massive bloody snake; more yellow I suppose, than orange. But I don't know what kind of snake it could be."

I think the snake will have to wait for a future investigation, I do have a little experience of native snakes here in the UK. Where I used to live at Old Denaby there was marsh and swampland and grass snakes were common. I spent many hours catching them as a boy. One thing I have observed, I do know that snakes are creatures of habit and the same snakes can always be found in the same places.

If by some amazing chance, this exotic-sounding reptile has managed to find somewhere warm enough to survive the British winter, there would be a good chance it is still living close to where the couple have seen it.

White house:
"There is one more thing I want to say before you go. Before we saw that panther, we were overrun with rabbits. I mean there were hundreds, but they all just seemed to disappear not long after seeing that cat. I remember one morning, I went out and looked into the fields around us and saw dead rabbits everywhere. Most of them had been bitten and chewed, but it was the number that shocked me, there were loads of them. We don't see many rabbits anymore."

I thanked the couple for sharing their stories and I arranged to speak with them again after the weekend. I gave them my word that I would never reveal their identities.

The Cayton Panther Revisited
March 26th 2018

This was by far the warmest day of the year so far, and I could think of no better place to spend the day than at Star Carr. I had arranged to meet Christine once more, and the couple from the white house - so it promised to be an interesting trip.

I had planned to meet up with her at 12:00pm close to Cayton Cricket Club, then she was going to take me to the farm where she kept her horses. Thanks to Christine, I was able to walk with her through parts of Star Carr that would normally have been out of bounds to me. Much of the land is private and off-limits unless you know the land-owners. It was good to see that the drainage ditches extended deeper into the Carrs than I had previously seen. Their depth and size seemed to be consistent and fuelled my theory that if this big cat was real, then this could be how it travelled around undetected.

Christine wanted to show me a series of fields that ran along the railway line, and said that a few years ago a horse had been found dead in a nearby dyke one morning. We walked part of the way and she explained how the horse had always been a calm and good-natured animal, but suggested that something must have spooked him during the night.

Christine told me that the horse ran the entire length of the field, crashing straight though a barbed-wire fence and on into the next field. Undeterred, it carried on running through another barbed-wire fence, only coming to a stop when it jumped a hedgerow and landed face down in one of the dykes. The poor animal was found dead the next day; its body cut to ribbons from the ordeal it suffered.

Christine said, that on the farm, all they could do was speculate about what could have created so much fear, that the horse panicked and acted the way it did. The fields are miles away from any roads and no trains would have been running after 10pm. Not that a train should have bothered the horse; it would have seen and heard them pass by every day.

Christine drove us back along the narrow dirt road from the farm and stopped the car briefly to speak to a man with his dog. They obviously knew each other and spoke about the horses and a few other things that were happening on the farm. Then she asked the man if he had seen anything usual in the area over the past few weeks. When he asked her what she meant by unusual, Christine began telling him that she had seen a big black cat in the nearby fields and wondered if anyone else had seen it.

She introduced me into the conversation by telling the man that I wrote books about strange and unexplained things, and that I was interested in sightings of the big cat. He told us that he hadn't seen anything himself, but said that Christine's sighting did not surprise him, adding that, over the years, other people had spoken about seeing a big black cat on the Carrs.

UFO at the Carrs

However, the dog walker did have an interesting piece of information to share. This is what he told us, in his own words:

Dog walker:
"My wife never believed in things from 'up there'. You know; aliens and spaceships."

His eyes fixed on us both and he pointed to the sky. I said that I didn't think they were from 'up there', assuming he meant outer space.

Paul:
"If people are seeing them, then I think that they are already here."

Dog walker:
"Well, my wife used to laugh at anyone who said they had seen such things, until one night a few years ago. She went down to see our horses and came back in a state of absolute fear. Whatever she saw had turned her from non-believer into a believer that night.
She told me that something appeared low over the fields; a round, red, spotted thing is how she described it. She said it was a pulsing light that was silent and just seemed to appear out of nowhere. It hung in the sky for a while, long enough for her to realise that it was like nothing she

had ever seen before - and it scared her so much, she just couldn't believe it. I never thought she would change, but she did after that night. She has never laughed or made fun of anyone since, who says they have seen a UFO. It has certainly made her think twice about going to the Carrs alone at night. Oh and its speed - she said that it accelerated away at incredible speed and was gone. My wife never laughs at anyone now who says they have seen aliens or spaceships, because she says she's seen one herself."

Whenever possible I use first-hand witness accounts, but this random story seemed detailed enough and appropriate, given that so many unexplained things are seen and experienced at Star Carr.

All the Strange Creatures

A short time later Christine drove me back to my car at the cricket club and my next stop was to visit the couple who lived at the white house. I was looking forward to chatting with them again and gathering a few more details about the big cat sighting. I had phoned them in the morning to say that it would probably be mid-afternoon by the time I reached their home. They said that wasn't a problem and told me I could park on their drive when I arrived.

The couple, whose names I have changed to Jack and Ann for this account, greeted me at the door and inviting me into their spacious living room. I had learned most of the story when we had spoken before the weekend, but I felt sure they had more to tell. I also needed to see their garden, to form a picture of where the cat had been seen.

The only extra information I learned from them about the cat, was that when Jack first saw it, he said it was sitting at the bottom of the garden. I pushed him to tell me about its size; because I had to be sure it was a genuine big cat.

Jack:
"I didn't know what it was at first. I thought another dog had got into the garden. It was just sat there you see, like a dog; bolt upright. Then when it stood up and I got a side view, I knew it was no dog."

I really liked how open and honest this couple were. Despite wanting to remain anonymous, they did not mind telling me about the things they had seen. After telling me everything he could remember about the cat, Jack's wife said, "Tell Paul about the worm you saw in the garden."

I thought this couple would be interesting to talk to, but I never expected to be talking about a worm - and I soon learned that this was not the same creature as the snake they had told me about when we last met.

Jack:
"Oh yes, well that was a strange thing. I can tell you that after I saw it, I never lay on the grass again."

I had an idea of what he was going to talk about, but I didn't say a word. When you immerse yourself in the world of the strange and unexplained, you hear about many things. And as crazy as it may sound, I had already heard about a larger worm-type creature before, so I just listened to him patiently.

Jack:
"I'm not exactly sure when I saw it, but I reckon it was at least four or five years ago. I remember walking down the garden one summer and seeing this thing sticking up out of the grass."

At that point Jack showed me his thumb and said the thing was about three times thicker and it stood straight up in the grass about twelve inches.

Jack:
"It's hard to explain it really, I remember thinking, 'What the hell is that?' It was sort of translucent, not see-through exactly, but getting that way. And if it does not sound too crude, it looked like a condom. I looked at it for a few seconds, I don't know what I thought really, it just looked so odd. Then I took a few steps towards it and I don't know if it saw me or it felt my footsteps getting closer, but it suddenly seemed to suck itself back into the ground, it was very fast.

When I looked there was just a small round hole, nothing like as thick as the worm-thing that had been sticking out of the grass. I have never laid down on the grass since that day."

I had been told about a similar worm-type creature by a man who lives in Bridlington. He almost stood on it while out walking. He believed it was basking in the sun like a snake, and it was also translucent. The only thing different in his description was, he said it had a diamond-shaped head. He also saw it retract into a hole in the ground. The man compared the creature's speed and movement to that of a razor clam on a beach; and anyone who has ever tried to catch one at low tide will know exactly what he means.

In a matter of days the reports from Star Carr had moved from alien big cats and UFOs to giant snakes and now, translucent worms. I just wonder how many other unexplained happenings are waiting to be discovered on the Carrs.

FILEY'S GOLDEN SANDS

The small fishing town of Filey is just over six miles up the coast from Bridlington, as the crow flies. And over the years, information has slowly seeped out about a strange phenomenon observed in Filey bay. I had been told about the golden sand, or lights seen in shallow water, on more than one occasion, from people who have no connection to each other. Yet the stories are remarkably similar, which suggests to me that something is definitely taking place.

The last time I heard about it was on May 9th 2018, when I was contacted by a man named Jason Stonehill. He wanted to tell me what he witnessed while he was out sea fishing in Filey Bay a few years ago. He said this was in 2011, but admitted that it could have been a year earlier or later.

Jason told me that he was with a group of other anglers who were out night fishing, when they all observed golden-coloured lights moving beneath the water. The thing that puzzled Jason the most about this, was that the lights seemed to be beneath the sand. He said they must have been, because he saw them close to the shore, where the water is shallowest. He also said that some of the other anglers that night said they had observed the same light phenomenon in the past, and none of them had a clue what it was.

After listening to Jason relate his account, and remembering my own sighting of lights under the sea off Bempton, I decided it was time to do some additional research into the lights beneath the waves of Filey Bay.

The Filey Lights

Glowing lights beneath the waves are something I witnessed myself back in 2017 with my good friend Bob Brown, when we saw them from Bempton Cliffs. But lights seen under the waves are nothing new around this coastline. They have been reported around the area for decades - so I know these exotics are a very real phenomenon. The descriptions of the Filey lights however, are slightly different to the lightforms seen over the sea. And although the lights that I saw were in deep water, I think there has to be a connection.

One of the first people to tell me about them was a professional photographer named Charles, who used to live in the town. He contacted me in 2016 because he wanted to share a collection of UFO reports gathered by his own family. One of the accounts describes a sighting of golden lights seen beneath the sea, at the end of the peninsula known as Filey Brigg.

I have since discovered that other locals; including trawlermen and people fishing from the beach, have also seen them. Some of those accounts have been handed down over many generations, but like many close-knit communities, the information is hard to obtain. Quite why that is I don't know. It is almost as though there is an unwritten law, where things that run deep are rarely shared with outsiders.

This does not just apply to local fishing communities; it is the same in villages and towns all over the UK. You usually have to play an active part in the life of these communities to be accepted. And even then you are still reminded, from time to time, that you were not born and bred locally. These traits are often ingrained in families with a history of working at sea and can go back hundreds of years. It was not so long ago that people entering Flamborough did so at their own risk, because residents were genuinely hostile towards strangers. In fact, some locals are still very guarded around outsiders who become part of the community.

Even the larger fishing towns like Bridlington, where I live, seem to work by this same unspoken code. Bridlington folk call themselves *'Bollington Jackdaws'* and refer to people from outside of East Yorkshire as *'Wessis'* or *'Comfors'*. They say a Wessi is someone who comes from the west of Yorkshire and a Comfor is someone who 'came for' the day and stayed. It is a different world when you get beneath the surface and meet people who genuinely believe they been infiltrated by outsiders. Genuine first-hand accounts from these locations are hard to obtain, but they are always welcome.

A New Contact

Below is an extract from a long email that I received back in 2016, from my contact named Charles, the professional photographer from Filey.

"Dear Paul,

I hope this email finds you well and the Truth Proof project is running smoothly. I hope you are still turning up interesting and engaging narrative, as part of the wider mystery surrounding the phenomena that has occurred in the Yorkshire region over the past decades.

After hearing your recent interview with Howard Hughes I felt compelled to reach out and make contact with you to relate my own accounts of odd goings on in and around Scarborough, Cayton and Filey whilst growing up in the area during the 1990s.

My mother also had a number of strange encounters and sightings, as well as third-party anecdotes relayed to her by trustworthy members of the community; the likes of police officers, fishermen and lifeboatmen in Filey... Likewise, my father, now passed, had several strange tales which I heard him recount many times through our all too few years together. Most of the stories I have are brief in nature, but have left a profound mark on my family and I, such that, the passing of years does nothing to change our minds that what we have seen was inexplicable.

My father was an engineer, a 'no-nonsense' man from Hull. He was the son of a signalman, had a grammar school education, and had been to war and back; so as a rule he would always seek out logical explanations in place of conclusions based on surface observations and fantastical assumption. My mother - a hairdresser by trade (now retired) and daughter of widowed single parent - whilst not having the same experiential and mathematical mindset as my father, still considers all logical reasons for an observed phenomena rather than assuming something to be paranormal.

Their logical, yet open-minded, nature has been distilled into myself, a career professional photographer with a strong technical understanding of physics affecting visual phenomena, giving me a balanced outlook which allows for the consideration of experiences, as yet unexplained by science and psychology. For me, the paranormal is something that I have grown up knowing to be an existential constant, which is often overlooked by those less willing to admit that they simply do not know enough about the universe to adequately explain what is staring them in the face.

I have, of late, considered that I should commit our combined memories to some form of permanence and would be happy to share them with you as I go. Though I understand that third-party anecdote is imperfect and lacking in evidential quality for your purposes as an investigative author..."

After his first email I realised that Charles was potentially an excellent source of information, and he would form an honest and intelligent opinion of what he was presented with. When I first heard about the Filey lights I always suspected that I would eventually find out more. I felt sure, from Charles's early correspondence, that he was telling me the truth about what he and his family had learned over the years.

More from my witness Charles:

"Good Evening Paul,

...it's definitely an interesting locale; my mother has told me many times of the strange goings on off Filey Brigg and she remembers the fishermen telling stories of glowing objects under the water that often broke the surface and flew away, but seemed to come and go from alleged submerged caves at the end of the rocky outcrop.

The older residents of the town used to tell her about the folklore of a dragon, that lived in the supposedly hollow cliff and how they'd seen odd illuminations beneath the waves. It certainly makes you reconsider our lore of dragons, faery folk and imps; which seem to feed into latter-day reports of unexplained aerial phenomenon, such as ball lightning, ILFs and fully physical craft.

All the best,
Charles."

Suicide Vehicle

One of the most interesting stories that Charles told me was during a phone call, when he talked about a bizarre incident witnessed by his mother and father in the late 1970s.

Charles:
"My mother distinctly remembered having conversations with fishermen and police officers who were coming out with strange stories. One of them concerned these lights in the water off the Brigg - but then there was something that she and my father witnessed themselves.

Whilst out walking on the seafront at Filey, they saw a craft of some kind - my mother always described it looking like a long wheelbase 4x4 vehicle, which had several rows of seats - and they saw it travelling along the top of the Brigg. Now this is impossible because there was always huge trees there, which stopped vehicles getting through - unless they had driven through some big steel gates, which only the police and coastguard had keys for. Not only that, it would be difficult for any vehicle to negotiate the rocks and boulders up on the Brigg.

My parents told me they saw figures sitting inside this vehicle or craft, and they watched it travel all the way along to the end of the Brigg. From their vantage point on the seafront, they could see the silhouette of the Brigg clearly in the twilight. Then they saw this thing go straight off the end of the Brigg.

The police were called out because it appeared as if this had been a group suicide. There were people inside after all. The coastguard were also called out to search the water off the Brigg, but nothing was found.

This occurred around the same time the police had been called out to different sightings of lights or objects, which they even chased around the Filey area one evening. They finally saw them fly _into_ a gasometer; which is one of those large collapsible gas storage containers."

The Filey Dragon

The town of Filey has a centuries-old legend of a dragon, which was eventually sent to its death from the Brigg by a local family. The story tells us that accounts like these run far into the past. I have wondered if these old stories about dragons actually originate from ancient encounters with the lightforms. I would imagine that the sudden appearance of glowing orange and red lights out at sea would have surely caught the imagination of the people who saw them in days of old

- people who believed in fiery dragons. There is a large black stone inside Bridlington Priory known as the 'founder's stone'. The carvings on this ancient piece of marble are quite interesting, in that they show two fiery dragons or 'wyverns' above, what looks like, Bridlington Priory. The people of Bridlington and Filey must have seen the same lights in the sky as we do today, but could those lightforms actually have been thought to be dragons?

Below: The Founder's Stone at Bridlington Priory

The two dragons or wyverns seen on the Founder's Stone

In 1934 a coastguard named Wilkinson Herbert claimed that he saw a sea monster up close while he was out walking on the beach at Filey. Here is his account, as published in *The Daily Telegraph* newspaper on March 1st of that year.

"Suddenly I heard a growling like a dozen dogs ahead. Walking nearer I switched on my torch and was confronted by a huge neck, six yards in front of me, rearing up 8 feet high! The head was a startling sight - huge eyes like saucers, glaring at me. The creatures mouth was a foot wide and [its] neck would be a yard around. The monster seemed as startled as I was.
Shining my torch along the ground, I saw a body about 30 feet long. I thought this was no place for me and from a distance, I threw stones at the creature. It moved away growling fiercely and I saw the huge black body had two humps on it and four short legs with huge flappers on them. I could not see any tail.
It moved quickly, rolling from side to side, and went into the sea. From the cliff-top I looked down and saw two eyes like torch-lights shining out to sea 300 yards away. It was a most gruesome and thrilling experience. I have seen big animals [when] abroad, but nothing like this."

Interestingly, this vintage report appeared just weeks before a news story of the Loch Ness monster was seen in national newspapers. The story was accompanied by the famous surgeon's photograph, which showed the head and neck of what looked like a huge sea monster, and was published in the *The Daily Mail* on April 21st 1934. So who inspired who?

The following two pages:
On May 19th 1934 the strange sighting of a bird 'as big as a man' was reported in the Bridlington Free Press

and in 1706, a shoal of 'monsters' arrived in Bridlington Bay only to be attacked by locals, according to this vintage report from 1930.

FREE PRESS, SATURDAY, MAY 19 1934

GARDENER GETS A SHOCK

Mistook Eagle for Aeroplane

BIRD AS BIG AS A MAN

A sound resembling the noise made by an aeroplane heralded the approach of a huge bird near Bridlington School on Saturday evening. From a description given a reliable eye-witness of the strange spectacle, it is now considered almost certain that the bird was a golden eagle, king of birds, and one of the rarest of visitors south of the border.

The golden eagle, in its natural haunts, is a huge creature, preying on animals and smaller feathered creatures. The legendary stories of its adventures are countless.

Mr. C. Dowson, 152 Brookland Road, was digging in his garden when he became aware of the presence of something strange. There was a noise like a plane flying high and he was impelled to look up. Hovering over a plantation in the distance, east of the meteorological tower in the grounds of Bridlington School, he saw IT.

"AS BIG AS A MAN"

He describes it as being almost "as big as a man." It was flying slowly and as though tired or injured. On approaching, it swooped down as though to alight in a field at the rear of the garden in which Mr. Dowson was working. It was then that the watcher caught a clear glimpse of reddish tinted wings wide-stretched for the dive and a fish-like tail jutting out from a greyish body.

In an interview with a "Free Press" reporter, Mr. Dowson, who is a railway ticket collector, described the phenomenon in the following manner.

"On Saturday night, just when it was becoming slightly dusky, I was working in my garden. (The garden borders the Bridlington School grounds). Hearing the sound of something flying in the distance, I looked up. I thought it was a plane and nine times out of ten I would not have bothered. Coming from beyond the plantation was a huge bird. It appeared to be as big as a man but slightly smaller than I am. Some men came running from the plantation and the bird hovered around above the field. Two ladies were passing in the street and I called them in to see the bird which swooped down as though it was going to alight in the field.

"Its body was grey and the wings were red. It had a tail just like a fish and a curved beak."

DISAPPEARED FROM VIEW

"I thought it was a huge owl and when the bird vanished in a downward sweep, the men continued to run across the field. It appeared as though it was landing, but disappeared from my view."

Mr. Dowson omitted to discover the names of the ladies who had observed the presence of the bird with him, but there is no doubt that the incident was observed by several other people in the vicinity. A party of men apparently working in the School grounds searched the field for some time, but failed to find any sign of the bird.

Several local amateur ornithologists have visited the scene of the appearance of the bird, and without exception, they are inclined to the opinion that the visitor was of the golden eagle species. Its size, colour and general appearance coincide perfectly with descriptions of the king of the eagles.

The golden eagle is in the habit of making its eyry in high hills or in cliffs which it is impossible for human beings to reach. In Scotland it is known to exist, but except for the extreme north of England, in this country it is practically unknown. It lives to be a hundred years of age and has been known to beat deer and sheep into insensibility with its massive wings. Golden eagles have been known to reach a length of over three and a half feet from head to tail. Their wing-span is enormous.

A Bridlington postman named Sawdon claims that he saw a golden eagle at Cottam some years ago.

THE BRIDLINGTON FREE PRESS,

SATURDAY, APRIL 12, 1930.

MONSTERS IN BRIDLINGTON BAY.

Vivid News-Sheet Description.

Strange monsters in Bridlington Bay are described in a statement from which Brother S. Purvis quoted at a meeting of the Augustinian Society in the Bayle Gate on Monday evening. The Prior, Brother F. U. Leadis, presided.

The heading of the article is little less fearsome than the monsters described. It runs as follows:—

"A strange, wonderful, and amazing relation of 30 terrible sea monsters of dreadful and unusual shapes, and of vast bigness, who to the great affrightment of many of the inhabitants, came into Bridlington Bay in Yorkshire, on the 23rd of January, last, 1706, of which 24, of them were killed and taken, after some hours of fighting and contending, roaring horribly and casting up floods of water and blood, turning the water into a sanguine complexion, with a true description of them in all their forms, parts, and proportions, the like never having been seen in any age, with some remarks on such an unusual wonder in nature as it may signify according to the event or observation of the antients."

"The above," said Mr. Purvis, "is the heading of a very rare little tract or news sheet of which few in Bridlington have even heard. Startling as are the details we are assured that: 'The truth of this relation is credibly attested by Mr. Samuel Arneby, Mr. Jackson, Mr. William Thompson, masters of ships, now in town (London), who lodge at the King's Arms at Execution Dock, and by one Mr. Robinson next door to the Golden Ball at King Edward Stairs, who came lately from thence and saw these monstrous fishes, where there were several thousands of spectators.'"

The Tumbling Lightforms
Mid-November 1994, 5pm

Another sighting that my friend Charles shared with me occurred in Scarborough in 1994 and had multiple witnesses; including himself. Here is an extract of an email he sent recently, detailing his experience:

"...my mother, father and I resolved [to] give our family dog a longer than normal walk before dinner... As we exited the estate and walked up the hill toward the (A165) coastal road we passed a number of people, families out doing the same...Nearing the top of the hill we crossed over the road to where the [children's] park was situated...It was the darker side of twilight and the street lights had been on for a while...

As we stood and allowed the dog to take deep sniffs of the ground... our attention was caught by a small cluster of red/orange lights which resembled Christmas tree string lights at a distance. We watched as the cluster of four or five lights appeared to slowly tumble toward us, moving slowly in from the sea toward the coast.

Before long the cluster grew to perhaps seven or so individual points of light which had increased slightly in magnitude as the object, or objects, moved toward us. The street was fairly busy and several other people had now noticed the lights that hung against [the] hazy night sky... As more people stopped, one in a car whom had pulled over to watch, the lights seemingly gathered momentum...

[They were] now a group of around ten points of light, with the tumbling effect becoming more pronounced. The best way to describe it visually is to ask you to imagine a transparent spherical fishbowl or hamster ball with a bundle of Christmas tree lights inside being rolled across a pitch black velvet sky... It was impossible to determine height or scale with any certainty, but it didn't seem to be that far away from us.

It's tumbling motion gave each of the points of light an almost orbital appearance, that is to say that they were fixed on an orbit around a central, lightless, invisible point. Each light was on a different axis without any notable uniformity to their spacing, giving the object an intentionally random motion and therefore making it difficult to distinguish the true shape, scale or directionality of the phenomena.

By now the object cluster was rolling almost directly over us in complete silence and appeared to shift to become a more reddish hue. It had moved, I would guess, on a north-northwest vector and continued to do so as it tumbled away inland with the points of light disappearing gradually one by one as it went on it's way; still tumbling but decreasing in the number of points until it appeared to vanish entirely.

I would estimate that the whole experience lasted no longer than a few minutes, though it felt much longer at the time."

Charles's sighting is as peculiar as they come and I cannot recall hearing anyone describe the lightforms moving in this way before.

THE WEREWOLF OF FOX WOOD

I could not write another *Truth Proof* book without including even more truly incredible accounts of werewolf-type creatures. The fact that such reports keep coming my way makes me believe there is more than a tiny grain of truth to them. As to what these creatures are, any opinion is as valid is as mine. I don't think every account can be put down to witness misidentification or an overactive imagination. What is more amazing, is that most of the accounts I have collected are of sightings from repeat areas; where people, who are unconnected to one another, see these creatures in the same remote patches of woodland.

The village of Grindale sits on the outskirts of Bridlington. It is mostly farms and a few cottages. It has no shops or amenities and is quite isolated. The following account was given to me by a man who used to live in the village over twenty years ago.

Back in the 1980s Rob was often out and about in the fields and woodlands surrounding Grindale. At the time he was actively poaching; setting snares and out hunting - in places he shouldn't have been. I have spoken to him many times about what he saw on the edge of Fox Wood that day and it is clear from his description that it was no ordinary animal. I recorded our interviews as he shared his account with me and I also made notes at the time, so what you are about to read is exactly what Rob told me during our face-to-face meetings in 2015. Rob is a blunt-talking man who uses the local dialect, so I have added standard words where needed, for ease of reading.

Rob:
"Right. Am gonna start by saying I don't ever want my full name to be seen anywhere with what am gonna about to tell you. I know what I saw and I will take that to the grave, but we were on land we shouldn't have been on. We was poaching.

It was late in the year, November I think, and about 1983. I remember there was snow on the grund [ground] *and we was up around Foxy* [Fox Wood] *checking me snares. It was really odd, we hadn't caught anything for weeks and believe me, I was good. Before this, I used to go up there and could always get phesys* [pheasants], *rabbits or hares. But there* was nout [nothing]. *The woods had been cleared out, or something had scared most of the game away. And something was beating me to the snares. I could see where we had caught something, but something else had ragged [stolen] what we caught out of the snare. It was really starting to piss me off."*

Rob had my full attention as I listened carefully to his story unfold.

Rob:
"Well I was up there early one morning, it was just getting light. Me and another lad was walking along the edge of a field towards Foxy [Fox Wood], but the wood was dead. Nothing made a sound; no birds, no game, nothing. And our snares had either not been touched or whatever was caught had been taken. It was really strange. I know it sounds daft, but it actually felt creepy.

We stopped at the edge of the field and had look round. I remember turning to talk to my mate and seeing movement at the other side of the field. Something caught my eye and I turned to look.

Well let me tell you, I have never seen anything like what I saw in my life. I didn't know what I was looking at first. I thought it was a young hoss [horse]. I thought 'what's a hoss doing over there?'

*Then this f***ing thing jumped clean over the hedge and landed in the field. It was massive. And it cleared the hedge without any problem. But it was the way it landed that got me. It landed on all four feet just like a cat. And it never moved after, and that hedge was high. If a dog or a hoss [horse] had jumped over something that high it would have run forwards a bit when it landed. But this f***ing thing just landed and stopped dead.*

*Now my mate, he started whistling the f***ing thing."*

I looked at Rob in disbelief. What he was describing sounded strange enough, but to hear him tell me that his mate began whistling it sounded truly crazy.

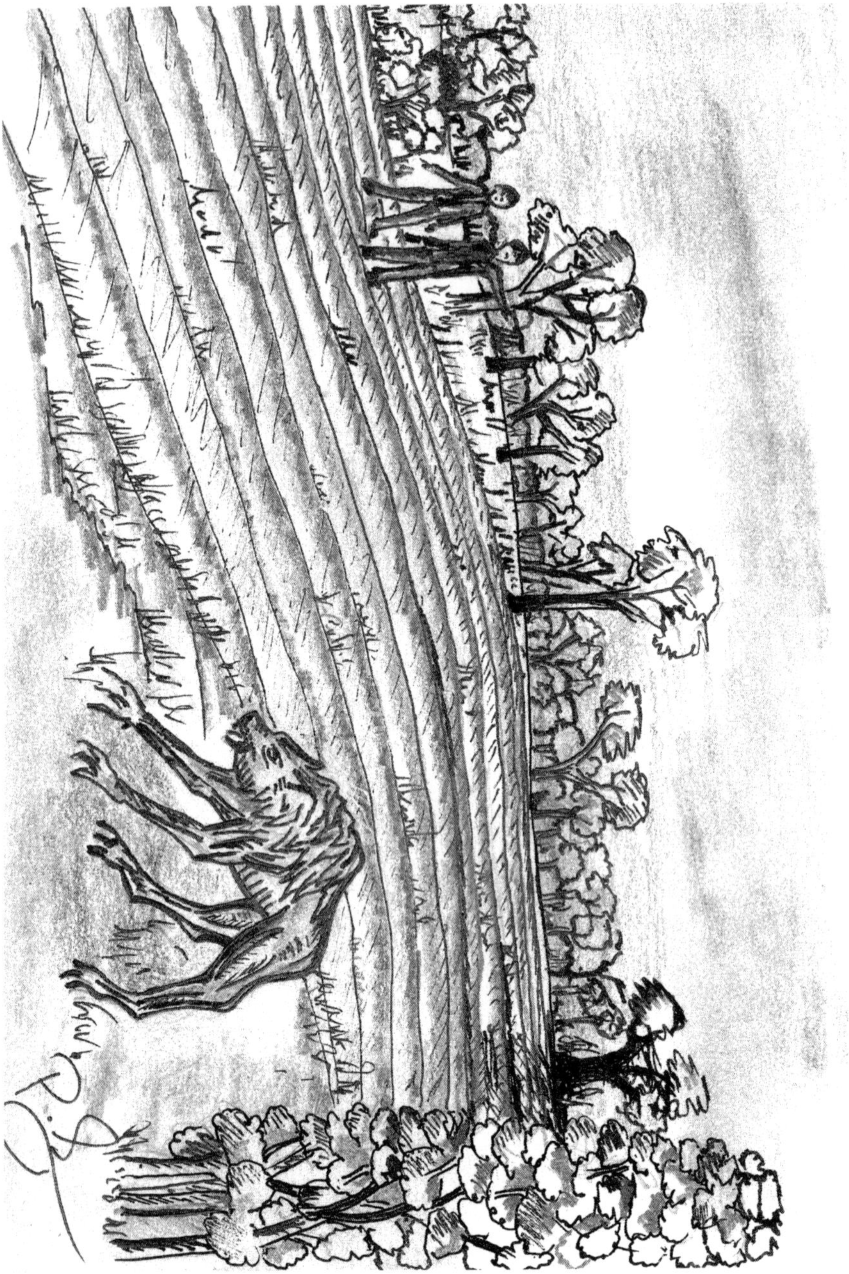

"Yep, he started whistling it. I could have battered him [hit him] *myself* Paul. This thing was looking at us. I told him to shut his gob [mouth] and then I started scrambling around in the hedge bottom to find a fence stake or something. Not that it would have been any use."

Before Rob went into the details of what the animal looked like, I asked him to tell me how far away it was from their position.

Rob:
"It was on other side of field, a ploughed field. You could see all the snow, frozen in rows on top of the land, with the striped ridges of soil lower down. I would say it was about 200 yards away, but we could see it clear. It was massive mate, and the hedge that it cleared was about eight feet high and it landed on all fours just like a cat. It was the weirdest thing I ever saw. It was all chest and no arse; like a bodybuilder. No...like a male lion; all front. It's hard to explain. It had this massive chest, shoulders and arms - and I would call them arms."

Paul:
"What colour was it Rob?"

Rob:
"It was brown, but like a brindle. Kind of light and dark brown. But it f***ing saw us, that's for sure. Soon as that silly bugger started whistling, it glared at us. Oh, it knew we were there alright. Its eyes fixed on us for a few seconds then it set off running along side of the field; in great big long strides."

Paul:
"What? It was running on two legs?"

Rob:
"No it was on all fours, but it moved in giant leaps... yes giant leaps. Sort of sprang off its back legs, landed, then repeated it. That f***ing thing was fast mate. If it had wanted to, am sure it could have killed us in the blink of an eye."

I asked Rob to tell me about its face. I knew he only saw it for a few seconds, but I wanted to know if he could tell me what type of dog it resembled.

Rob:
"It was no dog mate. If you had seen size of it, you would know what I mean. It was massive. I don't know any dog that looks like that thing. I might have only got to look at it for a short time, but I saw enough to know it was different to anything I had ever seen before. It looked like it had a baboon's face, in the middle of massive shoulders and arms. It ran across that field from Foxy Wood to the woods at the other side and we never saw it again.
I went up there the next day and took a shotgun. If I had seen it I would have shot it."

Paul:
"Did you see any signs of where it had been; did you find any prints?"

Rob:
"Didn't see anything; no prints, nothing. That's another strange thing. Something that big should have left prints when it landed on other side of that hedge, but I couldn't find anything. The grund [ground] was frozen, but something that big would have left prints."

Rob's account is impressive, and the creature he describes does not sound like any known animal in the UK - or any other country for that matter. In my opinion we are left with two possibilities: either Rob is lying about what he saw that day on the edge of Fox Wood (and if that is the case, then so are all of the other witnesses who have described seeing a similar type of creature) or, however impossible it may be to accept, Rob and all of the other witnesses are telling the truth.

Rob's account makes no sense in a world where we are supposed to know all there is to know. So once again, I am left wondering what we are dealing with. Some of the accounts that have emerged over the years from nearby Flixton and the surrounding area, describe a beast the size of a small horse. In other parts of the country, folklore tells of a creature known as the shag-foal; a goblin horse with flaming eyes and canine teeth, that was said to terrify people from time to time. The village of Grindale is only six miles away from Flixton, as the crow flies, and the land between the two consists of remote fields and woodland.

THE CAYTON CARRS WEREWOLF

This next account came my way in February 2018 while I was contacting various farms about sheep mutilations. I was not actively looking for anything to connect 'werewolf' accounts to the sheep phenomena, and I still have nothing to link the two, however, interesting pieces of information do crop up when you least expect them.

When looking for information that could shed light on the Bempton sheep killings, I made enquiries miles out of the affected area. It was whilst speaking to a farmer fifteen miles away, in Ganton, that I was told about a very old werewolf account. Ganton is less than four miles away from Flixton and this story proves, once again, that location is key.

The farmer, who is in his late 60s, told me a story that he was told when he was about twelve years old. He believed the story when he first heard it and he still does today. At that time he was working on farmland out on Cayton Carrs. I explained in TP1 that the Carrs are an area of fertile wetland that stretch for miles across Cayton, Seamer and Flixton. It is an ancient land where stories of wolfmen go further back in time than anyone living can remember.

The farmer I spoke with told me that when he was twelve he worked for an elderly farmer named James Keith, or Jimmy to his friends. Jimmy claimed that he had seen a werewolf out on the Cayton Carrs, and described it as a huge hairy man, that was terrifying to look at. He said that it stood over seven feet tall and was covered in thick brown hair.

The farmer who told me this also said that many generations of Jimmy Keith's family also claimed to have seen a werewolf on the farmland around Cayton and Flixton - with accounts in the family going back at least 200 years. At some point in the future I want to visit the area where these sightings occurred. I don't think anything in the form of evidence will be found, of course, but walking on the land where these creatures have been reported would be an amazing experience.

A more recent sighting of the Cayton Carrs Werewolf came from a farmer who lives in Folkton. In 2015 he claimed to have seen a huge man covered in hair running across the Carrs in broad daylight. From where he stood, he could see the village of Cayton half a mile away. The farmer told me that he lost sight of the creature when it left the open fields and entered woodland known as the Spell Howe Plantation.

The Cayton Carrs and the Flixton and Folkton Carrs are virtually one in the same. It is only the village names that separate them. So what is it that keeps on appearing around this area? Some people believe there is a breeding population of huge bipedal beasts roaming the woods and open fields. I cannot support any such notion, but there has to be more to this than just random sightings. I believe these creatures are real. The only trouble is, I just don't know what 'real' means anymore. The creatures certainly operate in ways that we cannot understand, but that does not have to mean they have superior intelligence.

Witness sightings are random and they are often years apart, which makes it impossible to predict any future appearance - and when they are seen, the unfortunate witnesses are usually scared to death.

I sometimes wonder if these things have always been here and they can somehow render themselves invisible. Some people believe they arrived here along with occupants of UFOs - the same has been said about the appearances of big cats that are reported. Other people claim that the creatures are descendants of 'fallen angels' who came to Earth and bred with humans.

The list of explanations is endless, but at the end of the day, they are all just theories. No one really knows the truth and most people would not accept the possibility or the reality that these things even exist.

The following pages contain a vintage report from the Bridlington Free Press of the phantom hound of East Ayton near Scarborough, also known as the 'Bargheist'.

(This is the clearest copy possible from the original image)

WEDNESDAY, FEBRUARY 9, 1927.

BARGHEIST.

The Phantom Hound at Brompton & East Ayton.

[By HARWOOD BRIERLEY.]

Many villages in the three Ridings of Yorkshire furnish odd creepy tales about a fearsome black dog or hound called by such names as Barguest, Bargheist, Guytrash, Padfoot, Flay-boggart, Black-a-Bogle, etc. I am not yet in a position to write the life-story of the diabolical "Black Dog of Brompton Carr" or the "Bargheist of Hungate" (main street) at Brompton. Repeatedly have I heard about strange doings and untoward happenings as a result of this supernatural animal's reappearances. On no occasion does its behaviour appear to have been praiseworthy.

AN OMEN OF DEATH.

Bargheist surely belongs to the folklore of the Ancient Britons. By them it would be handed on to the Celtic race, our first word users. Their language was not innocent of demons, who were responsible for tempests, pestilences, monstrosities, and mysterious deaths. If bargheist be a dictionary word it is made to pass as of Teutonic or Germanic origin. That theory I shall oppose. Bargheist must have been a four-legged ghost which made its home in a "howe," bury, burk, or burial mound of the Ancient British people; which mounds could be seen on nearly all our moors and wolds till the ploughman or forester upset them. Although so widely distributed over village streets, by woodland walks, old lanes, and river sides, this spectral hound's place of origin must have been the prehistoric burial mound. It came out usually on dark stormy nights as if to warn the inhabitants that somebody was going to die. In several Yorkshire places its visitation was regarded as an omen of death. At Horton, near Bradford, I heard that Bargheist was once seen by several honest people at the very moment that old Squire Sharp died at Horton Old Hall.

A STRANGELY BUILT HOUND.

Now I am anxious to make Bargheist's acquaintance in the Scarborough district. Perhaps I shall be so favoured before long. He is still about as big as a sheep. From his somewhat lean flanks hangs a shaggy long coat of black hair. Terror untold was inspired by his flaming, glowering eyeballs as big as saucers, which dilated in the midnight darkness. He favoured the witching hour of 12, of course, but quite often appeared on the scene as soon as public-houses were closed.

Strange, but I cannot hear that it was this awesome hound's habit to growl at anybody. The name Padfoot originated with the light pad-padding sound of his cushioned paws, but this sound was usually drowned by the clanking of a heavy chain which trailed along the causeway or winding lane. As at the other end, it was something like a collar. Padfoot was seen by some in the light of a ferocious beast which had broken loose from a menagerie. The phantom hound was noted nowhere for speed or fleetness of foot; at any rate he rarely overran any of his victims in the Town Gate or tree-shaded Loverslane.

LEGEND OF HUNGATE.

There are scores of old towns and villages, like York and Brompton, which have a Hungate, named either (like Hunmanby itself) after a pack of hounds or a flay-boggart like barghest the death-hound. The legend must have been circulated by pot-house frequenters, by undesirable story-books, by careless parents and nurses—perhaps, in the latter case, with a view to keep young children out of darkened streets, churchyard walks, and riversides. You hear a tale at East Ayton that a certain prolific pear-tree belonging to one Barnabas, or Barney Taylor, was every fruitful year a source of considerable temptation to the village lads. They recognised that if said pear-tree was to be raided, it must be done during daylight hours. To go near it after dark was dangerous, on account of the wholesome belief that Barguest might be prowling about. Barguest, if encountered, would certainly give the little thieves a fright.

MONSTERS ARE REAL

One of the most rewarding things for me, as a researcher of all things strange, is when I make contact with a first-hand witness to something truly remarkable. The biggest problem I face is when a witness is so affected by what they see, they don't want to speak about it.

I was first told about the Foxholes Werewolf in January 2018, by a friend of the person who saw it. I was given a brief outline of what happened and an email address to contact the witness. The story sounded so incredible; like something from a horror film, that I knew instantly I had to contact this person. I sent an email the same day, explaining that I was researching accounts of the Flixton Werewolf and would love to hear more about his encounter at Foxholes.

Foxholes is only five miles from Flixton, as the crow flies, and just nine miles from Grindale, so it is fairly well placed within the zone of activity. The encounter happened on the B1249 road from Driffield; a stretch of road that leads up to the A1039, which is connected to many of the Flixton werewolf accounts.

I checked my emails closely for several days afterwards, hoping I would receive further information about the encounter, but I heard nothing. I was initially told that the witness was a very busy man and I might have to wait a few weeks before I got a response, so I remained hopeful and waited. But when no reply came, I resigned myself to the fact that this would be another account that had slipped through my fingers.

Then in June 2018 I was told about a farmer who claimed to have seen a huge wolf-like animal run out from some fields and keep pace with his vehicle for a short time. The information was a bit sketchy and I never got to speak with the farmer face-to-face, but what caught my attention was the fact that his encounter also happened on the B1249. Now I had learned of two sightings of a huge animal on the *same* stretch of road, but neither witness wanted to talk.

I decided to try again to establish some kind of contact with the first witness. I still had his contact details and, despite feeling as though I was pressuring him, I thought it was worth another go. My first job was to message his friend to say that I had not received a reply and ask if he could contact the witness again for me, and give him the assurance that I would not reveal any personal information. I even asked if he might get the story for me, presuming the witness did not wish to speak to me directly; but in the end, that was not needed.

In late July 2018 I finally received a short email from the Foxholes witness, with a phone number. So I agreed to give him a call the next day at the time suggested. Now that I have spoken to this man I can say that I believe him to be very genuine and, above all, truthful. To protect his identity I am simply referring to him as Peter.

Foxholes Werewolf Sighting on the B1249
November 2017

Peter:
"It happened last year. I was driving home from Scarborough after visiting my parents. I think it was November, although I cannot be any more specific than that. It was dark but there was moonlight and I remember it had been raining. I think the time was between 9 and 9.30pm. It was a journey home much like any other. I think I was doing about 50mph when I became aware of something moving at the side of me. You know, when you catch something in your peripheral vision? It was on my side of the car and when I eventually turned to look, I could not believe what I was seeing. I was shocked."

Paul:
"What did you see Peter?"

Peter:
"I'm not sure what it was. I had never seen anything like it before in my life. It was a huge animal and it had a mane like a lion. It was very frightening and it was right next to the car window. This thing was running at 50mph and what was even more scary was that it was staring at me. It had big glowing yellow eyes."

I could hear the unease in Peter's voice as he relived the encounter. At this point, what I found incredible was how this creature was able to run alongside of a car travelling at 50mph and look directly into the vehicle. How was it able to do that and not focus on the road?

Peter:
"I remember it had been raining and this thing looked wet, the mane was black or dark brown and very thick. It tapered off to shorter fur that looked shiny, but that could have been because of the rain. I still struggle to understand exactly what I saw. The creature's back was at least as high as the car door and its head was high enough to look into the window at me. It was huge."

I asked Peter if he remembered hearing any sound as this thing ran alongside of his car.

Peter:
"No, I never heard a thing. I only became aware of it because I saw something out of the corner of my eye. I looked and it was there. It kept pace with the car for about thirty seconds, until I put my foot down. I could see it in my mirror as I sped away. It had stopped running and was just standing still in the road. The way it looked at me was terrifying; those big yellow eyes staring right at me."

Paul:
"Did you feel scared due to its sheer size and appearance Pete or did it somehow instil fear into you."

Peter:
"I'm not sure, I didn't hang around to find out. It's still unbelievable when I think about it. Its teeth were huge, as long as my thumbs and curved. And its face didn't really resemble any animal I had ever seen before. It looked a bit like a baboon, but bigger. I just don't know what it was. I was so relieved when I put my foot down and pulled away from it."

Peter's account fits with some of the most bizarre stories that I have ever heard. He had a thirty-second sighting of an animal that could have been the Flixton Werewolf and during that half minute of time, its face was no more than twelve inches away from his.

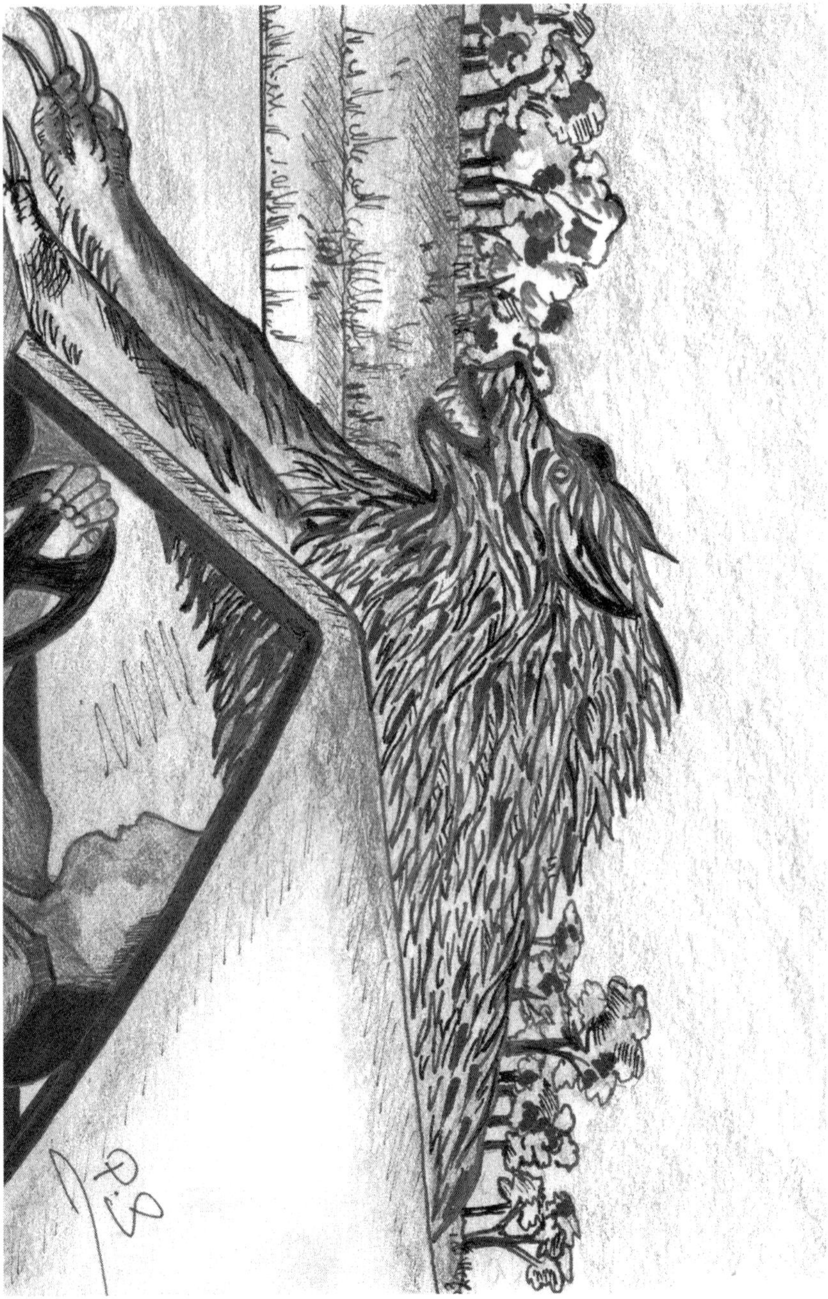

Peter said the animal's back was at least level with the top of his car door, below the window. The car he was driving was a Jaguar and from the bottom of the window to the ground they measure thirty-nine inches. If the creature had been simply standing and not running by the side of his car, I think we could probably add a few inches to that measurement.

I thought about the glowing yellow eyes that Peter had described. He had been driving at night with his headlights switched on, but they would have been out in front and unable to illuminate the animal's eyes, especially when it turned to look at him. They could not have been picked up in the headlights, so maybe they were self-illuminating in some unknown way? I also wondered what the animal's intention was; it obviously had enough intelligence to look directly at the driver of the car - and how was it able to run at 50mph and still look into the car? There were so many questions and no answers. Peter's description is very much like the creature seen in the 1970s at Grindale; which looked like a male lion with a face like a baboon. So could this be the same species of animal?

Incredibly, there are over forty years between the two sightings, and some of the Flixton Werewolf accounts go back much further in time than that. Enough witnesses have stepped forward to say they have seen these beasts to discount them as misidentification, so just what *are* people seeing? I very much doubt that we have a breeding population of werewolves in East Yorkshire! But whatever these witnesses have seen, I just cannot imagine such large beasts remaining undetected in today's world, where mankind seems to be encroaching on everything. And there seems to be no reason for their appearance - it is almost as if they are able to 'switch into' and 'out of' our reality in some strange way.

From witness descriptions, these beasts sound more like something from a horror film. I think we can say, without a doubt, that they are like no ordinary dog. Mastiffs are among the heaviest dogs in the world, with adult males weighing as much as 250 pounds. Yet they are not tall enough at the shoulder to reach the height of a Jaguar car door. And what breed of dog is able to run at 50mph for thirty seconds? No dog has ever been recorded running at 50mph, let alone sustaining that speed for so long. Moreover, the fastest breeds of dog are all sleek and lean and the animal Peter saw was a huge and powerful beast with the mane of a lion. His description is of something that should not exist, but clearly it does on some level, beyond our current understanding.

This is only my opinion, but I believe these creatures are interdimensional and they slip into and out of our existence. I have no idea if such creatures are able to do this at will or whether many factors play a part in creating the perfect conditions for them to make an appearance. Regardless of the details, once they are seen they are never forgotten.

Somewhere, there has to be a key in all of this confusion to unlock more clues. The witnesses have nowhere to turn for answers and no one is able to explain what has just flipped their understanding of the world and its reality on its head. This is typical of such accounts of the strange and perhaps why the vast majority of reports are never told. They leave nothing but confusion in the minds of the people who remember them.

Some Things Are Better Left Undiscovered: The Towthorpe Beast

In early 2018 I interviewed a man from Scarborough named James. We have met on several occasions and each time he retells his story, the fear in his voice remains the same. I have his surname, but have been asked not to use it. I did, however, have his permission to record our interview, when he told me about a terrifying experience he had at Towthorpe.

Towthorpe is between Sledmere and Fimber and only nine miles from Foxholes and because James's experience happened around the same time as the Foxholes encounter, I think there is every chance that they are connected in some, as yet inexplicable, way.

When James entered a secluded field at Towthorpe with his metal detector, one night in early 2018, he believed nothing could possibly scare him. After all he was the proud owner of a Caucasian Shepherd dog, which never left his side on his night time excursions.

These large dogs were originally bred as guard dogs to protect livestock and defend homes against wolves and bears. They are loyal, courageous and fiercely protective of the people they come to trust and love. Their strength comes from their massive proportions and they will not back away from a fight, even against wild predators. The fact James was accompanied by a dog like this, is one of the reasons why his account is even more interesting.

James:
"It happened just after Christmas 2017. I decided to check out a few places with my metal detector. I didn't have permission to be on the land, so I went during the night. I was going into a remote area, but I do not scare that easy. Plus, I had the dog with me and she is not scared of anything, or so I thought."

I asked whether the dog stayed close to him at the time.

James:
"Yes she never leaves my side Paul, she is incredibly protective. The first night I went to the field I dug up two hammered silver coins, but something was wrong, I could feel it. There's a long narrow wood that runs along the length of the field and there was something in there watching me. It was strange. Then I could hear something walking through the foliage and I realised it was quite close. The dog knew something was in there with us, but she stayed close to me. But then it began getting vocal.

I have heard deer in rut and I have seen and heard badgers and foxes. This noise was none of them. It sounded like a cross between a deer and a Bassett hound. I have never heard anything like it."

James stopped talking and rolled up his sleeves to show me his arms. The hairs were standing up as he was speaking to me; an example of the emotional reaction to the fear he felt while retelling the story.

Paul:
"Whereabouts were you James? And don't worry, I understand if you would rather not say."

James:
"No I don't mind mate. We were at Towthorpe; it's slap bang in the middle of nowhere. Whatever was in those woods that first night was stalking me - well that's what it felt like. It's a narrow wood that runs

along the side of the field where I was metal detecting. It was dark, but when I walked, it walked and I could hear it breathing. So it was close. It was the growling sound that made me think 'what the hell?' It was a good place though, because I found some hammered silver coins there that first night."

Paul:
"So how did your dog react James; did she bark or growl?"

James:
"That's the thing Paul, she was quiet. Nothing scares that dog, but she did act different to usual.

Despite being a bit unnerved I decided to go back a few days later. Those coins were hard to resist! You need an off-road vehicle, and so I parked up out of the way and entered the field. It was after midnight so no one was about. I doubt anyone ever goes there much, not even in the daytime. And I still felt safe because I had the dog with me, but I was wary of the woods though, after hearing that sound a few days before."

Paul:
"Can you describe the sound? What made it so different to the other animal noises you have heard?

James:
"Well for a start, that was just it - it was different. I have never heard anything like it before or since. I know what a deer sounds like and I have heard foxes and badgers. But none of them make a sound like this thing did.

I hadn't been walking along the edge of the field for long before I heard movement in the woods. Then it began to howl. Sort of deep and guttural. Like the deepest bark you will ever hear, followed by what sounded like a Bassett hound. All that sound came from the same animal. It was hair-raising. That's when I decided to let the dog go into the woods. I figured that she would sort it out or scare it off, but I was wrong.

She went charging in there like a maniac, there was a bit of commotion and I heard her yelp a few times. Next thing, she came running out of that wood whimpering like a baby, with her tail tucked between her legs. She proper sh*t herself. I have never seen her behave like that before. And that thing in the woods, whatever it was, kept making those screaming, barking howls. It really was terrifying.

I didn't hang around. We got back to the car as fast as we could and we were out of there. I have never been back and I don't mind telling anyone, who wants to go looking for those coins, where it is. You will never get me to go back there again, not even in daylight. Whatever was in that wood didn't want us there. I bet it is still around. No one ever goes to that area, maybe that's the reason why."

With most of these accounts, we have to rely on the witness being genuine and truthful, because we have nothing for proof except their word that anything actually happened. But the sheer reluctance of some witnesses to talk about their experience must tell us that the vast majority of them are genuine.

More on the Foxholes Werewolf

I am always careful to not over-pressurise witnesses to talk about their experiences; however, I realised after writing up the account of the Foxholes Werewolf that I had a few more questions to ask the witness named Peter. After all, he did have a much closer encounter with the animal than most people have ever had.

In our first communication Peter and I spoke on the phone, and I could tell he was very nervous about relating his story. Even though it *was* his truth, it also went against the grain of everything he believed possible. So instead of phoning him again, I sent him the following short email containing just six questions.

Email to Peter - February 2018:

"Hello Peter,
thank you so much for talking to me on the phone the other day. I do not want to pester you with phone calls, but I do have a few more questions. It would be a big help if you would answer them for me.

1. *Could you guess the animal's weight? And compared to the head of a mastiff or bear, how big would you say was its head?*

2. *Did you notice its ears?*

3. *How large were its eyes (compared to human eyes or the eyes of a cow)?*

4. *Do you think the eyes were self-illuminating?*

5. *Do you think it was actually running? (In TP1 I published an account of a similar creature, from some men at Harwood Dale, but they thought it was moving too smoothly to be running.)*

6. *Have you ever seen another animal with teeth as big as that creature's before? If so, what type of animal was it?*

I really appreciate your help. It really makes a difference to my work.
Regards
Paul"

Within a few days I received a reply from Peter:

"Hi Paul,

1. The head was about size of a grizzly bear.

2. I didn't notice its ears - a lot of hair / mane would have concealed them.

3. Not sure if the eyes were actually illuminating - it was only a foot or so away from me at the side of the car, but I could see them clearly.

4. It was definitely running on all fours - like a dog in full chase.

5. I've travelled a lot and have seen monkeys/apes with big canine teeth, that they show when on the attack. Can't guess the weight very easily because of the hair, but it was very powerful and strong looking.

Hope this helps,
Peter"

Can you imagine something that has a head the size of a grizzly bear pacing your car? It sounds incredible and that is exactly what it is. But Peter is one of many witnesses who have described a similar creature. His encounter may have been during the night, and it may have only lasted thirty seconds, but so far, I have not spoken to anyone who has been closer to this animal than Peter.

For me, the yellow eyes are still the biggest puzzle, and the fact that this monster was able to look into a car window whilst running at 50 mph. Was this an ancient beast with advanced abilities? I'm not sure how that works.

The Flixton Werewolf is something that appears to only exist the moment it is seen, after which, it is gone without trace. I think it is clear that what we think of as real in this world, is only one level of something much deeper. Sometimes monsters and demons don't just live in our minds, sometimes they jump out of our nightmares into what we call reality. Only the people who see them truly know that monsters are real.

WALLABIES AND GIANT LEAPS INTO THE UNBELIEVABLE

When I found an interesting article in the Bridlington library archive from June 2011, I had no idea at the time that it would open up so many doors of investigation. The words 'high strangeness' reached another level while I was investigating these accounts. They were so strange and may even have connections to events on the other side of the world.

I think of all of the sightings and accounts covered in the *Truth Proof* books with an open mind, and at all times I am careful not to influence or steer the reader in any one direction. However, the plain truth is, that some cases are at the *highest point* of high strangeness, and although I may not have answers, the evidence revealed in the following story points in the direction of a true unexplained phenomena.

I love looking through old newspapers for reports of the strange, but one thing I have learned over the years, is to expect the unexpected. In the winter of 2014 I was once again seated in front of the microfilm viewer at Bridlington library archive. Studying the old newspapers can often reveal a bigger picture; over months, years and sometimes decades, and it is possible to learn many things that were impossible to know at the time the events were unfolding. It is a bit like looking at an area you have been familiar with for many years, but from higher ground.

The article that first stirred my interest came from the *Bridlington Free Press* on June 30th 2011. It described how zoo keepers at Sewerby Park Zoo in Bridlington had found four of their Australian wallabies had been decapitated. I thought the account was fascinating and immediately suspected that something highly unusual had happened to these small kangaroos.

If someone had told me that I would be researching the deaths of wallabies, before I had found this story, I would have laughed at them, but my research did eventually reveal links to similar animal decapitations in Australia.

The Coffs Coast Connection - New South Wales

Before covering the wallaby decapitations at Sewerby Zoo, I would first like to share an account from over 10,000 miles away, on Australia's Coffs Coast. In January 2011, Coffs Coast wildlife rangers reported that three wallabies had been found decapitated and their mutilated bodies had been discovered on a golf course at Emerald Heights.

These strange deaths appeared to be nothing more than macabre killings, carried out by a sick individual or individuals. But this was more than one random act of madness. It was the meticulous precision of the killings that stood out and in the absence of any other explanation, the rangers suggested that a fox could be responsible. Whatever *was* responsible for taking the heads off these wallabies, their deaths show remarkable similarities to the Sewerby Zoo killings.

<u>Coffs Coast Advocate: January 14th 2011</u>
Wallaby Beheaded 'With A Sword'

"A samurai sword or machete may have been used to behead a wallaby in another brutal mutilation on the Coffs Coast..." stated the first news report that I came across on the Australian wallaby mutilations from 2011.

The newspaper went on to say that the authorities were continuing to investigate some disturbing wallaby mutilations; the most recent of which was found at Emerald Heights. Wildlife rangers and animal welfare officers thought that a samurai sword or machete had been used to decapitate the small marsupials, in what was alleged to be the third such attack in the area (after some similar killings at Safety Beach in the past). Investigators had no real clue why anyone would want to harm such placid creatures. The regional inspector for the RSPCA, Andrew Kelly, said, *"This is extremely troubling behaviour and not the first attack we've seen on kangaroos or wallabies in the area... What is most concerning is the motivation behind these attacks."*

By publicising these attacks, wildlife rangers were hoping that some information might come in from the public to help the police identify those responsible. The article went on to quote Coffs Harbour wildlife ranger Ann Walton, who said, "'We can't work out why the bodies of the animals are always found, but not the heads... We thought fishermen were responsible, but those we spoke to said anglers would most likely use a whole animal in their crab-pots, so we just don't know why someone would do this."

The report ended by stating that whoever was responsible could face a fine of up to $10,000 and five years imprisonment, for animal cruelty and use of a dangerous weapon, as well as other offences. It was clear to me that no-one mentioned in the article had a clue what *was* responsible for the deaths of these animals. Although it was suggested that a sword-wielding lunatic had chased the wallabies across a golf course, I don't believe for one second that this was the case. I think this was an apex predator of unknown origin.

Wallabies are renowned for being hard to catch and the article suggests that the wallabies had been killed instantly. I have not read of any toxicology reports suggesting that the wallabies were drugged or incapacitated before death, but if they are genuinely difficult to catch, how else could this have been done to the animals?

I have spoken with keepers from different animal parks around the UK who inform me that wallabies are very fast, agile and strong. The general opinion is that if captive wallabies ever manage to escape, they are rarely caught, and they have no problem surviving in most environments. The Coffs Coast wallabies are wild animals so we must assume that they would be even harder to catch. There appeared to be no pattern to the killings and no clues were ever found. Placing the blame on a fox seemed to be the only plausible explanation, even when the apparent method of killing was nothing like fox behaviour.

The Australian authorities were convinced the animals were being killed in one location and their remains left out in the open on the golf course afterwards. I think this has to be the case, since there has never been any reports of sightings of a samurai sword wielding lunatic, chasing wallabies across Emerald Heights golf course.

Let us assume for a moment that someone could get close to a wild wallaby - which in itself would be a near impossible task, since these small kangaroos can reach speeds of up to 30mph - but let's imagine a person could get close enough to cut off a wallabies head with one full swipe of a blade, severing main arteries leaving the heart pumping out blood at an alarming rate. Since no blood was reported at the scene, the animals must have been killed elsewhere. Their heads were never found and no other marks or signs of trauma were present on the bodies. It just does not make sense.

I very much doubt anyone has ever considered there could be a connection between wallaby deaths from opposite sides of the world. But because of the close similarities between the Australian wallaby deaths and those killed at Sewerby in the UK, could it mean the people responsible were globally connected? So far I have found no evidence to suggest that such a group exists, but then I wondered if the Australian wallaby deaths could have been the work of a cult, although I am not so sure this was anything more than a crazy notion.

There is no evidence to connect any cult activities to wallaby deaths either, but the list of animal body-parts known to be used in ritualistic magic is quite extensive. So, since no real suspects stand out, should we throw the net wider and dare to suggest that another phenomenon is responsible?

Around the same time as the Coffs Coast wallabies were being discovered in New South Wales, there were UFOs being reported just fifteen hours away at Bendigo near Melbourne. The Bendigo Advertiser reported that a forty-eight year old man spotted an unidentified aerial object, between midnight and 5am, on Saturday January 8th 2011. The witness, who is a retired camera operator, said he was standing at his back door, facing west, when he noticed something strange in the sky.

"At first, I thought it was a bright star..." he said. *"But I kept watching and once the sun started to come up it remained very bright and I realised I was looking at something very different."* He said there was, *"definitely something unexplainable hovering overhead,"* The witness also commented that he had always been sceptical of UFO sightings, but this extraordinary encounter had turned him into a believer.

I am not suggesting that unidentified aerial objects or their occupants are responsible for killing wallabies, but if we are looking for highly unusual killers, then we have to consider highly unusual suspects. Bendigo is approximately 870 miles away from the Coffs Coast, and although the distance is considerable, if the UK killings are linked to the same phenomena, such a distance is nothing.

This following short report contains the only information I could find on some other wallaby deaths, in Lysterfield. It is worth noting that these killings are also close to water and, although Lysterfield is roughly 870 miles from the Coffs Coast, it is just 120 miles from Bendigo.

Star News for Berwick & Beaconsfield: May 5th 2011
Wildlife Decapitated, Mutilated

"Wildlife in Lysterfield Lake Park were decapitated and mutilated this week. A small kangaroo or wallaby was decapitated near the boat launch area and another was killed by the cutting of its neck and skull. Police are searching for information about the decapitation and mutilation that took place between 6pm on May 2nd and 8am on May 3rd."

This short but interesting report, highlights additional wallaby mutilations along the south and eastern coast of Australia. After talking with wildlife experts I also discovered that other areas along this coastline had reports of decapitated wallabies. Many of those reports failed to reached the media.

The Wallaby Deaths at Sewerby Park Zoo - East Yorkshire

The intriguing news story I found in the Bridlington library archive, on the strange deaths of wallabies at Sewerby Park Zoo, received no more coverage after it was published in the *Bridlington Free Press* on June 30th 2011 - but I knew that it warranted more research.

Bridlington Free Press: June 30th 2011
Wallabies Killed at Sewerby Park

"Four of the five wallabies at Sewerby Hall's zoo have been killed. A fox is thought to be responsible for the killings, which all but wiped out the

zoo's collection of wallabies; according to East Riding of Yorkshire Council. The only surviving wallaby has now been re-homed for its own safety. A concerned visitor to the zoo, who wished to remain anonymous, said she did not believe a fox could have killed the wallabies – and had heard that a severed wallaby heads had been found in the animal's enclosure.

'I think it must have been a person,' she said. 'Wallabies are fairly large animals and I can't see a fox wanting to take them on. I think it's more likely that some cruel person is responsible.'

However, a spokesman for the council said all the evidence pointed towards a fox attack. He said: 'It is with great sadness that Sewerby Hall and Gardens has to confirm that four of its wallabies have died. Evidence suggests that a fox is responsible.... Sewerby Hall and Gardens has had...the perimeter fencing checked and has secured the other animals at the zoo. Despite this tragic incident, Sewerby Hall and Gardens remains open for business...'"

After learning about these animal deaths, my first job was to contact Sewerby Hall. Although the story was six years old and I realised the staff may have changed in that time, I wanted to try and arrange a meeting with the head zoo keeper. On Monday August 4th, I called Sewerby Zoo and explained what I was researching. The staff I spoke with were intrigued by what I told them and were open to discuss the matter. They were kind enough to arrange a meeting for me at 1pm later that day with John Pickering, the head zoo keeper.

I arrived at 1pm on the dot, and was greeted in the front courtyard by John himself. After introducing myself, I followed him inside and was led to an upstairs room overlooking the zoo.

My first impression of this man was that he was a professional who took his job very seriously. John already had an idea about why I wanted to speak with him, so with that in mind, I asked if he could recall anything unusual leading up to the events of June 2011. He said he couldn't recall anything out of the ordinary happening, until the day the wallabies were found. At this point, I did not know if he was aware of the other wallabies that had been found in similar circumstances throughout the year. I suspected that zoos in the UK might be connected by some kind of networking facility, where information was passed between them, but from John's reaction, this was obviously not the case.

John Pickering:
"I remember it well Paul. They were killed over a few nights. It was very odd. We did think a fox had killed them, because CCTV showed a fox in the park. But that's not unusual if I am honest. I think the reason we suspected a fox was because someone had dropped two cockerels over into the llama enclosure a few weeks before. These things happen from time to time, but they seemed happy enough living there with the llamas."

Paul:
"So someone left two live cockerels in the zoo?"

John:
"Yes. Like I said, it happens. Their owners must have been fed up with them and they probably didn't have the heart to kill them, so we ended up with them. They were no bother, so we just left them in with the llamas. Then I remember coming to the enclosure one day, there was snow on the ground, and we saw a few spots of blood on the fresh snow and the cockerels had gone. There was nothing; no feathers or anything to suggest they had ever been there.

I do remember wondering why I could not see any paw-prints around the spots of blood, but I never thought much more about it after that.

I think that was the start of it really. From that point we just thought a fox was responsible. It is strange though, we never had a problem with foxes before. In the past the wallabies were in an open enclosure, with much less protection than they had in 2011. So it does make you think if it really could have been a fox.

The first wallaby killed was a baby and when we looked on the CCTV we did see a fox walking around the zoo. We just assumed it was responsible after the cockerels had vanished. Then we found the first headless adult wallaby. It was shocking, but we thought the fox had got brave and started taking the adults."

Paul:
"So you never saw the fox take anything from the zoo or attack any animals."

John:
"No. We saw nothing in the wallaby enclosure, we just assumed the fox had got brave and took the adults."

Paul:
"I know wallabies are smaller than kangaroos, but I didn't think they were so small that a fox would take them on. Do you think a fox would tackle a fully grown wallaby?"

John:
"It was the only thing we could think of Paul and now you say that, it does make you wonder. I agree, they are smaller than normal kangaroos, but not that small, not the ones we had. They were Bennett's wallabies and they are about 24kg. I remember that I once had to catch one of them and I had hold of it by the tail. It lashed out with its feet and tore right through my uniform. They are very powerful for their size and not easy to catch."

Paul:
"I was told by someone that no meat was taken from the wallaby bodies. I find it strange that a fox would not eat their kill. Like you say, they would not have been easy to catch, yet all they did was decapitate them?"

John:
"Yes I agree, it was strange behaviour. The local pub, The Ship, kept a few animals as well and I seem to recall that they had some decapitations around the same time."

I did contact The Ship Inn to ask about these animal deaths, but they did not want to comment.
I took the opportunity to ask John if he was aware that a large black cat, similar to a panther, had been seen by numerous people around the area at the time of the wallaby killings. To my surprise, he had heard about the panther and told me that one of the girls who worked at the zoo

claimed to have seen something similar around Bempton Cliffs. What he said next surprised me a little; he told me that the girl described it as looking like a black lion. The number of people who claim to have seen such an animal, with fur that resembles a lion's mane is quite high, so I do believe such a creature exists or *manifests* in the area. When so many witnesses come forward, who are independent of one another, and they all describe the same thing, it has to be taken seriously.

I asked the John if he knew about the vagrant who lived in the woods at Danes Dyke. I told him that he had also seen something like a black panther on two occasions, both times in the early morning. John said he knew nothing about this. He wasn't even aware that anyone was living in the woods, so he was surprised when I told him the man had lived there for over nine years.

Danes Dyke is only about two miles from Sewerby and if this big cat was real, the zoo would easily be within its hunting range. This does not mean that the cat was responsible for the wallaby deaths, because there is no evidence to suggest that a big cat had killed them. Whatever *had* killed these animals did so for reasons we have yet to discover. It is, however, another interesting and unexplainable element, when added to the strange mix of events in this area that I call 'exotic nature'.

John:
"Once the six wallabies had been killed Paul, it all stopped. You would have expected the killing to continue, but it just stopped."

Paul:
"Six?"

I never realised that this cloaked killer had removed the heads from *six* wallabies at Sewerby Zoo. It certainly was not the behaviour of a normal predator, but the article from the *Bridlington Free Press* had been vague. It stated that four or five wallabies had been killed, but after speaking to John Pickering, it was clear that over a number of days six wallabies had been decapitated.

Whatever was responsible had cut the heads clean off these poor animals, but had done nothing else. The wounds were clean and precise, which I think rules out a fox - unless they now go around carrying sharp blades?

I told John about some other strange cases I had discovered in the *Free Press* from 2006; articles about mutilated roe deer found on Bempton Lane, Short Lane and Wold Gate. These killings were very strange in that, it was reported, the deer meat had been pared from the bone in an unusual way, but no meat had been removed from the scene. I also told him that deer carcasses had been found in Danes Dyke with meat removed clean off the bone in a similar way.

These reports went back to 2006, so where had the killer been from 2006 to 2011? Moreover, where would it have gone after the wallaby killings stopped? The condition of each deer was same with each one that was found, so what kind of predator could mutilate another animal in such a way and why? To my mind no known animal acts this way, these killings are on another level. John said he knew nothing about the deer killings from 2006 and I still had not told him anything about the coincidental wallaby deaths in Australia.

I don't think my job is to try and convince other people. If the research reveals an undeniable truth then it has to be considered, even if it cannot be understood. The proof that these killings were affecting one species in different parts of the world has been established. How and why it happened has yet to be understood.

The similarities in these killings are striking, but the distance aspect is the real mystery for me. If we believe in coincidence then there is nothing unusual in any of this. I don't have the answers, but I can say right now that I do not believe in coincidences of this magnitude.

We should consider that distance does not deter the phenomena. But are we really so closed-minded to believe that one species, from different parts of the world, just happened to die in the same way in 2011. Just because we do not understand how it happened does not make it any less real.

More Australian Animal Deaths

Further research revealed that more wallabies had been decapitated in New South Wales during 2011. Even though Australia is 10,000 miles distant from the UK, I believe there could be a connection between these deaths. The phenomenon appeared to be jumping from one part of the world to another and every time, the victims were kangaroos.

Canberra Times: October 7th 2011
Just 70 Miles From The Coast

"Several decapitated animals have been found in bunkers at the Queanbeyan Golf Club, after a deer head was located in toilets at Riverside Plaza last month."

This was the opening paragraph in a long report in *The Queanbeyan Age* newspaper - which went on to say that two dead rabbits, a headless kangaroo and another kangaroo's leg, had all been found at the club recently. The finds began after security guards found, what they thought, was the head of a deer in Queanbeyan shopping centre. Then a few days later, the remains of a decapitated kangaroo was found in one of the bunkers at the nearby golf club.

The superintendent of the golf course, Jason Ferry, said, *"We're finding the bodies, but the heads are nowhere to be found... We kept the body of the kangaroo for the forensic guys, but they didn't come down."*

The article also stated that staff at the golf club were amazed at the precision of the killings - and this intrigued me the most, because they thought this was the strangest aspect of the animal deaths. They assumed the dead rabbits had probably been trapped, but the lack of marks on the dead kangaroo was a mystery. It was *"spotless,"* said Mr Ferry, *"It didn't have a mark on it... and its head had been removed cleanly."*

Does all this reveal a pattern to the Australian and UK animal killings? The bigger picture seems to indicate a common thread running through them all, which is the way the animals heads are removed with such precision. Again, wildlife experts continually blame foxes for the deaths, but no one seems to challenge the fact that the animal's heads were 'removed with surgical precision' - which rule out foxes altogether.

The London Wallabies

Ealing Times: October 29th 2011

"Police are still on the hunt for the thug who decapitated a wallaby in Brent Lodge Park, Hanwell. Park keepers were appalled to find the beheaded animal in its enclosure last Thursday morning, October 20th."

This report, from the London newspaper *The Ealing Times*, speculated that someone broke into the wallaby enclosure at Brent Lodge Park, by cutting through a perimeter fence. According to a vet report, the culprit is accused of attacking the park's Parma wallaby with a knife and removing the animal's head.

Brent Lodge Park had become home to the wallaby, named Bruce, just six months earlier, after the animal had been relocated from another zoo in Norfolk. But unfortunately the Brent Lodge did not have CCTV, so no film of the attack exists. Local councillor Bassam Mahfouz was quoted in the news report as saying that he was, *"completely sickened by this attack on a defenceless animal... the whole community will be equally shocked."*

Thankfully, although the park's other wallaby was left in a distressed condition, no other animals were hurt during the incident. Police described the attack as unusual and said they were determined to find out who was responsible, but it was later suggested that a fox could be blamed for the attack.

The Mail Online: November 24th 2011

Four weeks later *The Mail Online* carried a report of more animal deaths at Brent Lodge Park. The park had brought in three more wallabies to provide company for Rolph, the wallaby left traumatised after his companion Bruce was killed. But in a matter of days, two of them were dead. The report stated, *"One animal was found with its throat cut, while all that remained of the other were limbs scattered across the park..."*

According to Scotland Yard, investigators were keeping an open mind, but they were considering whether foxes were responsible for the attack. The report quoted Acting Detective Inspector Steve Mayes, who said; "We are increasingly concerned regarding the incidents in the park... These sorts of incidents are very unusual and we are determined to find the person or people responsible. Our wildlife team is investigating."

Council member for the environment, Bassam Mahfouz, confirmed that the wallabies were now being locked up overnight and a new CCTC system was being installed, with a security detail patrolling all night. He suggested that, "if a person was responsible for the attacks, they may have been keeping an eye on the news and learned that more wallabies had been brought to the park."

Once again the investigators believed a knife or blade was used to kill the wallabies, but they also suggested that a fox could be responsible. This only suggests to me that they had no real idea who or what was responsible.

London Evening Standard: November 24th 2011

News of these wallaby deaths was also reported in *The London Evening Standard*, with the headline, "A children's petting zoo has called in private security guards after the slaughter of three wallabies."

The full report carried virtually the same details as the other newspapers, but this one included the lines, "the perimeter fence had apparently been cut" and "police strongly believe foxes are to blame..."

The newspaper stated that that wallabies and other park animals were now being kept in brick-built sheds overnight and park manager, Jim Gregory, explained that when he first came to work at the park two years earlier, the animals were spending sixteen hours a day locked in the sheds. He said, "We worked so hard to change that, but now we're back to square one."

Counsellor Mahfouz, was quoted as saying, "...we brought in vets to check if it was an animal attack and they said it was more likely to be a human attack. It's absolutely sickening. The park is a real jewel and we want to keep it that way."

The newspaper made a point of stating that the park's perimeter fence had been cut, but that still does not explain how the perpetrator entered the wallaby enclosure, which would have had its own boundary fence.

These mutilation incidents bear remarkable similarities to those that were happening 10,000 miles away in Australia, and it would appear that no has even dared to consider there could be a possible link.

The Shell Cove Swamp Wallaby

On December 19th 2011 the Australian newspaper *The Illawarra Mercury* reported that, "*A dead female swamp wallaby has been found in a roadside reserve in a bizarre case of mutilation at Shell Cove.*"

The animal was first discovered by a member of the public who contacted local wildlife services. The wallaby was found to have had its ears cut off. A volunteer on the scene also found a badly injured young wallaby by the roadside. Illawarra wildlife rescuer Cathy Joukador speculated, "*...the mother may have been hit by a car and thrown the joey, but then someone came back later and moved the [adult's] body and cut the ears off, which is bizarre.*" Miss Joukador described the wounds as "*totally clean cuts*" with no evidence of bite marks. She also stated that if a fox had been responsible it would have gone for the belly and not touched the ears.

The following day, before the animal was removed, the Illawarra wildlife rescue were called about a decapitated wallaby found at the same location, but this was the *same* animal which was now found with its head removed. Then, after returning to the site the carcass was gone. Miss Joukador said, "*I don't know whether someone found it and disposed of it or whether something else awful* [occurred]. *It's bizarre, it's absolutely bizarre...*" Apparently the female's young joey did not survive.

I wish the researchers luck in their search for the killers of these animals and in their investigations of any similar deaths in the future. I don't have any answers, but I do hope I have opened a few eyes and minds to the possibility that an unknown predator could be at work. I have also considered that a combination of more than one predator could be responsible. Or could the practise of dark magic have connected with something unnatural? The animal deaths show traits of ritualistic occult-type killings, but I still have to question how identical incidents were taking place on opposite sides of the world. And why would small kangaroos be the animals of choice? It all seems so unlikely.

I have highlighted that a fox has been the standard explanation used throughout the media in the UK, but who could be feeding them this line? Or is it simply that a fox is the biggest predator we have and they could not think of anything else?

During September 2017 I phoned most of the major zoos and animal parks in the UK to inquire if any of their wallaby population had been harmed during 2011. After I had explained what had been happening, some of the zoos were quite open and happy to talk with me. Others refused to comment, even when I pointed out the similarities in the killings, they did not want to know. I think this was because of a combination of reasons. Foxes or people using sharp blades were always the prime candidates for the killings. It is clear that no one could think of a better explanation. If I had suggested the crazy notion that I believed the killer could be something unrecognisable to science, I am sure people would have laughed. Yet no one seemed to question how ridiculous the theory was that the killings were done with sharp implements, and at the same time suggesting that a fox could be responsible.

The fact that similar acts were being carried out 10,000 miles away in Australia went unnoticed in the UK. And even if someone *had* made a connection, I'm sure it would have been a scenario that seemed impossible to the media, and therefore not worth considering. The bigger picture shows that these things *did* happen throughout 2011, although I don't think they will ever be believed. This is over-science.

More Thoughts

On September 13th 2017 I had an interesting conversation with a zoo keeper from the New Forest Wildlife Park in Southampton. I told him that the animals killed at Sewerby Park Zoo were Bennett's wallabies and that a fox had been named as the suspected killer. The keeper told me that he did not believe a fox could or would attempt to kill a Bennett's wallaby. He explained that they have had Bennett's wallabies in their wildlife park for many years and foxes live around the enclosures. He said that in all the years they had been at the wildlife park, none of them had ever been attacked, not even the young ones.

I don't think foxes cannot be 100% ruled out, but it is an interesting observation when added to the evidence that suggests the animals had their heads removed with a sharp implement. The wildlife experts I contacted in Australia were also of the opinion that a fox would not attack a wallaby. Other evidence that points away from a fox being responsible is the condition of the carcasses. Whilst it is true that foxes can remove the heads from some of their kills, they do it with their teeth - not a samurai blade.

In December 2011 the volunteer at the scene of the Shell Cove killings described how the swamp wallabies had been found. The report says the female wallaby's ears had been cut off, then a day later a second animal was found with its head cut clean off. This was clearly not the work of an ordinary predatory animal; not one that thinks and acts in the way we expect.

It was thought that the first wallaby had been hit by a car, but the report went on to say that the animal's severed head was removed with a clean cut, using something like a samurai sword. So many of these cases appear to involve blunt force trauma, such as collisions with motor vehicles. But for me that assumption fell flat as soon as I read about the wallabies ears being cut clean off. Is it also possible the carcasses are being dropped from the air after death? It would explain the blunt force trauma and the lack of blood at the scene.

Human Understanding

An explanation that best fits into human understanding always has to found. But what we see when the evidence is laid bare, rarely fits the explanations put forward. I'm sure the experts who have studied the evidence must realise this, but I wonder how many of them realise something else is responsible.

The biggest problem we face when researching and writing about the unexplained is a lack of knowledge. We simply do not have the capacity to describe and educate, when we cannot see beyond the horizon. This applies to just about everything I have ever researched, including my own experiences. Our understanding simply hits a dead end after the experience ends. The wallaby mutilations are no different. The killer or killers were never seen, so we try to interpret what could have killed them, based on the evidence left behind. No one dares to suggest the answer might be beyond the horizon.

The Shell Cove witness said they thought the first wallaby had been hit by a car which threw the joey away from its mother - but they don't *know* if that was the case. This explanation fits into a framework we can understand, and if the rest of the account does not make sense, we forget about those bits. Such an impact would surely have caused extensive injuries to the adult, yet the report only mentions the young having severe injuries.

If a fox was responsible for the killings, surely it would it have gone for the wallaby's softer belly area. Why a fox is mentioned is beyond me, but there is nothing normal about these killings. What predator kills for nothing? And if humans were responsible why was it only in 2011. Why stop early into 2012?

Elermore Vale, NSW, Australia: January 7th 2012
Mutilated Wallaby Found in Elermore Vale

"On Saturday 7th January, in the early hours, fire fighters rushed to Elermore Vale Shopping car park to extinguish a car fire. The fire brigade stumbled across a mutilated brush-tailed rock-wallaby. The disfigured wallaby had its throat cut and also had its tongue cut off."

This was the opening paragraph of a disturbing report of an incident outside an Australian shopping centre in January 2012. It was believed the mutilated wallaby was part of a possible revenge attack after some drunken teenagers had allegedly attacked a nearby mosque.

On its own, this strange killing does not appear to be anything more than a macabre death carried out by a sick individual or individuals. But less than seven days later, 230 miles north on the same stretch of coast, a second wallaby was reported killed at Emerald Heights on the Coffs Coast. The accompanying news article tells us that three wallabies had been killed and that the killer had removed the heads of its victims with such precision, that they believed a samurai sword was being used.

Ealingtoday.co.uk: January 11th 2012
Finger of Suspicion Points to Ealing's Nocturnal Predators

In the UK, in the same week, came a report from the *Ealing Today* news website, which stated, "*Police have closed their investigation into the deaths of three wallabies... they now believe foxes were most likely to blame.*" Police were quoted as saying; "*Our enquires have concluded that the deaths were most likely to have been caused by animal behaviour, for example attacks by foxes.*"

A member of the local council said; "*We will continue to ensure that the enclosures are secure to prevent any access to the animals, by either people or foxes. We have also installed CCTV cameras around the animal centre which are monitored 24-hours a day.'*"

The report says that a knife was used in the attack yet I have been told there was little or no blood at the scene. Other reports blame a fox, but regardless of who or what was responsible, I cannot imagine how there could be little or no blood after cutting through an animal's main artery. This attack is a little different to the others, in that the park's perimeter fencing was cut to gain entry into the enclosure. The report goes on to say that the surviving wallaby, Rolph, wasn't hurt in the attack, but had been visibly distressed by what happened. I could accept all this, but the opinions constantly change with the reports.

Did the Suspect Change in 2012?

Early into my investigation I wondered if a big cat could have been responsible for the Sewerby killings, but after speaking with staff at the zoo I soon realised that it could not have been a cat.

However, in other parts of the UK, mutilated wallabies were still being found, along with other animals, such as roe deer. A big cat was considered to be the main suspect in these reports. Reading the news reports, with more than just mild interest, it became easy to realise that a cat was not the killer.

MailOnline: January 25th 2012
Three Wallabies Found Savaged to Death by Big Cat

"A mysterious blood-thirsty wild cat is feared to have struck again after three wallabies were found devoured on farmland..." This report from the *Mail Online* website described wallabies that had been found *"stripped to the bone"* with their internal organs placed neatly *"beside their bodies"*. The mysterious 'Wildcat of Woodchester' was blamed for the deaths after the three wallabies were found to have suffered puncture wounds to the neck. The Mail Online compared this to an attack by *"a panther-like creature"*.

The report went on to say that three mutilated deer carcasses had also been found in previous weeks, near Stroud in Gloucestershire, just twelve miles from the site of the wallaby deaths. DNA samples were said to have been taken and test results were *"expected to be revealed over the next few days"*.

The news site consulted an expert, sixty-five year old Frank Tunbridge, who said he was convinced that a large feline predator was responsible. *"There could be no creature other than a big cat that could bring down and kill these wallabies..."* said Mr Tunbridge, who said that the killer must have leapt over the seven foot fence that surrounded the wallaby enclosure. The first wallaby was found stripped of its skin, the body of the second was discovered hidden under a pile of leaves and straw. Both showed signs of being eaten. The third animal was killed the next night and a fourth wallaby, found uninjured, was thought to have died of shock. Mr Tunbridge said the wallaby carcasses *"have all the hallmarks of a panther or puma kill."*

Photographs of the wallabies, who were found by their owner on January 6th 2012, revealed similar wounds to the three roe deer. The first deer had been torn open and major organs were missing, the animal's fur was found beside the body and the snout was also missing. This particular clue might indicate the natural behaviour of a big cat, which can often hold onto it's kill in this way to suffocate it.
A second deer carcass was found ten miles away near Cirencester by a dog walker and a third was discovered fifteen miles north west, a few days later.

Professor Allaby of Warwick University said he was, *"prepared to believe in the existence of big cats in the UK"* and was in possession of the DNA samples which he hoped would contain cellular evidence to prove the killer was a big cat. Could the killer really have been a big cat? Professor Allaby told me himself by email that cat DNA was not found in any of the samples that were tested. So in my opinion, the killer was not a cat.

I think it is highly likely that the same kind of predator was responsible for all the wallaby mutilations worldwide in 2011. I have since learned that mutilated carcasses of roe deer were also found around the same time the Sewerby wallabies were decapitated. If I am right, this places the suspect into a category of over-science that few will accept and no one understands.

An Unknown Something

Without doubt people are seeing big cats roaming in the UK countryside. However, many things about the various mutilations point to the killer not being a cat.

Besides the lack of DNA evidence, big cats usually suffocate their victims by clamping their jaws over the muzzle - especially if the neck is too thick; such as a cow or large antelope. This would not have been the case with a wallaby. The article also states that some of the animals had puncture wounds to the neck - but would a cat puncture the neck of its victim, then suffocate it via the muzzle, only to eat the muzzle. The lack of blood is also an unusual aspect, in view of the massive trauma inflicted on the victims.

I would also have expected to read about claw marks, scratches or other signs of trauma; because no animal in the throes of death would give up without a struggle, yet there was no mention of any kind of resistance.

People have always been desperate to give the killer a label. In the past, if someone had even mentioned seeing a big cat roaming through the British countryside, they would have been laughed at. Suddenly, people seem quite happy to blame the mutilations on a panther or puma-type cat - except there are other points that rule out a big cat being responsible for these attacks.

Leopards, jaguars and pumas don't usually leave their food source in the place that they killed it; they prefer to store food off the ground and out of reach of other carnivores – and most big cats usually start eating their kill from rear, not the stomach. The skin is much easier to open from there and the point of least resistance is always their best option. And I know for a fact, that gamekeepers in the Malton area of the UK have photographic evidence of deer carcasses found in trees. But this was not the case with these kills. I also think that if a big cat were present in the area for any length of time, we would find other evidence; such as claw marks, paw prints and scent marking. I have not heard of anyone taking about finding any such evidence.

If none of the above information seems convincing, we have to ask what hungry animal leaves its victim's internal organs, placed neatly beside the carcass? These unexplained cases are examples of an exotic science that cannot be touched or understood. I think we are looking at an intelligence that does not even consider us in its modus operandi.

Perhaps the best indication that no normal predator is responsible, is the fact that the internal organs of the some of these animals were placed neatly beside the carcasses. One of the wallabies was even reported to have died of a heart attack. The victim's heads were removed with surgical precision, which is very unlike the behaviour of a predator. The fact that the attacks appeared to have occurred under the cover of darkness also makes the results even harder to comprehend.

For now, all I can do is highlight the high strangeness I find, in the hope that one day more fragments of truth come to the surface and begin to make sense. Bizarre cases such as these and others I write about in the *Truth Proof* books, rarely give the definitive proof that the general public would find easy to accept. Unanswered questions and soul searching are often all that anyone is ever left with.

I suppose I could provide elaborate theories that suggest many different types of aliens are visiting us, or that through some weird kind of mental channelling I have been given the answers to all of this. But I would rather tell the truth and simply present the facts of what I see happening - even if the source of these things is beyond my grasp.

THE MONSTERS OF WHARNCLIFFE WOODS

The frightening account you are about to read came my way on Sunday June 24th 2017. The story conjures up images that could come from the most terrifying movie, and proves to me that monsters are real.

I had not been on my computer for over 24 hours that day; which is rare in this world of social media and the interconnecting lives we lead. It was the morning after I had attended the *Awakening* UFO Conference in Manchester, and I planned on having a lazy day because I did not get home until the early hours the night before. However, some things never change and, as usual, I was up early and sitting at my laptop, writing. The conference was a disappointment and fell short of my expectations for the £50 I paid for the ticket - but that, as they say, is another story.

I was looking at a long list of messages and comments that had arrived via email and social media. There were also a few new friend requests, including one from a man called Jason Jones. I usually look at a person's profile page to check if they seem legitimate before adding them as an online friend. But I could see right away that this new contact was genuine. Jason had sent a short message with his request, and as soon as I read it I knew that he was on the level and that we had to talk.

I replied immediately and a short time later, he sent me another message asking if he could speak with me, if I had the time. I messaged him back to ask if he wanted my number so we could speak on the phone, but he suggested it was probably better to talk via *Skype*, because he would be calling from Australia. I agreed and within five minutes we were talking as though we had known each other years. It turned out that Jason came from Sheffield in the UK, but had emigrated to Australia in 2002. He told me that he had just been listening to my voice in a recorded interview from Vic Cundiff's *Dogman Radio*, in an episode where I was talking about the Flixton Werewolf.

Jason said he wanted to tell me about something terrifying that happened to him and two of his friends, in Wharncliffe Woods on the outskirts of Sheffield, when he was a young man. The encounter happened in September 1987 and Jason was now forty-nine, but in the thirty-one years that had passed he had never spoken to anyone about what happened. This is Jason's account in his own words:

Jason:
"Hi Paul and thanks for taking the time to talk to me. After I heard you talking about the Flixton Werewolf on the Dogman Radio show, I wanted to tell you my own story. I'm not sure it's a Dogman account, but whatever it was I never want to see anything like it again.

After hearing you telling other people's stories I decided it was time to tell mine. I've said nothing about it all these years, but I know it was real. I can remember what happened as if it was yesterday and it still scares me to think about it. You will be only the second person I have ever told. I have only just told my wife.

I was eighteen at the time. There were three of us and I was the youngest. Scott was the oldest, he was twenty-four I think and Mark was twenty-two. Mark and Scott used to love exploring and they spent lots of time camping and foraging in the woods and fields round Sheffield. It was the first time I had ever gone with them and I was excited at the thought of spending a few nights out in the wilds. I suppose I looked up to them a little bit, with them being older than me.

I remember it was just starting to get dark when we arrived at Wharncliffe Woods. We had planned to get there in daylight, but that didn't work out. We followed one of the trails through the woods for about a mile until we found what we thought was a suitable place to set up camp. By this time it was very dark and we could not see anything between the trees and the thick vegetation. I began collecting dry wood with Mark, and Scott was busy scooping out a patch of earth so we could build a fire. We were ill-equipped and only had one torch between the three of us. Battery torches were nowhere near as good in 1987 as they are today.

I think it was September. I do remember it was still quite warm. We were all in high spirits so nothing really bothered us. After lighting the fire, we settled around it laughing and joking. The darkness added to the excitement of spending a few nights in the woods.

I remember I was sitting with my back against a large tree. Mark was on my left, at my 9 o'clock, and he was laying on some bracken, and Scott was in front of me at my 12 o'clock. He had brought a plastic groundsheet and fixed half of it up to some trees behind him to create a windbreak of sorts, although we didn't really need it.

We were just sitting around talking and having a laugh. As far as I was concerned this was a great adventure. We didn't feel frightened or sense anything untoward. I suppose at that age I must have felt invincible.

At some point after midnight we must have all drifted off to sleep. I'm a very light sleeper and remember waking up with my back to the tree and looking at my watch. It was about 2am. Something must have woke me, so I just sat there listening to the silence. You know that feeling you get when something is not quite right? Well that was the feeling I was getting. Then I had an overwhelming sense of fear come over me, even though everything seemed so still and silent. I glanced over and in the firelight I could see Scott was still sleeping. That's when I heard the sound of a small twig snapping behind me. I sat there for a moment listening, it was really weird.

Suddenly all hell broke loose. There were branches and trees cracking and breaking everywhere, and the next thing I heard was Scott screaming and shouting in the dark. It was terrifying. I looked over to where he had been laying and I saw him suspended in the air.

I could not work it out at first. He was upside-down and two or three feet off the ground. It was terrifying. By this time we were all screaming, but I could not take my eyes off Scott. I could just see his arms and legs violently thrashing about in the glow of the fire. I had never been so scared in all of my life. To be honest, I've never felt so scared since. I honestly thought we were all going to die.

But that was only part of it. I could see this big black fur-covered arm reaching down and it was holding onto Scott by the ankle, at least I thought it was his ankle. It actually had hold of him by his calf. Something was holding him up in the air with one arm, but I only saw its arm. Scott was hanging upside down screaming and crying and all I could see was a huge dark arm in the darkness. I have never seen anything like it before in my life. It was massive. Its hand was wrapped round Scott's lower leg like it was holding up a baby.

Scott used to train on the weights and did body-building. At that time he was about fifteen or sixteen stone, but this thing, whatever it was, just held him up in its outstretched arm as though he weighed nothing. It's impossible to say how long this whole thing lasted - maybe not even a minute - from when I heard the twig snap to seeing Scott suspended in the air. But in that time we all thought we were going to die.

Suddenly it just dropped him and we heard it running off. We heard trees and plants smashing and breaking as it crashed through the woods like a tank. Then, as it got further away, we heard a sound like a gunshot or like we could hear a tree exploding. Then just complete silence.

Scott was scared out of his mind. He wanted to run - run anywhere he could. He wasn't thinking straight. Me and Mark had to jump on top of him and hold him down, he was hysterical. It was hard to make sense of what had happened. That thing that got hold of Scott was a monster and it freaked us all out. But if we had tried to get out of the woods, I think we would have got lost. There was nowhere to go and nothing we could do, so we had to try and stay calm. We couldn't risk going anywhere until it started to get light. And that thing, whatever it was, was still out there.

We built up the fire with anything we could get hold of, keeping it going all night. We even burnt the plastic groundsheet. That's how desperate we were to keep that fire going. Everything went quiet for a while and although we were still very scared, we began to relax a little because the thing had gone.

About half an hour later we heard a noise that came from deep in the woods. It was another loud bang, like a tree exploding or a gun shot. It's really hard to explain that sound. Seconds later there were trees and branches breaking and smashing all around us. It was terrifying. I was still sitting in the same place, with my back against the tree, trying to understand what was happening. Then I heard branches breaking behind me.

That's when I realised there must have been another one, because I heard movement coming from more than one direction. We couldn't see them - they stayed just out of sight, right on the edge of the darkness. It was as if they were enjoying scaring us. I really thought we were going to die that night.

These terrifying attacks continued throughout the night. Everything would be quiet for about half an hour then it would start again - crashing and thrashing about in the darkness, with branches snapping and trees breaking. Then there was silence, until it started again. It only stopped just before daylight entered the woods. I think they could have killed us at any time, but for some reason they chose not to. I now think all they wanted to do was scare us to death. The one that held Scott could have easily ran off with him. As soon as it was light enough to move, we were out of there. I never went back to Wharncliffe Woods after that.

The sight of Scott dangling from that huge fur-covered arm has haunted me all of my life. I was the only one who saw it, but I know what I saw Paul. Until I heard you talk about people who have seen the Flixton Werewolf, I never wanted to speak about this to anyone."

I could sense the fear and emotion in Jason's voice as he retold his story of the monsters of Wharncliffe Woods. And it was obvious to me that this incredible experience left an impression which still scares him.

I suppose an encounter with a large bear or primate would be terrifying enough, but Jason had witnessed an assault by a creature far more frightening than something known to be living on earth. His description of the creature's behaviour is different to that of any known predator. Its actions show an intelligence that is outside of expected and accepted animal behaviour.

Following page: an impression of Jason, Scott & Mark's experience, drawn by my daughter Gemma

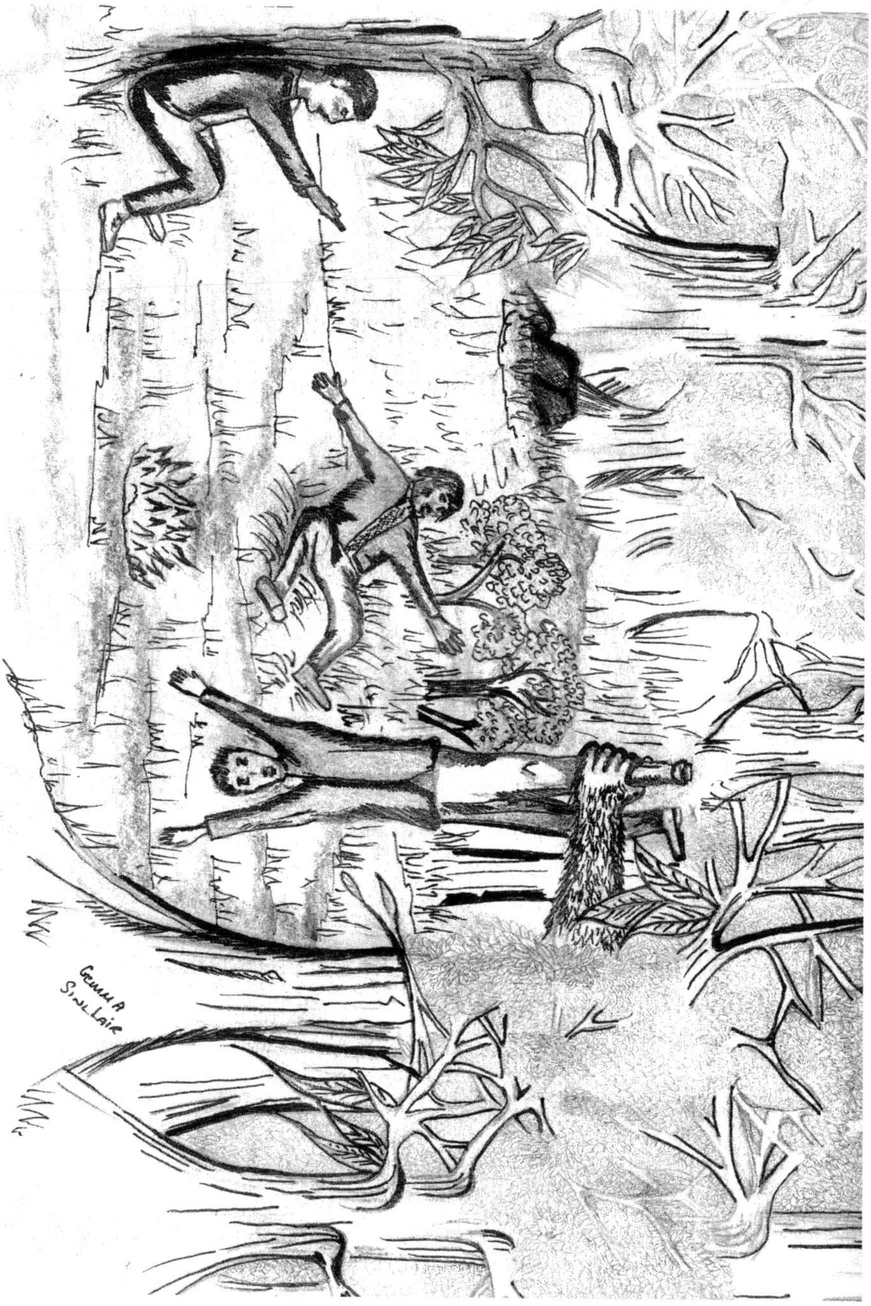
GEMMA
SINCLAIR

Although we may never know what these things were, Jason's recollection of hearing what sounded like a gunshot or an exploding tree, intrigues me. It conjures up visions of a monster that was entering and re-entering our world from some altered reality. I cannot explain what happened, but for me, the sound he described is a most interesting point. I'm not sure why, but I think something was 'displaced' in some way, which made that sound. A bit like when we reach altitude in a plane and our ears pop or when a jet breaks the sound barrier.

His friend Scott was six feet tall and weighed sixteen stone and although Jason may only have seen part of the creature, it was strong enough to hold Scott at least three feet off the ground, with one hand. We have to assume that the creature's huge arm was attached by a shoulder to a fully formed body; which must mean that whatever was holding onto Scott, was over ten feet tall.

North American grizzly bears can stand up to ten feet tall and weigh over a thousand pounds. The largest primate on Earth is the eastern lowland gorilla from central Africa, which stands up to six feet tall and weighs over five hundred pounds. The bear is the only one of these two huge mammals close enough in size to fit Jason's description, but there are no wild bears or gorillas in the UK. To suggest such a thing would be ridiculous, but people *are* seeing and experiencing something, and that something is very real.

The way Jason described the animal's movements also meant it had explosive power, and was very fast. The amount calories needed to sustain such an animal would be vast. So what would it have needed to consume to maintain itself? We may never know, but this massive presence in Wharncliffe Woods was definitely something physical and powerful - breaking trees and taking hold of a fully grown man tells us this.

Jason's account is full of interesting details - enough to keep any researcher busy for years. Clues about this encounter lead us in strange directions, but then, like a steel trap, the trail snaps shut. It is here one moment and gone the next, almost as though it drags any trace of its existence back to where it came from. And as much as I try, I cannot bridge the gap in my understanding and figure out how these phenomena appear and disappear. This is why I have said so many times, that our acceptance of these unknown 'somethings' has to come first.

There has to be something about the locations that are unique, because there are no large predatory animals living and breeding in Wharncliffe Woods - or the Flixton Wolds for that matter - but people *are* seeing them.

Proving any of this is impossible; because science will not normally accept theories without proof, and the only traces of proof are trapped inside the heads of those who witness these things. But Jason did describe hearing trees breaking and crashing, and he told me that the next day, Scott's calf was swollen and blue from where he had been grabbed and held up in the air by the creature. He said the bruising went all around the upper part of Scott's calf. So is this the kind of evidence that could back up his story?

The bruising Jason described must mean that these creatures have hands very much like our own. Most other animals have paws and claws, but only something with hands similar to our own could take hold of a sixteen stone man by the leg and dangle him up in the air. For me, this throws even more confusion into the mix, because the only creatures with grasping hands are primates, and besides zoo animals, we are the only primates inhabiting the UK. None of this adds up, so therefore it cannot be true. But Jason's account tells us that it must be.

In TP1 I shared stories about the Flixton Werewolf. One account told the story of two young boys who encountered a large creature, covered in fur, with a head not unlike a dogs. They saw it around the burial mounds found at Sharp Howe at Staxton Wold, and said it was looking at something in its hands. But dogs don't have hands.

The creature Jason saw holding his friend up in the air must have had hands similar to our own; the only difference being that the hand must have been enormous. When he first told me about seeing Scott hanging upside-down I thought he meant something had taken a hold of him by the ankle. I later discovered that was not the case; this thing had grabbed him around the upper calf. Due to Scott's size it would be no exaggeration to suggest that his upper calf must have measured at least sixteen inches all the way around. So the creature that took hold of him must have had hands so big that they easily wrapped around his calf.

What the three young men experienced was powerful enough to kill them all, so why didn't it? Did the creature have more than basic animal instincts? Was it just playing? Could there even be a universal law that stops them from taking a life?

I cannot begin to imagine the place they come from or what it is like - or how they arrive and depart, unseen. They are a complete unknown and do not naturally exist in our world. For now, it is pointless speculating how they come to be here, we just have to accept that they *are* seen from time to time; as transient unknown somethings, that enter our sphere of existence, to terrify anyone who is unfortunate enough to see them, until they slip back into non-existence.

BRITISH BIGFOOT

The following accounts were kindly shared with me by researcher Deborah Hatswell, who manages the *British Bigfoot Sighting Reports* website, which has a network of research team members across the UK.

The first account comes from an area north of Sheffield, ten miles north east of Wharncliffe Woods. The witness is named Liam and he contacted Deborah Hatswell in April 2018

Growls and Howls in the Night
Strange Experiences at Bolton-upon-Dearne

Liam:
"I have been experiencing some strange howls and noises close to home....the first time I would have been about 10-11 yrs old. It was just after I'd gone to bed, at around 9pm. I remember it being around summertime as it was still pretty light outside. There were dogs barking everywhere along the streets and I was at my window listening to all the noise and commotion. After around half an hour, all the barking stopped suddenly and I could hear a faint howl that sounded as if it was kind of distorted - not a howl you would expect to hear like foxes or dogs, this howl was really strange.

So I went and got my Mum so she could listen too. She was at the window with me, to humour me as I was young, but then she heard it herself and her face immediately dropped and she quickly said 'Oh it's nothing'. I almost believed her, but as soon as she said it, she went all around the house checking the doors were locked and closing all the curtains... but that was back then and we still live in the same house.

The second time was quite a while after, as I'm 21 now. I started to notice things again late last year, around September time. It started with minor things, such as, what sounded like a dustbin being dragged down the street at a ridiculous speed. Then later in the night there were obvious sounds of things being thrown and hitting the wire fence across the road. I think the strangest was hearing the horses in the [nearby] field sounding like they were petrified and stampeding around.

There were two nights when I heard long drawn out groaning sounds that would get closer to the house and then fade away, and this would repeat and get closer again. Both times they'd persist for around about an hour, maybe slightly longer - but during that time every animal, including the usually very loud dogs in the street, were completely silent. When the noise stopped, it seemed like every animal was in panic mode, or shaken up somehow.

One thing I will mention, but I'm not entirely sure if it has a reasonable explanation or not, was on a night in August last year...I could hear a toddler murmuring outside on the street as if it was upset. I shrugged it off because the folk across the road often have their grandkids round and they usually play in the garden till late. After I had tried to ignore it for probably ten minutes, it went from murmuring to absolutely stomach churning screaming. It didn't sound like kids playing at this point, so I jumped out of bed, got dressed and I grabbed the bar we use to open and close the loft hatch, without even realising, and I ran outside thinking some child was being hurt or abducted.

The moment I got outside, it stopped. Everything was deadly silent and no-one was around. That's when it hit me about hearing accounts from people with Dogman and Bigfoot encounters; where the creature may imitate sounds of children in distress or shout your name to lure people outside. I put that out of my mind and I tried to rationalise the experience. I ran up and down at least five different streets looking for whatever made the noise and I saw nobody. I didn't see anyone who had come outside because they heard the sounds too. There wasn't even a house with its lights on with people looking out of the windows or twitching their curtains. It was deadly silent.

The next day, I asked my parents about what had happened in the night and they didn't even know I'd gone out of the house, let alone hear a kid screaming - which I thought was strange, because I literally burst out of my room and sprinted down the stairs, not caring about making noise or waking anyone up.

I live in an area where's there is plenty of wooded places etc and we have a lot of water sources around. There are plenty of dykes and brooks, deep enough for probably something the size of a horse to move along undetected. Also, the area near my house, where the noises seem to have been emanating from, has now been designated as a nature reserve and they've gone to quite an effort to keep people out...

Liam supplied Deborah Hatswell with a sound clip of the 'groaning' type noise, which Deborah has included in this youtube video of Liam's accounts: www.youtube.com/watch?v=p_pTZp3xWH4

Deborah says that Liam is very interested in investigating the new nature reserve area close to his home, and tells me that his situation is ongoing. He has had further strange experiences which she has not included in her online reports.

The next two accounts contain similarities, but they are separate experiences. They both come from young boys who were playing in woodlands and they both occurred in locations within walking distance apart, and less than ten miles from Wharncliffe Woods. In the first report, the unnamed witness experienced multiple sightings of a dark figure with red eyes, the earliest was in the 1980s when he was a child.

The Ivy Den Creature
Dark Figure Seen at Hackenthorpe

Witness:
"Dave and I were about nine or ten years old and we were playing in what we called the 'ivy den', at Hackenthorpe in Sheffield. I was hanging onto a tree swing over a stream, when suddenly my friends and brother got up and ran across the stream, up the bank, then off as fast as they could go without saying a word to me. I was just hanging onto the branch of the swing and when I looked down the stream to see why they ran, I saw a six to seven foot dark figure with the brightest red eyes. It was running up the side of the stream, about twenty feet away, coming in my direction.
Then this thing jumped across the stream with ease (which is too wide for anything normal to jump) and it was heading straight towards me. I dropped off the swing and I legged it across the stream, running hard. Then I fell trying to get up the bank, and as I turned to see where 'it' was, it was just stood at the other side of stream staring straight at me. I set off shouting 'HELP!'

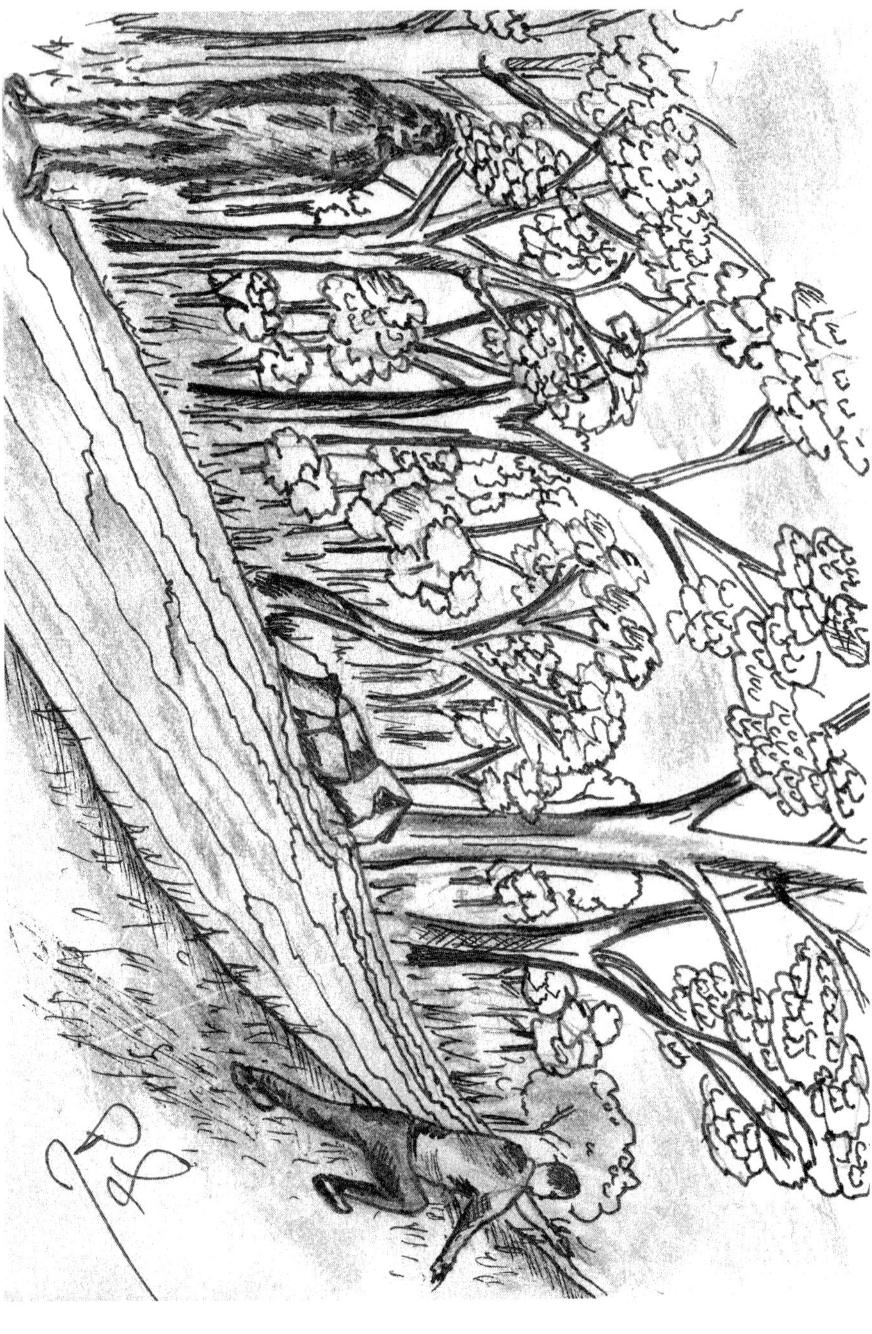

One of my friends heard me yelling and he came back and got me and helped me to get out. During the one to two minutes this was all happening, 'it' never made a sound. There was no thumping of running feet and no sound when it jumped and landed. This was my second sighting of this 'thing', but I have seen a dark figure quite a few times since; years later when at work and once, while driving, I saw 'it' by the side of my car."

The next account occurred in Cat Woods, a location south of Sheffield, nine miles south east of Wharncliffe Woods. The witness is Shaine Winfrow, who was a child at the time of his experience.

Howls, Figures and Footprints
The Bigfoot of Cat Woods

Shaine:
"When I was fourteen years old I was out in the woods close to home, in a place we went to all the time. We were doing the usual boy's games, and on that day I was with my brother and a friend and we decided to make a rope swing.

We were in Cat Woods in Sheffield. I have always called it this, but it doesn't show up on any maps. It must just be a local name I think. Anyway, we were swinging and making a noise, but over the top of that we could hear something close to where were. We couldn't see it, just hear it, but whatever was howling was getting closer.

We were looking around to try and see what it was, then we looked up the tree where we had our rope swing. Much further up the tree, in the branches above our heads, we saw something standing on the branches there. It was black and grey and stood on two feet; one foot placed on each branch. We also saw a smaller one, across from us, that was the size of small child.

We ran so fast to get out of there. We went back a day later to get our rope swing, but it was ripped apart in pieces and covered in black and grey hair. We never went back there again."

Today, Shaine is a member and active researcher in Deborah Hatswell's British Bigfoot group. He still carries his frightening experience with him and now collects other local accounts and related news reports.

Of his sighting, he says: *"If I had to explain it, I would describe them as Bigfoot; hair covered and ape like - almost like a man and a monkey at the same time."* But this was not Shaine's only experience. He also describes photographing a strange footprint he found in the area and once being chased on his bike by what he calls 'a green eyed cat', which he says kept up with the speed of his bike. Shaine is open to discussing his experiences and has gathered quite a knowledge of the subject.

A STRANGE OWL AND AN UNKNOWN TRUTH

I was told about the next account by Philip Morris, who lives on West Hill in Bridlington. I wrote about Phil's own sighting of a green glowing UFO in the first book. When Phil bumped into a couple of his friends, Ann and Martin, who live in the town, they began to discuss his UFO sighting. It turned out they had read both of the *Truth Proof* books.

Ann told Phil that she had also had a strange experience in the same area many years before. Her account may not sound as exciting as some of the incidents I have written about in my books, but if we are ever going to get closer to understanding what is going on, Ann's story is just as important as all of the others.

When I eventually spoke with Ann and listened to her account, I was reminded of the fact that certain places regularly exhibit unusual phenomena. In some areas, the less dramatic incidents are often overlooked, so I call these locations 'secondary areas of exotic nature'. The land around Bessingby is one of the secondary areas of exotic nature I am familiar with. Short Lane at Bempton is another - and like an old clock, they all seem to strike with random phenomena at any given time. I just want to understand what makes them tick.

Ann's experience happened between West Hill and Bessingby in 1967. She was with her boyfriend Alan and remembers that it was an unusually hot summer. Alan was in the RAF at the time and they had just got engaged. I asked Ann if she could recall the month:

Ann:
"I think it was June and we were walking on the path between West Hill and Bessingby. The area has changed beyond recognition. Back then it was just a dirt path; a cut-through between the fields. Now there's houses, shops and industrial units, where there was once open fields and woodland.

I remember it was late afternoon and sun was still shining. The air was warm and everything seemed normal. We were enjoying our walk, when suddenly we both stopped and looked at each other. We realised something had changed. Everything around us had gone totally still and silent. Even the air had changed and it suddenly felt very cold; like we'd walked into a fridge. It was a very odd feeling. I'm sure we both noticed it at the same time, but there was no explanation. We couldn't hear anything - even all the birds had stopped singing. I know I felt very frightened. It was almost like we'd opened a door and stepped into another world. It was the strangest feeling ever.

I'm not sure how long the experience lasted or quite how we knew it had ended. But that strange experience is something that both of us have never forgotten these past fifty years."

As researchers we are missing vital clues if we don't consider cases like Ann's. By only focusing on the truly amazing stories, many accounts like this can be overlooked or forgotten, but they can provide us with vital clues. The tangible silence and the sudden temperature change - these things and more are spoken about by witnesses all over the world.

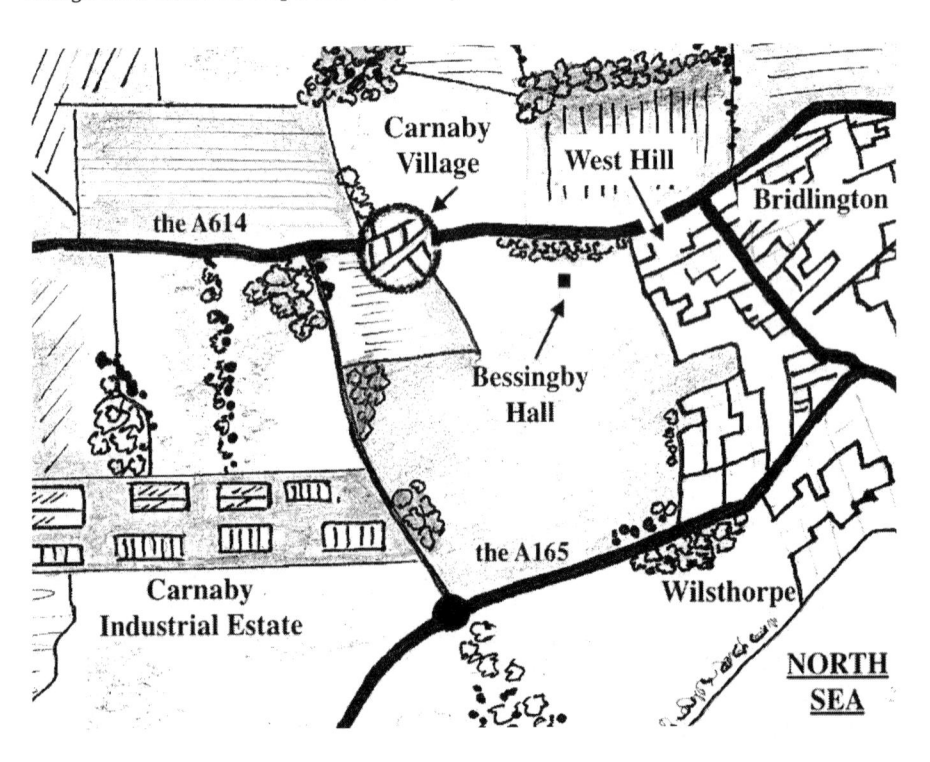

I wonder if the effects Ann and Alan felt, within that state of altered awareness, were actually intended for them? Perhaps they just happened to be in the right place at the right time, when a door to exotic nature opened and closed. Was this phenomena specific to the area around Bessingby? Or are there areas of exotic nature spread evenly all over the surface of the planet? Could these effects even move around, in some kind of sequence, affecting any living thing that happens to be there when they occur?

At this moment in time, I think it is a mixture of both questions. Past research reveals that this location is definitely a repeat area, but were Ann and Alan the catalyst that was needed to create the effect? Would it have happened with or without their presence? Some may say I am over-thinking, but over-thinking is the only thing we can do. Clues to the truth must exist somewhere within these historic accounts.

I have a report from the 1990s where staff at Bessingby Hall claim to have seen a spaceship hovering over fields, very close to where Ann and Alan had taken their walk back in 1967. The object was seen by multiple witnesses who were working in the Hall. They stood watching this dazzling oval-shaped craft, which seemed to be stationary above some trees.

There is also a report from 2002, of a dark hooded figure that suddenly materialized in front of a cyclist on his way to work at Carnaby Industrial Estate, near Wilsthorpe. Whatever he saw that morning scared him so much that he refused to cycle along the same road again, choosing instead to cycle an extra two miles to avoid the road.

In the 1970s, Phil Morris saw a glowing green UFO between West Hill and Carnaby, Lesley Buttle witnessed a spaceship over the allotments at Bessingby (which has to be one of the best close encounter stories ever told), and in 1966, Rob Fletcher and his brother had an amazing sighting of a spaceship close to West Hill. The list of unusual happenings seems endless.

All of these accounts have one thing in common; they were all from within a mile of each other. I wonder how many other strange incidents have gone unreported in this area. If it were not for my research, I think most of these stories would have died with the people who saw and experienced them.

I learned more about Ann and Alan's strange experience after Ann told me they had been discussing what happened on that day in 1967. Their conversation revived a peculiar memory, that for some reason, Ann had forgotten all about for over fifty years. During their conversation, Alan asked Ann if she could remember the owl? At first Ann told me that she didn't understand what Alan was talking about. Then as he recalled his version of the experience, Ann's mind went back and suddenly, the memory of him pointing to a white owl came flooding back.

Alan reminded Ann that when they had reached that strange, detached 'zone of silence' on their walk, they saw a huge white owl circling above them. I find it incredible that such a vivid memory can just leave a person's mind, but that is exactly what happened in Ann's case. She had completely forgotten about the owl until Alan reminded her of it. It is as though the memories were there, but they needed a trigger to bring them back.

I wonder why we often forget such important details? The white owl and the silence were part of their experience, yet Ann had forgot all about them. Alan had thought it was huge - larger that he expected a white owl to be. The only white owls native to UK are barn owls, which have a wingspan of around a meter. So what did they see?

Sometimes I think there is something that does not want us to remember. If we all had perfect recall we would be joining the dots. Even when the intelligence behind all of this leaves us with only fragments of an untraceable truth, those who have the experience will still change the way they think. Perhaps the memories are stamped into our DNA in some way, to be passed on to future generations, to potentially drip feed into our whole being over many lifetimes?

I do not think any new memories, from their short but amazing experience, are ever going to surface for Ann and Alan. However, seeing the owl whilst trapped in that cold unnatural silence could be a strong indicator that something else happened to them both that day.

This may be the last thing that Ann or Alan have ever considered, but owls have long been associated with alien abduction experiences. Witnesses often talk about seeing owls when relating such unusual experiences. It is thought they are used as 'screen memories' to mask something else entirely. Of course, this may not be true in Ann and Alan's case, but my interpretation of their story is that they had somehow briefly entered a kind of 'changed reality'.

My friend Whitley Strieber, who documented one of the most incredible and detailed alien abduction cases ever, said that before his abduction experiences, he remembers being watched from his back yard by a white owl. He published his account in the book *Communion*, which was eventually made into a film in 1989. Ann and Alan's experience took place over twenty years before Whitley Strieber's, but perhaps the owl is the thread that connects them both.

Seeing an owl is not such a rare thing, especially near rural areas. I remember seeing a large white owl flying over some flooded land at the back of our home when I was a child. This was immediately after I saw a silver pencil-shaped object, flying over the water. I think I was so amazed to see the owl afterwards, that I forgot about the UFO for many years.

Why do alien abductees see owls? I wish I knew. The fact that owls seem to feature in the recall of many witnesses has to mean something. These 'never-land moments' are so contrary to anything that normal life shows us, yet we choose to forget them.

I still say that location is key. Even though the events may not make sense, the same 'repeat areas' continue to present unknown phenomena. I am sure some important clues could be found, if it were possible to gather enough data; dates, times, weather conditions and so on. But saying there are repeat areas, does not bring us any closer to an answer. Until more researchers in different parts of the world begin to recognise and accept witness testimony, no serious studies of the data can be looked at and cross-referenced.

Science does not want to touch these unknowns, because there is nothing to work with; except witness accounts that makes no credible sense. All the sightings, experiences and happenings are so random, they are virtually impossible to study. It is difficult enough when none of the pieces of the puzzle fit and the only common link we have seems to be a location.

I call these places areas of *over-science,* where an unknown truth resides beyond the thinking mind, in a 'no man's land' where science does not want to look.

Recent Email From a Reader

"Hi,

I've been reading your Truth Proof books and its been making me think twice about something I once saw in the woods. It was when I joined the army in 2007. It was during an exercise in Staffordshire when we were sent out into the field for a couple of nights.

There must have been around forty of us in our dugouts. The first night we drew up a watch list and my watch was around midnight-ish.

After I got settled down for a two hour stint with the other guy (there's always two on at night), it wasn't long before we noticed two dim red lights in front of us; maybe 30-40m away.

We both watched for a long while and at first we thought it was one of the directing staff with two mini glow-sticks above his head. But we couldn't see anyone there, and especially we couldn't hear any noise and its hard to move in the woods without making noise. And anyway, why would someone stand there holding two mini glow-sticks above his head for over ten minutes?

We both concluded that they looked like eyes. But on the other hand, they could not be eyes, because eyes don't glow red - and if they were eyes, they were far too tall to be a person. The two red lights were moving around, but still in the same position - they weren't darting from tree to tree. They were moving, and thats what made us think that they were eyes, because they would naturally move if whatever they belonged to was moving too. But again, eyes don't glow red, and it was far too tall.

Neither of us were scared, but neither wanted to go investigate, mainly because of the cold we didn't want to move position. We really didn't know what it was. I do remember the woods being quiet because I remember thinking, it can't be directing staff, because there's no noise.

We watched it for maybe ten minutes. It was a long observation and neither of us said much to each other; only commenting on what it might be. The next day, it was forgotten about.

Only recently I began thinking again of that night in the woods, when I began to hear about 'dog-men' and some of your stories. A lot of the witnesses claim that they have glowing red eyes and stand very tall. It was the glowing eyes that got my attention, because that's just what the two of us thought we were seeing.

This was in 2007. I don't know where exactly it was, but the Army Training Regiment was Litchfield.

Gerry Thomas."

Paul Sinclair lives with his wife and family in the UK seaside town of Bridlington, on the east coast of Yorkshire.

He is a talented artist who creates huge surrealist artwork and enjoys countryside walks - and never leaves home without his camera!

He began his research in 2002 after creating the *ILF-UFO* sightings website. He has a Truth Proof channel on Youtube and a website; www.truthproof.webs.com

Paul can be contacted through the Truth Proof page on Facebook.